Samuel Adams

American Profiles
Norman K. Risjord, Series Editor

Samuel Adams

America's Revolutionary Politician

John K. Alexander

ROWMAN & LITTLEFIELD PUBLISHERS, INC.
Lanham • Boulder • New York • Oxford

ROWMAN & LITTLEFIELD PUBLISHERS, INC.

Published in the United States of America
by Rowman & Littlefield Publishers, Inc.
4720 Boston Way, Lanham, Maryland 20706
www.rowmanlittlefield.com

12 Hid's Copse Road
Cumnor Hill, Oxford OX2 9JJ, England

British Library Cataloguing in Publication Information Available

Library of Congress Cataloging-in-Publication Data

Alexander, John K.
  Samuel Adams : America's revolutionary politician / John K. Alexander.
    p. cm. — (American profiles)
  Includes bibliographical references and index.
  ISBN 0-7425-2114-1 (cloth : alk. paper) — ISBN 0-7425-2115-X (pbk. : alk. paper)
  1. Adams, Samuel, 1722–1803. 2. Politicians—United States—Biography. 3. United
States—Declaration of Independence—Signers—Biography. 4. United States—History—
Revolution, 1775–1783—Biography. 5. United States—Politics and government—1775–1783.
I. Title. II. American profiles (Lanham, Md.)

E302.6.A2 A54 2002
973.3'092—dc21   2001044998

Printed in the United States of America

♾ ™
   The paper used in this publication meets the minimum requirements of American
National Standard for Information Sciences—Permanence of Paper for Printed Library
Materials, ANSI/NISO Z39.48–1992.

For my favorite historian,
June Granatir Alexander

Contents

Preface

*S*cholars have pursued a dazzling array of approaches when examining America's colonial and Revolutionary eras. Despite the diversity, three lines of inquiry, which at times meld into one another, have gained prominence in recent years. One group of scholars emphasizes assessing how and why society and culture developed. These analysts usually insist that the thoughts and actions of those who typically lacked power—such as women, racial minorities, and the poor—must be considered. Thus scholars highlight the issues of gender, race, and class. Other analysts devote their energies principally to unearthing the philosophical roots of political thought or to deciphering the language people employed. The third major approach is hardly "new" since it is the most traditional form of history. It is the approach that glorifies the writing of narrative history, the telling of the story. The narrative approach should be placed alongside the "New Historiography" because, after coming under heavy assault, it is regaining favor.

This biography of Samuel Adams, who was arguably both America's first professional politician and its first modern politician, touches on many points raised by the New Historiography. For decades, the standard interpretation of Adams depicted him as the controller of a "trained mob." The people supposedly had no will of their own; they had no agency. However, most modern scholars maintain that colonial and Revolutionary crowds typically acted purposefully and for reasons that made sense to those in the crowds. While this study endorses the view of Samuel Adams as a skillful political organizer and emphasizes that he developed innovative ways of bringing ordinary citizens into the political process, the work supports the arguments advanced in the New Historiography. The less powerful members of society *did* have minds of their own; they *did* have agency. In addition, although the documentary record is frustratingly thin at spots, an analysis of how Samuel Adams related to women and of his efforts on behalf of opening educational opportunities to females provides important evidence to help answer the question, Did the American Revolution fundamentally transform the status and situation of women? The record is even thinner when it comes to race relations, but what little exists is revealing. Moreover, because Samuel Adams trumpeted the idea of creating a "virtuous" society to sustain America's republican governments, an assessment of him enlightens us about the development of society and culture in the era of the American Revolution.

Samuel Adams's life and thought are of special importance to those who explore political philosophy and the meaning of language. During his lengthy political life, Adams penned a wide variety of writings ranging from artfully crafted letters to official government documents to newspaper polemics. Adams's writings and political activities reveal the philosophical underpinnings that he and many others brought to the issues of the day and help us fathom the nature of rhetoric and propaganda in early America. Moreover, like modern scholars, Adams was attuned to the importance of language and sensitive to the meaning of vital terms such as "virtue." Here again, an exploration of Adams's career, including his too often neglected role in the 1780s and 1790s, meshes with recent trends in scholarly inquiry.

While an analysis of Samuel Adams helps answer a range of questions scholars now emphasize, his biography is particularly useful as a way of understanding the past through narrative history, through telling the story. Judge James Sullivan went too far when, eulogizing Adams, he claimed that "to give his history at length, would be to give an history of the American revolution." Still, Judge Sullivan was not far off the mark. Samuel Adams's contemporaries, friend and foe alike, agreed that he was perhaps the most important of those colonials who championed the movement toward American independence. He was America's revolutionary politician. So Samuel Adams's story—the story of a true political animal—compels us to think about how and why the Revolution occurred; it also forces us to confront the ideas and assess the actions of those Americans who opposed the Revolutionary movement. In addition, although Samuel Adams was not one of the framers or even an ardent proponent of the Constitution of 1787, his extensive role in the creation and defense of American governments again provides a useful way of exploring crucial developments in early American politics.

Because the story of his life opens a wide window on the nature and meaning of the American Revolution and life in eighteenth-century America, Samuel Adams's biography fits usefully into the New Historiography. Nevertheless, a study of Samuel Adams is perhaps most valuable not for how it fits with currently fashionable historical questions—after all, historical fashions, like other fashions, change—but for the timeless example he provides. Who can deny that the people—and not just Americans— have increasingly viewed politics and politicians with a jaundiced eye? Cynicism runs deep. In the United States the roots of that modern cynicism can probably be traced to Watergate. A host of additional political scandals, including a modern impeachment of an American president and the bizarre climax of the presidential election of 2000, kept the roots well watered. The sense of frustration accompanying this growing cynicism is illustrated by a bit of modern American popular culture: the *Doonesbury* comic strip, in which people who lived through the shocking and disturbing political revelations of the Watergate period now find it hard to be shocked and outraged by the sliminess of politicians. In the immediate aftermath of the horrors of September 11, 2001, Americans viewed politicians more favorably; however, that upswing in popularity might prove fleeting. Americans might reembrace the notion that virtually all politicians are scoundrels. Samuel Adams reminds us it does not have to be like that. Although Adams had his foibles and his weaknesses, as the following pages reveal, his story demonstrates that a lifetime spent in politics can be honorable and worthy of admiration. Samuel Adams offers the example of a political life built on a principled defense of liberty and on a nearly selfless concern for others. If one may borrow and slightly expand on a line from Jane Austen, such a person will always have attractions, and should always have attractions, for us.

Despite Samuel Adams's important role in the era of the American Revolution, scholarly interest in him has fluctuated dramatically, and so too have the interpretations of Adams. (For an analysis of the biographers' Samuel Adams, see the bibliography.) However they interpret him, those who study Samuel Adams must contend with the fact that eighteenth-century American English looks strange to the modern eye. In addition to English spellings, one encounters added letters (such as "republick" for "republic"), peculiar omissions (such as "observ'd" for "observed"), or seemingly missing letters (such as "pressd" for "pressed"). Writers often sprinkled their prose with capital letters; yet the word "negro" was rarely capitalized. In addition, many authors engaged in what might reasonably be called "adventures in punctuation." Still, what looks odd to the modern reader was not necessarily wrong by eighteenth-century standards. Accordingly, I have followed this rule when quoting: quotations are given without alteration and without any attempt to indicate "errors" through the use of "[*sic*]." Where it seemed necessary to add material for clarity's sake, it has been inserted in brackets. These points merit special comment because I have consciously striven to allow the people who lived in Samuel Adams's time, as well as the revolutionary politician himself, ample opportunity to speak for themselves.

Many people played special roles in helping me craft this work. Jesse Lemisch did not comment on the manuscript, but it was taking his course on the American Revolution at the University of Chicago and then being his research assistant that forever hooked me on the subject. Norman K. Risjord, the series editor of American Profiles, was a hands-on editor. He read drafts of the manuscript closely and offered truly constructive criticism. John P. Kaminski, the director of the Center for the Study of the American Constitution, performed a similar service. It was a pleasure working with the people of the Rowman & Littlefield Publishing Group. Lynn Weber, the managing editor, Mary Carpenter, the acting editor for history and politics, and Cheryl Hoffman, the copyeditor for the project, all contributed skillfully to the process that turned a manuscript into a book. Gregory M. Britton, who was then the director of Madison House, suggested I write this biography. Even after he became director of the Minnesota Historical Society Press, Greg continued this interest in what we called the Samuel Adams Project. Since doing this work allowed me the opportunity to think and write about the nature and meaning of the American Revolution, a topic to which I have devoted my scholarly life, I shall be forever grateful to Greg for asking me to do a biography of Samuel Adams. June Granatir Alexander, my wonderfully talented historian spouse, poured enormous time and energy into the effort. Having over the years already engaged in innumerable discussions about Samuel Adams, June scrutinized drafts of every chapter time and again. Changes made at her suggestion have materially improved the work. June once teased me about liking the second Elizabeth Adams so much in part because I thought she and Samuel's "Dearest Betsy" were so much alike. As usual, June was right. I believe that in important ways Samuel Adams came to rely on Elizabeth's wise counsel; similarly, I rely on June's wise counsel. Moreover, Samuel realized how fortunate he was to be able to share his life with such a marvelous, loving woman. I have the same privilege and, like Samuel, am grateful for having it.

1

The Failure of Promise

*S*amuel Adams was born to a life of promise. Although his merchant father lacked a gentleman's education, he had a knack for making money. In 1712, when only twenty-three years old, Samuel Adams Sr. could afford to buy an impressive residence in Boston, the largest town in British America. Sitting on a substantial parcel of land that extended from Purchase Street down to the harbor, the house had a garden, an orchard, a rooftop observatory, and an unobstructed view of the harbor. In April 1713, the senior Adams wed Mary Fifield, and the Purchase Street house became their home.

Religion played a central role in the couple's lives. Mary Adams devoutly followed the Puritan faith, and her husband answered to the title of Deacon Adams because of his lengthy service with the Old South Congregational Church. In 1715 he helped lead a successful petition effort asking the Boston Town Meeting for a parcel of land on which to erect a church. The New South Church, located a mere two blocks from the Adams home, opened its doors in January 1717. Samuel Adams was baptized there on September 16, 1722, the day of his birth.

One can only catch glimpses of the personal side of the Adams family. What Samuel thought about his pious mother has not been preserved, but he remembered his father as "a wise man and a good man." Young Samuel's relationships with his siblings—and perhaps to a degree with his parents and especially his mother—could not help reflecting a grim demographic fact. Mary Adams bore a dozen children between 1716 and April 1740, but only three lived past their third birthday. In addition to Samuel, Mary (born in 1717) and Joseph (born in 1728) survived to adulthood. So the rigors of pregnancy and the sadness of death regularly visited the Adams home as Samuel grew up. The frightening child mortality that afflicted the family made Samuel the eldest Adams son from the day of his birth. By Samuel's own account, his sister Mary, who possessed her mother's fervent religiosity and was five years his senior, exerted an important influence on him. As a mature man, he observed that it "is a happy young man who has had an elder sister upon whom he could rely for advice and counsel in youth."

1

Samuel's parents started him on the road to acquiring a gentleman's education by enrolling him in the Boston Latin School. As Samuel traveled that road, his family continued to prosper. The senior Adams improved the quality of his mercantile operation by acquiring a wharf, and he also owned a malt house. Through the 1720s and 1730s he purchased additional lands and houses, presumably to lease. Continuing a process begun before young Samuel's birth, the elder Adams's role in Boston's political affairs also kept expanding. In 1710 the town meeting elected him a tithingman, a post that centered on enforcing laws concerning public houses. He moved up the political ladder when he served as a constable in 1718–19. At that time, a constable's duties included collecting fines and taxes, responsibilities that made the post so burdensome many paid a fine to avoid the job. But Adams accepted the position and the next year was again made a tithingman. In the 1720s, the elder Adams ascended to higher levels of politics. The town meeting routinely elected him a tax assessor, and in March 1729 he became a selectman. This executive position made him one of the leaders of the town meeting.

The political rise of Samuel Adams Sr. did not happen by chance. The eighteenth-century historian William Gordon asserted that by 1724, or even a little earlier, Adams and about twenty others met in caucus and formulated strategies to get their candidates into positions of power. This organization, later called the Boston Caucus, gained political favor by championing economic issues that mattered to common folk. Because hard money was in chronically short supply, the caucus advocated the emission of paper currency. The group supported tax officials, often caucus members, who typically overlooked delinquent taxpayers suffering hard times. The caucus also strove to protect the political rights of citizens. It fought to ensure the integrity of Boston's town meeting government, a system that gave the citizens a direct say in determining how their city functioned. The system's democratic features came at a price, though. The town meeting, which relied on elected committees rather than a few officials to set policy, often proved less than efficient, and that prompted calls for incorporating Boston as a city. Under the leadership of the caucus, the town meeting thwarted various incorporation schemes during the 1730s that would have significantly diluted the voters' power by eliminating the elected committee system. To further protect the citizens' political clout, the Boston Caucus also ardently supported the legislature's successful efforts to deny the royal governor a guaranteed salary. (Because the British government followed the practice of letting the colonies pay the salaries of most colonial officials, the Massachusetts Charter of 1691 gave the colony's legislature the power to determine and pay the salary of the royal governor as well as the salaries of other royally appointed officials. That system saved the Crown money in the short run, but in the long run it gave the colonial legislators the power of the purse, an advantage they used to pursue their own, not necessarily Britain's, interests.) By the time young Samuel Adams entered Harvard in 1736, his father, as a result of being appointed a justice of the peace, had become Samuel Adams, Esquire.

In those days a Harvard undergraduate's class ranking reflected his father's attainments, not the student's performance or even his academic promise. So it is hardly surprising that Samuel Adams, the son of a wealthy justice of the peace, was placed sixth in a class of twenty-three. Even that high ranking was, in fact, unusually low. Had the normal system been followed, young Samuel would have been second—not sixth—in his class. The reason for the demotion is revealing. The president of Harvard, Benjamin Wadsworth, apparently disliked the idea that the top two positions in the class would go to the sons of men who, although justices of the peace, possessed neither a gentleman's education nor other special distinctions; so Wadsworth arbitrarily decided to rank the sons of clergymen ahead of the sons of justices of the peace. Nothing in the sparse records that have survived from Samuel's youth suggests he or his parents knew about, or even would care about, this snub. Still, the ranking process and the snub are important. They illustrate how elite members of Massachusetts society strove to keep social distinctions sharp and clear. The slight in ranking Samuel reveals that wealth and even important political standing could not, in the eyes of some, transform his father into a gentleman. Deacon Adams, it seemed, lacked the proper education that marked a true Massachusetts gentleman.

Attending Harvard would give young Samuel the education his father lacked and also prepare him for the ministry, the profession his parents expected him to follow. Samuel took courses with Edward Wigglesworth, a professor of divinity, and he did so amidst the early rumblings of religious enthusiasm that soon exploded into the Great Awakening. Nevertheless, and despite his own lifelong religiosity, Samuel did not fancy becoming a clergyman. The ancient Greek and Latin authors and the writings of English political philosophers proved more appealing than theology. Perhaps it was his growing interest in politics that led Adams to arrange a general debate among classmates on the topic of liberty.

Samuel Adams received his bachelor's degree on schedule in 1740 and returned home to a promising, if uncertain, future. Having decided against the ministry, he had to select a new career. As Adams family descendants later recounted, Samuel, urged on by his father, eagerly began studying the law. But for some unrecorded reason, his mother opposed this course. A new plan emerged: he would become a businessman. Samuel soon found himself in a countinghouse under the tutelage of Thomas Cushing, a leading Boston merchant. Cushing quickly decided that the recent Harvard graduate was not merchant material. As Cushing reportedly saw it, young Samuel worked hard and was intelligent, but he lacked business sense, in part because politics dominated his thoughts. In an effort to jump-start his son's business career, the senior Adams loaned him £1,000, an impressive sum for the times. The effort fizzled. Young Samuel loaned a friend half his start-up fund, and the friend never repaid the money. The other £500 soon disappeared as well. Perhaps realizing the accuracy of Cushing's judgment about his son's lack of business talent, Adams effectively became young Samuel's employer by making him a partner in the family malt house business.

While it hardly explains the younger Adams's false career starts and failures as a businessman, Thomas Cushing may have voiced the vital point when he spoke about young Samuel being distracted, almost consumed, by politics. Such a preoccupation would have been natural because the political intrigues of the early 1740s were of immediate, pressing concern to all the Adamses. Indeed, the Adams family found itself sucked into a political firestorm that threatened to incinerate its prosperity. To understand the formative years of Samuel Adams, the revolutionary politician, one must examine what was called the land bank controversy.

The political turmoil sprang from a chronic problem faced by Massachusetts and the other British colonies in North America: the lack of a medium of exchange, literally an absence of money in circulation. As New England's economy grew, its money supply needed to expand. Since hard money—gold and silver—was always scarce, colonies wanted to issue paper money. However, to protect merchants who routinely advanced credit to colonial merchants, the British opposed the issuance of legal-tender paper money because of the likelihood of depreciation. Still, on occasion, chiefly during wartime, England reluctantly allowed some colonies to print currency. Massachusetts began issuing paper money in 1690, and it circulated throughout New England. Under orders from the British government, however, the many issues of Massachusetts currency, which depreciated rapidly in the 1730s, were being withdrawn from circulation. So the Massachusetts currency could not meet the region's money-supply needs.

At this juncture, Rhode Island entered the picture. Because that self-governing corporate colony was not as tightly regulated as the royal colony of Massachusetts, Rhode Island found it easier to issue paper money and in the late 1730s flooded New England with its currency. In 1738 and again the next year, the Boston Town Meeting sounded the alarm in instructions issued to its representatives in the colonial assembly. The town meeting maintained that Rhode Islanders were stealing Massachusetts's trade because the colony lacked a medium of exchange. The situation worsened a year later when the British government decreed that all Massachusetts paper money must be retired from circulation by 1741. Faced with what it perceived as imminent economic ruin, the Boston Town Meeting, in instructions Deacon Adams helped draft, renewed its call for legislative action. The Massachusetts House of Representatives responded in June 1739 with an almost plaintive cry for help. Agreeing that Massachusetts desperately needed some form of currency, the representatives established a committee to receive proposals from "any persons whomsoever" to create a medium of trade.

Samuel Adams Sr. did more than help write instructions for the Boston representatives. Realizing that England's prohibition against Massachusetts's issuing paper currency did not extend to *private* ventures, he and other leaders of the Boston Caucus proposed creating a land bank. It issued currency and loaned it to private individuals who secured the loans by mortgaging their land. The land bank was also called the manufactory scheme because it accepted payments of interest and the principal of the loans in marketable items such as hemp, flax, cordage, and bar or cast iron. The land bank benefited the colony in important ways. It provided a desperately needed money supply. It was designed to promote manufacturing ventures, and that, in turn, would provide more jobs. Adams and other caucus leaders became directors of the land bank.

Eventually over a thousand people became land bank subscribers. The plan enjoyed widespread support, in part because virtually all landowners could subscribe and by subscribing obtain what amounted to a loan. Thus men on the rise could use the land bank to improve their economic opportunities. If Thomas Hutchinson, a prominent member of the long-established, politically powerful, and conservative merchant family, was right, the economically vulnerable found the land bank appealing. Hutchinson, who considered the idea of a land bank repugnant, claimed that "the needy part of the province in general favored the scheme." Those who actually subscribed to the land bank were, Hutchinson sniffed, not much better off. The subscribers were "generally of low condition . . . and of small estate, and many of them perhaps insolvent." Still, Hutchinson conceded that a few men "of rank and good estate" backed the endeavor. Samuel Adams Sr. would certainly belong in that more esteemed group.

Many other leading Boston merchants joined Hutchinson in recoiling at the thought that a medium of exchange would be based on something other than gold or silver. Ten merchants, headed by Edward Hutchinson, a cousin of Thomas, quickly established a silver bank that issued currency based on silver holdings. These merchants openly proclaimed their opposition to the land bank by announcing that no silver bank subscriber would accept land bank notes.

The political battle lines formed quickly. The backers of the land bank typically came from what was, over time, labeled the popular or country party. The leading Massachusetts supporters of the royal governors, often aristocrats such as the Hutchinsons, became known as the court party. Each faction dominated a branch of the colony's legislature, the General Court. The popular forces held the lower house, the House of Representatives. The House, which contained several land bank directors, supported the idea of private ventures like the land bank. The court party controlled the Governor's Council, the upper house of the legislature, and several silver bank directors sat on the Council. The Council and the royal governor, Jonathan Belcher, worked to destroy the land bank. Using the veto powers granted by the Massachusetts Charter of 1691, Governor Belcher played rough. Having rejected the house's selection for speaker because the man chosen was a director of the land bank, Belcher then vetoed appointments that would have placed land bank men on his Council. The governor pressed the attack by dismissing justices of the peace and militia officers who were prominent supporters of the land bank. Samuel Adams Sr., who in addition to being a justice of the peace was a captain of the Boston militia, thus lost two significant and prestigious offices. The worst was yet to come.

Responding to lobbying by Governor Belcher, his Council, and leading Boston merchants, the British government, which on principle opposed anything like the land bank or the silver bank schemes, took action. In late March 1741, reports reached Massachusetts that the House of Commons had enacted a bill to dissolve the private banks and ensure that no such ventures could be launched in the future. Weeks later, Belcher confided to Thomas Hutchinson that unnamed champions of the land bank had supposedly declared they would defy any anti–land bank act Parliament passed. These people, said Belcher, had grown so brassy and bold that they planned to rebel. No rebellion occurred, but Belcher rightly sensed the deepening anger festering among many Massachusetts citizens.

Parliament's antibank bill reached Massachusetts in July 1741. Parliament made it obvious its chief target was the land bank, not the silver bank. This extraordinary legislation was demonstrably unfair. Moreover, although the British constitution was an unwritten entity built on traditions, laws, and precedents and thus especially open to conflicting interpretations, the law was also demonstrably unconstitutional. Adopting a flagrantly ex post facto (after the fact) position, Parliament decreed that a 1720 law that would have made the land bank illegal in Great Britain also applied to the American colonies. Despite Parliament's assertion, the 1720 law clearly did not apply to the colonies. Parliament took special aim at the leaders of the land bank by decreeing that anyone who possessed its currency could demand that any partner or director immediately remit the value of the notes *plus* the applicable interest. If the partner or director refused to pay, he became liable for triple damages. Thomas Hutchinson reported that some land bank supporters wanted to fight Parliament's actions but the directors—and that would include the senior Adams—argued to end the scheme. The directors did that, Hutchinson pointed out, because they faced economic ruin if they continued the venture.

By employing draconian methods embedded in unconstitutional legislation, Parliament successfully crushed a popular program designed to help Massachusetts and its ordinary citizens. The Adams family had more reason than most to dislike Parliament and Massachusetts's anti–land bank forces. Although the senior Adams cooperated in the dissolution of the scheme, the legacy of the land bank controversy inflicted pain on his family for decades because Parliament's 1741 law proved an open invitation for anyone who disliked them to harass the senior Adams or his son. Indeed, efforts to seize the family's property continued even after the elder Adams died. So the danger the Adams family faced, to say nothing of the suffering and anger, did not fade when the land bank was dissolved. It burned itself into Samuel's consciousness.

Writing years after the fact, Samuel's second cousin John Adams, who was only six years old in 1741, maintained that the fight over the land bank raised "a greater ferment" in Massachusetts than the Stamp Act did. Considering the turmoil the Stamp Act unleashed, John's pronouncement seems hyperbolic. However, Thomas Hutchinson also believed the land bank controversy created long-lasting bitterness. John Adams and Hutchinson agreed on another vital point. Both said the land bank fight marked Samuel Adams's introduction into the public arena. John mentioned Samuel's "earnest efforts" to help the land bank subscribers, while Hutchinson assessed Samuel's defense of the Adams family itself. These analysts could have added that, in numerous ways, Samuel's efforts in this conflict foreshadowed political battles he would fight in the 1760s and 1770s.

Samuel Adams thus grew up in a politicized atmosphere where he watched his father assume a leading role in the Boston Caucus and its efforts to defend the common people against abuses of power by both the British Crown and the local gentry. The political firefight over the land bank not only threatened to destroy his family's economic security but also exposed the danger posed by the rich merchants of the court party. They seemed more concerned with self-advancement by wedding themselves to British power than with supporting their native colony. And parliamentary power exercised in an arbitrary way to crush the needs—to savage the very rights—of the people formed the core of the problem. This was the political world in which young Adams came of age. When he took a master's degree in 1743, Samuel proposed to argue the affirmative of the position "Whether it be lawful to resist the Supreme Magistrate if the Commonwealth cannot be otherwise preserved." Samuel's choice revealed his increasing focus on the crucial issue of defending basic rights.

Samuel began his own career as an officeholder in March 1747 when the Boston Town Meeting selected him as one of its clerks of market. In the wake of explosive riots against impressment—the practice whereby the British navy forcibly rounded up men to serve on its ships—that rocked Boston later in 1747, Samuel and some of his friends created a club for discussing public issues. Although it is not clear whether they provided financial support for the venture, Samuel and his friends did supply the political essays that became the chief fare of the *Independent Advertiser*, a weekly newspaper that first appeared in January 1748 and continued to offer political commentary until it ceased publication in 1750.

Two *Independent Advertiser* essays attributed to the younger Adams are extraordinarily important. They show that issues Samuel stressed as a college student—the questions of "liberty" and a citizen's right to resist the government's "unlawful" actions—became deeply embedded in his thinking. Commenting upon "Loyalty *and* Sedition," he asserted that "True Loyalty . . . is founded in the Love and Possession of Liberty." For Adams, "the true Object of Loyalty is a good *Legal Constitution*" that allowed a citizen "to remonstrate his Grievances." The people must know how their constitution worked, and they must display "a becoming Jealousy of our Immunities, and a steadfast Resolution to maintain them." Anyone who tried to subvert the constitution, or "even to weaken it," was disloyal. Slashing at the aristocrats who formed the backbone of the court party, Adams also denounced anyone who "despises his Neighbor's Happiness because he wears "a *worsted Cap* or a *Leathern Apron*" or who "*struts* immeasurably above the *lower* Size of People, and pretends to adjust the Rights of Men by Distinctions of Fortune." Adams returned to that theme in another essay that praised the Massachusetts Charter for protecting the people's rights. He opined that "it is not infrequent, to hear Men declaim loudly upon Liberty, who if we may judge by the whole Tenor of their Actions, mean nothing else by it, but *their own* Liberty—to oppress without Controul, or the Restraint of Laws, All who are poorer and weaker than themselves."

Adams's *Independent Advertiser* essays reflected his reading in political philosophy and more particularly his study of John Locke, the seventeenth-century political theorist revered both in England and in the colonies. In fact, sections of Adams's second essay read like extracts from Locke's influential *Second Treatise of Government*. Samuel's commentary also suggests that the traumatic land bank struggle may have helped convince him that haughty aristocrats, such as the Hutchinsons of the court party, were especially prone to trample on the people and their rights. Even more important, these essays outlined the fundamental political ideals Adams steadfastly followed throughout his long political career. He believed the people deserved a constitution that protected their rights and that gave them a legal way to redress grievances. Once such a constitution had been established, the people must vigilantly guard it against attack from *any* source. And while a threat to the people's fundamental rights could come from any direction, the people must be particularly wary of the aristocracy.

As Samuel staked out his philosophical niche in the political world, his father, long known as a leader of the popular party, continued as a role model. In the aftermath of the land bank dispute, Samuel Adams Sr. again consented to serve as a selectman. He held that post from March 1744 until June 1746, when the town meeting elected him to represent Boston in the house of representatives. He would have taken a seat in the prestigious Governor's Council had not Governor Belcher quashed the appointment. Deacon Adams also continued, as he had for years, to provide Samuel with something more than a political role model. When the *Independent Advertiser* began publication in January 1748, Samuel still depended on his father for employment and still owed him £1,000.

Samuel's supportive father died on March 8, 1748. The *Independent Advertiser*, in words his son might have written, proclaimed Deacon Adams "one who well understood and rightly pursued the Civil and Religious Interests of this People [of Boston]—A true *New-England* Man—An Honest Patriot." Even in death, the elder Adams extended special help to his namesake. The estate passed to Mary Fifield Adams and upon her death would ultimately be divided equally among the three Adams children. However, noting Samuel's position as the eldest son, his father's will stipulated that the £1,000 loan should be stricken from the accounts so Samuel could receive his full share of the estate.

With the passing of his father, Samuel assumed control of the family's financial affairs. Shortly thereafter, he took a major personal step. In October 1749 he married Elizabeth Checkley, the daughter of the Reverend Samuel Checkley, a friend of the family and the pastor of the New South Church. In the next seven years, the couple had six children. Only two—Samuel, born in 1751, and Hannah, born in 1756—survived to adulthood. The other children died in infancy, and the last was stillborn on July 6, 1757. Adding to Samuel's grief, Elizabeth died less than three weeks later, almost surely owing to complications from that stillbirth. Assessing her life, Samuel gloried that Elizabeth had "run her Christian race with remarkable steadiness, and finished in triumph!" "To her husband," he continued, "she was as sincere a friend as she was a faithful wife." Perhaps all too aware of his own meager financial skills, he boasted that everyone who knew Elizabeth admired "her exact economy in all her relative capacities." Now in his midthirties, Samuel Adams suddenly faced the daunting task of raising two small children without their mother and his loving and frugal wife. The future seemed anything but bright.

Fortunately for Samuel, he had recently acquired a political position that could support his family. In March 1756 the Boston Town Meeting had chosen him one of its four tax collectors and, as usual with such posts, reelected him the next year. For their service, tax collectors received 5 percent of what they garnered, provided the collection of the taxes occurred within a specified period. So Adams's economic fortunes stood on a firmer footing even as his personal life crumbled. But as Adams knew all too well, as long as the land bank accounts remained unsettled, his family's economic foundation could deteriorate quickly.

Samuel's contemporaries stressed that he was not materialistic. Far from it. But, the lingering effects of the land bank controversy meant that as the 1750s unfolded, he had special reason to fret about his family's economic future. As early as 1751, he twice had to defend his father's estate against commissioners the Massachusetts General Court had authorized to settle the land bank's financial affairs. And with bothersome regularity throughout the 1750s, Adams had to fight to keep his father's estate from being sold at public action to settle land bank accounts. In mounting those defenses, he used tactics and voiced arguments he would draw upon again in the movement toward revolution.

Adams employed a lengthy 1756 newspaper essay to recount his travails and link them to a denial of basic English rights. He groused that, although Massachusetts had created a commissioner system in 1743 to settle the land bank's finances speedily and equitably, the accounts remained unsettled thirteen years later! Worse yet, in 1748, after a fire destroyed most of the commissioners' land bank records, the General Court passed legislation that pitted land bank directors, such as Adams's father, against others in the land bank scheme in a way that "touch'd the New-England Constitution in its tenderest parts." According to Adams, the land bank commissioners had adjusted his financial statements and, without giving him a full hearing, somehow turned a balance into a debt. "Would any Man of Virtue and Candor say," he asked, "that a due Regard was had to Property, or even to natural Justice?" Surely "natural Justice" required the commissioners to hold a full hearing, yet they did not. Adams said he next tried petitioning the legislature, but it refused to act. None of this should have happened, since, according to Samuel, the commissioners had admitted that their assessment of the Adams account "was grounded on Mistakes." The commissioners' persistent hounding thus constituted "an Injury to the innocent." Proclaiming his determination to keep fighting against the possible seizure and sale of the Adams estate, Samuel closed by trumpeting more than his own injured innocence. He carefully linked his struggles to the idea of defending basic rights by asserting: "In the whole of these Affairs, I have never ask'd *Favor*, nor taken *undue Methods* to obtain it.—I have ask'd for *Justice*, and God be thanked, in an *English* Government we have a Right to expect it."

Adams's rhetoric may have forestalled action in 1756, but the land bank settlement nightmare recurred the summer after Elizabeth died. On August 10, 1758, Sheriff Stephen Greenleaf, acting on a warrant from the land bank commissioners, advertised that segments of the late Samuel Adams's estate would be sold at public auction on August 25. All the buildings and lands as well as the wharf and dock would be offered for sale. On the very day that announcement appeared, Samuel penned a response. Observing that the estate had been put up for sale four times since 1751, Samuel asserted that each time it happened, the persons attending the sale had become persuaded of "the inequity and illegality" of the whole proceeding. As Adams pointedly added, once the potential bidders realized the risk to themselves, no one entered a bid. He again emphasized, as he had in 1756, that the commissioners had allegedly admitted their claim against the Adams estate rested on mistaken calculations. That fact, according to Adams, justified his resistance to the whole process. Again donning the mantle of an injured innocent, he proclaimed that he could not understand why the commissioners continued to hound him *"so contrary to their own Apprehension of Justice."* The truth was, Samuel stressed, the commissioners knew he always stood ready to submit the case to arbitration or to the ordinary courts of justice. With a flourish, he asserted, "this I have a Right to contend for as an English Freeholder." He closed with an appeal that made any further action by Sheriff Greenleaf appear both unfair *and* a threat to fundamental rights. "I shall only," he remarked, "beg Leave to caution the Sheriff against taking such Steps as will have a Tendency to weaken the Security of English Property."

To strengthen his position, Adams authored another essay for the press. Following the standard practice of adopting pen names, he signed it "A Freeholder," a signature that invited all landowners to consider how the problems associated with settling the land bank accounts might touch themselves. Observing that the commissioners received compensation for their work, Adams suggested that they kept dragging their feet as a way of milking their lucrative posts. He described how the commissioners' actions might reduce "many good and loyal Subjects" to a pitiable uncertainty "with Respect to our Rights and Estates." Adams implied that that uncertainty hung over anyone associated with the land bank company. Obviously the commissioners were acting "contrary to all Reason, and the Spirit of the common Law, by which British Subjects are secured in the *quiet* Possession of their Property." Having invited all landowners to share his fears about an outrageous attack on property rights, Adams further disparaged the commissioners by asking: "I would be glad to know whether these Commissioners are accountable *in this life* for their Conduct?" Adams's complaints produced tangible results. The commissioners were fired. That pleasing outcome surely helped Adams realize the value of political mudslinging and of emphasizing how political opponents allegedly threatened everyone's basic rights.

But Adams's strong political missives could not stop Sheriff Greenleaf. On August 17, 1758, Greenleaf again announced the upcoming auction of the senior Adams's estate. Adams responded by moving beyond rhetoric. He threatened legal retaliation against anyone who participated in the sale. Probably timing its appearance to achieve maximum deterrence, on August 24, the day before the scheduled public auction at the Exchange Tavern, Samuel had a statement inserted in the newspaper right below Greenleaf's advertisement. Adams maintained that former Sheriff Benjamin Pollard had not tried to force such a sale. Why? Because he and Adams had been advised by a lawyer that the sale would be "illegal and unwarrantable." Realizing his own estate might be endangered if he took illegal action, Pollard, according to Adams, "very prudently" declined to proceed. As for Sheriff Greenleaf, almost menacingly Adams pondered, "how far your

determination may lead you, you know better than I." Lest Greenleaf, or
any potential bidder at the public action, miss the point, Samuel warned, "I
would only beg leave . . . to assure you, that I am advised and determined
to prosecute to the law any person whomsoever who shall trespass upon
that Estate."

Although it is not clear why, the scheduled sale did not occur. In a published notice of September 21, Sheriff Greenleaf announced the
"adjourned" auction was again being postponed until September 29, when
it would be held at the Royal Exchange Tavern from noon to one o'clock.
This time, Adams did not place a counterannouncement in the press, quite
possibly because he took more direct action. Thomas Hutchinson's recol-
lections reveal that somewhere in the process of stopping the sale of his
father's estate, Samuel moved beyond publishing threats. Recounting the
sheriff's efforts to sell the estate, Hutchinson proclaimed that Adams "first
made himself conspicuous on this occasion. He attended the sale, threatened the sheriff to bring action against him, and menaced all who should
attempt to enter upon the estate, under pretense of a purchase; and, by
intimidating both the sheriff and those persons who intended to purchase,
he prevented the sale, [and] kept the estate in his possession."

In the process of thwarting what he considered the land bank commissioners' unwarranted actions, Samuel Adams learned the value of carefully
escalating efforts and of putting opponents on the wrong side of a basic
rights issue. When his offer to adjudicate the matter fell on deaf ears,
Samuel sought legal advice. Once armed with a favorable legal opinion, he
broadcast that opinion in word and print. He maligned his opponents,
depicted the issues as involving basic rights, and invited people to see the
attacks on him as potential future assaults upon themselves. Adams already
understood what in later years he repeatedly declared to be a good maxim:
"to put and keep the enemy in the wrong." When physical intimidation
seemed necessary to prevent what he interpreted as an assault on basic
rights, he accepted the challenge and personally stopped the public auction. Samuel's bold efforts saved the day more than once in the 1750s.
Thus, the land bank controversy, in all its complexity, led Samuel to understand the importance of blending philosophy and action in ongoing political struggles. It also demonstrated the value of using the press to respond
quickly to important developments. Moreover, the continuing threat of
attacks on the family's property served as a constant personal reminder that
Britain's power over the colonies could be exercised in arbitrary and
destructive ways.

If John Adams remembered it accurately, Samuel's fear of British power
had fully matured by 1758 when he tangled with the commissioners and
Sheriff Greenleaf. Samuel's cousin asserted that, based on his own personal
knowledge, he could testify that from 1758 onward, Samuel diligently
sought out and courted the friendship of bright young men with political

talent (including, eventually, John Adams himself). More important, Samuel worked with each man "to cultivate his natural feelings in favor of his native country, to warn him against the hostile designs of Great Britain, and to fix his affections and reflections on the side of his native country." When writing to a friend in 1771, Samuel said that for over a decade the Crown had acted to weaken the Massachusetts House, "the Democratical part of this Government." Samuel had ample reason to stand watch and be ready to sound the alarm if the Parliament, aided by the court party, challenged the rights of the colonists.

Adams did not stand watch alone. As the 1750s unfolded, Samuel, like his father, became an increasingly influential leader of the Boston Caucus, a vital component of the Massachusetts popular party. As it had in the days when Samuel's father helped make it run, the caucus continued to champion the economic and political rights of ordinary citizens. In 1760, members of the caucus claimed their organization had *"from Time immemorial"* zealously defended *"our ancient* Establishments in Church and State." The caucus's opponents offered a different interpretation. In 1763, court party members derisively called the caucus "the Junto," denounced its members for supposedly adopting an antigovernment position, and accused them of pursuing selfish motives.

John Adams, then a country lawyer from Braintree, received a report of how the Boston Caucus worked in early 1763. As he recounted it, the caucus met in a member's home and deliberated in a large, smoke-filled room. Copying the town meeting, the caucus selected a moderator, who ran the meeting. The members then voted for nominees to office, ranging from house representatives and selectmen, to tax assessors and collectors, to wardens and firewards. Having chosen their candidates, the caucus sent committees to meet with the Merchants Club and, if possible, secure its backing for the men and measures the caucus put forward. As its name indicates, the Merchants Club, which by 1763 had been functioning for about fifteen years, considered itself the voice of the merchants. For its part, the caucus perceived itself more as the champion of the mechanics and artisans of the city, the people who manufactured various goods. The image of the caucus as what today might be labeled a political machine sharpens when one considers John's remark that James Cunningham, a glazier and militia captain, told him that he had often been invited to attend the caucus, and "they have assured him Benefit in his Business, &c." According to John, the caucus system worked so well that its members, rather than the town meeting, actually selected Boston's officials.

John Adams's description of the caucus as it functioned in 1763 can be compared to the analysis offered by "E. J.," a newspaper essayist. Although he admitted he now opposed the caucus, this penman claimed he had once been a member of the organization and thus knew how it functioned. According to E. J., the heads of the caucus met weeks before the town meeting and decided on candidates. Their choices got forwarded to a petty caucus, which debated them and settled points. Finally, the grand caucus convened just before the town meeting and formally approved what had already been decided. E. J. derisively pictured the caucus leaders beguiling the ordinary people with meaningless rhetoric about freedom and English liberty. As for those ordinary people, he depicted them as merely hunting for political offices and favors.

Although they voiced decidedly different views on the worth of the caucus, John Adams and E. J. agreed that the caucus of 1763, possibly using a two-tiered system, worked to control the major actions of the town meeting. The few existing minutes of a caucus, which cover a brief period in the early 1770s, confirm that depiction. By 1772, it had three branches, the North, Middle, and South Boston Caucus. Each branch chose nominees, formulated positions on important issues, and then sent representatives to the other caucus branches to reach a consensus on candidates and issues.

As he helped direct the caucus and went about recruiting potential luminaries to defend the people's rights, Samuel Adams cultivated the friendship of ordinary Bostonians. His daughter Hannah remembered him being so admired that he frequently served as an arbitrator when his neighbors became embroiled in disputes. Possessing a good singing voice and a mastery of vocal music, Adams founded singing societies of mechanics. Adams's popularity with common people can also be traced to the caucus's long-established lax approach to collecting taxes. Indeed, while Boston tax collectors were justifiably famous—or notorious—for less-than-vigorous collection of taxes, Samuel was the champion noncollector. In May 1763 a town meeting committee appointed to assess the situation reported that just over £4,000 of the 1761 tax had not yet been collected. Significantly, of the three tax collectors whose 1761 books remained open, Samuel stood responsible for almost £2,200; the other two collectors owed less than £1,000 each. Many Bostonians probably liked the way Samuel went about garnering taxes, and that probably enhanced his popularity. Adams, the caucus, and Boston could not, however, put off a reckoning forever. By the early 1760s, Boston faced a financial crisis that caused the town meeting to search for ways to reduce the colony tax levied against Bostonians, to speed up collection of taxes, and to cut the costs of government. In such a world, Adams's cavalier attitude toward gathering taxes could suddenly look less appealing.

Samuel Adams's lack of diligence extended to his personal finances. His cousin John, who admired Samuel immensely, remarked in late 1765 that Samuel's only real flaw was probably that "he is too attentive to the Public and not enough so, to himself and his family." Samuel received only a minimal income from his tax-collector post and the minor positions he may have held, such as serving as a clerk for land developers. So Samuel had little in the way of material wealth to offer in December 1764 when he married Elizabeth Wells, the twenty-eight-year-old daughter of Francis Wells, a merchant. In fact, by all accounts, Samuel gained a material advantage from the marriage because Elizabeth Wells, like Samuel's first wife, could manage a home effectively and run it on a limited income. In addition, she was an educated woman who came to share Samuel's commitment to politics. Elizabeth's friends might have questioned the wisdom of her marrying Samuel, but Samuel's friends could reasonably judge it a brilliant match for him. If Elizabeth's acquaintances fretted about her prospects for happiness as Mrs. Samuel Adams, events proved their worries unfounded. In July 1766, Abigail Adams, John's wife, noted that Elizabeth and Samuel had visited for a few days, and she found them "a charming pair" who showed "the tenderest affection toward each other."

The Samuel Adams who wed Elizabeth Wells was a man of average height, with a muscular build and light-blue eyes. His cousin John described him as having "engaging Manners." But to an outsider and even to many Bostonians, the Samuel Adams of 1764 probably cut a less-than-impressive figure. This Harvard-educated son of one of Boston's most popular and wealthy politicians had never shown skill as a businessman. He was just getting by financially. And because of his less-than-vigorous way of collecting taxes, by 1764 he faced possible economic ruin. Even his popularity might have been dismissed as a mere reflection of his failure to collect taxes. For all the promise of his birth, for all the advantages given by generous parents, Samuel Adams appeared to represent the failure of promise. Indeed, it would not have been unreasonable to judge Adams as little more than a political hack destined for, at best, an obscure future as a minor Boston politician.

Appearances can, of course, be deceiving. Although the scent of failure hung over him, Samuel Adams was a dedicated and skilled politician. He had long devoted himself to learning what contemporaries would have called the art and mystery of his craft, the craft of being a politician. He had also developed a clear political philosophy fashioned from more than abstract theory; it also grew out of his own experience, especially his struggles in the land bank affair. Adams firmly believed that once the people had a good constitution or constitutions, such as the British constitution and the Massachusetts Charter of 1691, they must jealously guard their constitutional rights. Steady vigilance was required lest the imperial government, quite probably aided by local elites, trample the people's rights. If defending their rights required it, the people must be willing to take decisive action. On the basis of his own experience, Adams distrusted both the British and the aristocrats of the court party. The motives of the Hutchinsons—especially Thomas, who kept accumulating more and more political posts—appeared particularly suspect. Moreover, Adams's unequaled political contacts and activities in the Boston Caucus gave him the potential to assume leadership in any effort to defend the people's rights. No one else, it seems, belonged to as many political clubs as Adams did. No other caucus leader rubbed shoulders with ordinary and poor Bostonians to the extent Samuel did. He had also publicly cast himself as a champion of the those who wore "a *worsted Cap* or a *Leathern Apron*" and of those numbered among the "poorer and weaker" segments of society. His cousin John realized the importance of Samuel's ties to the less powerful members of society. Writing in early 1765, John declared that Samuel understood "the Temper and Character of the People" better than any of Boston's other popular political leaders. Staunch loyalists, including Thomas Hutchinson and Peter Oliver, ruefully came to agree that Samuel was a consummate politician who possessed a special ability to reach those in the middle and lower ranks of society.

While Samuel Adams was transforming his personal life by courting and marrying Elizabeth Wells, the British Empire was also undergoing profound changes. In 1763 the people of the British Empire, Bostonians included, basked in the glory of having finally defeated France and her allies in the titanic Seven Years' War. It began in North America and eventually drew much of Europe into the expanding conflict. Winning the war made Great Britain the most powerful nation on the earth and greatly expanded the boundaries of the empire. It stretched from the Americas to India and now included more than two dozen colonies in the Western Hemisphere alone. Imperial victory did not come cheaply. Despite heavy taxation at home, the British national debt almost doubled during the Seven Years' War. With the British people groaning under an oppressive weight of taxes, the newly installed prime minister, George Grenville, cast his eyes on the Americans as a possible source of income.

As he looked westward, Grenville saw colonies that occupied a well-established economic niche in the empire. Everyone, colonists included, understood that colonies existed for the benefit of the mother country. The mother country had the right, which Britain had long exercised, of regulating the colonial trade for its own benefit. The colonists, who were expected to, and did, buy Britain's manufactured goods, were prohibited from manufacturing or growing products that might compete with Britain's home economy. Of course, the colonists had to prosper too, and the British imperial system offered the colonists many benefits. For example, the British required that the empire's goods be carried in ships built within the empire, and that regulation helped New England develop a profitable shipbuilding industry.

Politically, the colonists, like the inhabitants of the British Isles, were subjects of the British Crown and owed the monarchy unwavering loyalty. In fact, many North American colonists were more directly linked to the monarch than the people who lived in Great Britain. Over the years, Parliament had chipped away at the monarch's powers in the realm while leaving the monarch a freer hand in the colonies. That was especially true of royal colonies, whose governors the monarch appointed. And in 1763, most of Britain's American colonies, including Massachusetts, were royal colonies. In addition to pledging loyalty to the Crown, Americans acknowledged the supremacy of the British Parliament. Only a political fool would have challenged Parliament's right to pass the Navigation Acts that regulated aspects of the colony economy for the benefit of the mother country.

Despite holding a subordinate position within the empire, Britain's North American colonists were, as an English politician later phrased it, England's children, not her bastards. Economically that meant the colonists could engage in any commerce and manufacturing not prohibited by Britain. Politically it meant the colonists were British subjects. In practical terms, it meant that all the colonies had been allowed to develop their own legislatures, which the colonists saw as miniature parliaments. Of course, the colonial legislatures could not enact laws that violated the British constitution or laws, and colonial legislation could be disallowed in Britain. Moreover, in royal colonies such as Massachusetts, the governor appointed by the Crown had an absolute veto over colonial legislation. Although the colonies were seen as subordinate—as political children—none of the limitations placed on them aimed to, nor could they, obscure the fact that the protections of the British constitution covered the colonists as fully as they covered persons living in the realm. English politicians as well as Americans trumpeted and gloried in the fact that, as British subjects, the colonists had "all the rights of Englishmen." But constitutions and phrases like "all the rights of Englishmen" are always open to interpretation. That was especially true of the unwritten British constitution. Because it was built on traditions, laws, and precedents, it served as an open invitation for a family squabble over exactly what rights the colonists did have.

George Grenville and his political advisers understood the status of the colonists in the empire. And despite a surprising dearth of specific knowledge about the American colonies, the Grenville administration also knew that the colonists often evaded Britain's trade laws. Furthermore, the prime minister realized that the colonists had avoided heavy taxes. By the time he became prime minister in April 1763, Grenville had already decided the empire must undergo reform. He immediately ordered more vigorous enforcement of existing trade regulations. Then in March 1764, the prime minister proposed revising colonial trade duties, particularly those based on the colonists' extensive and profitable trade with the French sugar islands of the West Indies. What made this legislation, enacted in April and commonly called the Sugar Act, so significant was the precedent it set. Until that time, trade duties had been used to regulate trade, not to raise revenue. However, the preamble to the Sugar Act openly said its goal was to raise revenue, in effect to tax the colonists. When he introduced the Sugar Act, Grenville indicated that in approximately a year he would propose a stamp act that, modeled on the long-established British Stamp Act, would force colonists to pay an internal tax on most printed materials. Grenville knew many persons considered this direct taxation innovative. To blunt any future criticism, he made a bold offer to the MPs, as members of Parliament were called. Grenville announced that if *any* MP doubted the constitutionality of a colonial stamp act, he would establish a committee to determine its legality. No MP voiced a doubt. In the colonies, however, people like Samuel Adams had a very different response. As Adams saw it, Grenville's program of imperial reform directly challenged the constitutional rights of all American colonists. It must, therefore, be resisted with all the political skill he could muster. When Samuel Adams turned his attention toward defending the people's rights, the image of the failure of promise soon gave way to a recognition that he had a genius for politics and an unshakable commitment to preserving constitutional rights.

2

The People Shall Be Heard

$\mathcal{J}$amuel Adams's standing in the Boston Caucus, and consequently the town meeting, grew in the early 1760s. Each year the town meeting reelected him a tax collector, and he often served on committees that drafted documents for the meeting's consideration. In 1760 he helped fashion instructions for Boston's four members of the Massachusetts House of Representatives. Although addressed to the representatives, the instructions amounted to a political platform that informed the entire colony of the Boston Town Meeting's position on important issues. Because the instructions were reprinted in newspapers throughout the colonies, most Americans and even officials in Britain became privy to the meeting's pronouncements. The 1760 directives urged the House to hire a colonial agent based in London. Reflecting Adams's concern for protecting basic rights, the agent should have "natural Attachments to our Religious as well as Civil Rights." Those instructions helped produce results. In April 1762 the House appointed Jasper Mauduit, a religious dissenter from the Church of England, as the colony's agent in London. In May 1764, reacting to Prime Minister Grenville's tax plans, the town meeting again placed Adams on the instructions committee. He authored the directives, and the town meeting approved them with only minor changes. Those instructions, the first response crafted in America to Grenville's imperial reform program, systematically attacked the logic and constitutionality of Parliament taxing the colonists. As the author of the town's instructions, Adams emerged as a prominent spokesman for the colony's popular party.

Adams opened with a sketch of the citizens' rights and the duty representatives had to protect them. Representatives, he stressed, must constantly support "the invaluable Rights & Privileges of the Province." They had an obligation to safeguard the rights the colonists possessed "as free born Subjects" of Great Britain. Representatives must also remember their obligation to protect the rights set forth in the Massachusetts Charter of 1691.

Adams appealed to Britain's economic self-interest. Asserting that Massachusetts languished in debt because of its patriotic exertions in the late war, he argued that taxing the colony's profitable branches of trade would

19

ruin Boston and consequently injure Britain. Knowing most Englishmen would nod in agreement, Samuel observed that it was the colonies' trade that made them worthwhile to Britain. The commerce of Massachusetts had, he maintained, always been centered in the mother country. By paying cash for manufactured goods, the colonies provided the British with more income than parliamentary taxation might reap. As Adams depicted it, Massachusetts colonists already furnished the mother country with large amounts of revenue and were themselves just scraping along. In fact, if Parliament disrupted the colony's commerce, Bostonians would scarcely be able to earn their bread, much less buy the mother country's manufactured goods.

Adams also challenged Grenville's revenue plan on constitutional grounds. The issue was not money; it was the precedent such a levy would establish. "For if our Trade may be taxed why not our lands? Why not the Produce of our Lands & every thing we possess or make use of?" Adams sliced to the core of the matter by asserting that parliamentary taxation "annihilates our Charter Right to govern & tax Ourselves." By undercutting the powers of the assembly and the colonists' right to manage their own affairs, parliamentary taxation attacked the fundamental rights that citizens held as British subjects and as citizens of Massachusetts. Grenville's unjust policy must, Adams insisted, be reversed. For, "if Taxes are laid upon us in any shape without our having a legal Representation where they are laid, are we not reduced from the Character of free Subjects to the miserable State of tributary Slaves?" This argument clearly *implied* that parliamentary taxation was unconstitutional, but Adams did not use the term. Although he phrased his constitutional challenge gingerly, Adams just as carefully refrained from speaking of a subordination to Parliament. He merely acknowledged a dependence on, and subordination to, Great Britain. By doing that, Adams could later argue that an act of Parliament was unconstitutional and not be inconsistent.

To keep his challenge to Parliament's power from being labeled disloyal radicalism, Adams informed the representatives that they should have their agent reemphasize Boston's unshaken loyalty and unrivaled exertions in support of the king's government. Through a clever linkage of protecting the Crown's prerogatives and protecting the people's freedoms, he spoke of how the Massachusetts representatives had championed the king's rights in the colony. The British could also, Adams asserted, count on the Massachusetts merchants to follow "all just & necessary Regulation of Trade." Such properly deferential comments did not negate Adams's assertion that *any* parliamentary taxation of the colonists violated their liberties and was therefore unjust.

Adams also skillfully emphasized other fundamental rights. He observed that the people always had "the constitutional Right of expressing their mind & giving fresh Instructions" to their representatives. But Massachusetts could not instruct its MPs because, like the other colonies, it did not directly elect members of Parliament. Adams's words also implied that the colonists could never effectively be represented in Parliament. How could the citizens offer fresh instructions to representatives meeting an ocean away?

As future events demonstrated, Adams showed real foresight by also commenting on the issue of compensating judges. Although the British monarch appointed the colony's judges, the Massachusetts Charter made the colonial assembly responsible for paying them. By stressing that the judges depended on "the free Grants of the General Assembly" for their salaries, Adams underscored a cardinal tenet of the British constitution: taxes were voluntary gifts authorized by representatives elected by the people. Taxes levied by Parliament, where the colonists were not represented, could not meet that constitutional test. Adams's reference to judicial compensation also silently, but forcefully, underscored an important political reality: the Massachusetts legislature had, over the years, used its control over judges' salaries to keep the judiciary focused on the colony's, not the Crown's, interests. Adams's discussion thus touched on basic constitutional rights and also reminded the representatives of the need to retain their power of the purse.

The directives also offered a plan of action. After pressing the colony's legislators to show Parliament the folly of its plans for the colonies, Adams suggested that Massachusetts work toward formulating a unified colonial stance. A united approach made sense, Adams suggested, because Britain's new colonial initiatives threatened all Americans. If the other colonies joined Massachusetts in resisting, "by the united Applications of all who are aggrieved, All may happily obtain Redress."

When the Boston Town Meeting approved the Adams instructions on May 24, 1764, it became the first political body in America to go on record stating that Parliament could not constitutionally tax the colonists. The directives also contained the first official recommendation that the colonies present a unified defense of their rights. Even with the acknowledgment of subordination to Great Britain, Adams had staked out the colonists' bedrock political position: any form of taxation without representation was unjust.

The instructions Adams drafted helped link him with James Otis Jr., one of Boston's four members of the House of Representatives. Otis had become famous in 1761 when he opposed writs of assistance—general search warrants that allowed officials great latitude in searching for smuggled goods. Otis argued that writs of assistance violated "the fundamental principles of law." And, because "an act against the constitution is void," the writs were unconstitutional. His arguments did not sway a Hutchinson-dominated court, but they propelled Otis into the House and made him the acknowledged leader of Massachusetts's defenders of American liberties. In response to the Adams instructions of 1764, the House of Representatives approved a memorial, written by Otis, that was forwarded to Jasper Mauduit, the colony's agent. The House also sent Mauduit a copy of Otis's pamphlet *The Rights of the British Colonies Asserted and Proved,* which had been published in July and included an appendix containing the Boston Town Meeting instructions Adams had crafted. Within a year, Otis and Adams worked together so closely that members of the court party referred to them as a unit. Since Otis and Adams were considered a team, it is important to understand how their ideas and relationship developed.

In both his *Rights* pamphlet and the House Memorial, Otis took a bolder stance than Adams had in his town meeting instructions. Although he stressed the kinds of economic arguments Adams advanced, Otis pushed them harder and further. He warned the imperial authorities that the colonies might start smuggling on a wide scale and engage in the commercial production of wool if Parliament's offensive acts remained in place. Since smuggling was illegal and since Britain had decreed that colonists could not produce wool for export, Otis's threats infuriated British authorities. Adams, on the other hand, displayed a lighter, more skillful political touch. He merely suggested that parliamentary taxation would, by impoverishing the colonists, render them unable to buy Britain's manufactured goods. And he made it sound as if he rued the possibility. Thus Adams's appeals to British self-interest were less offensive and, as events proved, more likely to obtain revisions in British policies.

On the issue of political rights, Otis was again more inflammatory than Adams. He opened *The Rights* with a summary of what the philosopher John Locke had said about the conditions under which a people might legitimately rebel against their government. Otis did not, however, link Locke's analysis with the colonies' situation. Like Adams, Otis drew upon the Massachusetts Charter and the British constitution, but he also emphasized natural rights as he argued that the power of Parliament was limited. Parliament could not, for example, justifiably tax the colonists, since the colonists were not represented in Parliament. Otis, speaking as the voice of the Massachusetts House, bluntly held that acts of Parliament that went against "natural equity" or the fundamental principles of the British constitution "are void." Otis's bold, some would say reckless, pronouncements lost their potency when he tried to reconcile them with his acceptance of Parliament's supremacy. In fact, Otis maintained that the colonists could do nothing about Parliament's unconstitutional legislation. So while they might be justified in refusing to pay the taxes, the colonists "must and ought to yield obedience to an act of Parliament . . . till repealed." Although Adams's language was less likely to raise hackles, he actually took a stronger constitutional stance against Parliament. Adams could not be challenged, as Otis came to be, for conceding too much to claims of parliamentary supremacy.

The differences between the approaches of Otis and Adams illustrate why John Adams observed that Samuel was "always for Softness and Delicacy, and Prudence where they will do." John added the vital qualification that, while Samuel artfully employed a soft approach when possible, he was "starch and stiff and strict and rigid and inflexible" in the cause of protecting American rights. Thomas Hutchinson, who thought that Samuel Adams sought colonial independence from the beginning, offered a similar analysis. He claimed that Adams's public pronouncements were based on what he thought would help achieve independence. Thus Adams might sound moderate in public, but he was at heart a devious radical. The archloyalist Peter Oliver concurred and added a twist of nastiness. Samuel Adams was, Oliver thought, "a *Machiavilian*" who "was all serpentine Cunning."

Whether they praised or damned him, public figures from opposite ends of the political spectrum agreed on Samuel Adams's importance both as a political writer and as an ardent defender of American rights. Commenting approximately a year after Samuel composed the town meeting instructions of 1764, John Adams praised Samuel's "artful Pen." John added that none of Boston's defenders of America possessed Samuel's "thorough Understanding of Liberty"; none of them could match his "habitual, radical Love" of liberty. Discussing the same 1764–65 period, Hutchinson, the ultimate loyalist, declared that Samuel "had for several years been an active man in the town of Boston, always on the side of liberty" and had authored many of the publications championing colonial liberties. Hutchinson added a measured assessment. He described Samuel's earliest political writings as the work of an indifferent scribbler. But with grudging admiration, Hutchinson noted that practice had subsequently allowed Adams "to arrive at great perfection." He had, alas, acquired "a talent of artfully and fallaciously insinuating into the minds of his readers a prejudice against the characters . . . he attacked, beyond any other man I ever knew."

Adams labored hard to produce effective political writing. He was famous for working well into the night in his second-floor study. Joseph Pierce, whose business took him by the Adams house in the early morning hours, remarked that he usually observed light in Samuel's study. That indicated to Pierce that Samuel "was hard at work writing against the Tories." (This British term referred to those who favored the royal authority of the monarch; those who championed parliamentary authority were labeled Whigs. In the American colonies, "Tory" came to mean those who supported British authority while "Whig" signified those who championed the rights of the Americans.) As he wrote into the night, Samuel perfected a technique he had utilized in the lengthy land bank controversy. He put his political opponents on the defensive and hammered them. In modern parlance, as a political writer, Adams believed the best defense was a good offense. Equally important, both John Adams, the Whig and future rebel, and Hutchinson, the future loyalist, concurred: Samuel Adams was unwaveringly committed to safeguarding American liberty. They did not, they could not, say the same about Otis.

Despite their philosophical differences, James Otis and Samuel Adams both wanted to protect American rights, and they harmonized on many points. They certainly agreed that the colonies should work in unison to safeguard their interests. It was Otis who influenced the Massachusetts House to implement Adams's call for crafting "united Applications" from all the colonies so they "All may happily obtain Redress." The House agreeably informed the other colonial governments of its activities, including its efforts to get the Sugar Act repealed and to thwart passage of a stamp act. The representatives invited the other colonial assemblies to take similar action.

Merchants in Boston and elsewhere in the colonies added economic measures to the growing political resistance. In August 1764, fifty Boston merchants pledged to quit buying some British luxuries. And, following the lead of New Yorkers, groups in various areas, including Boston, promoted colonial manufacturing, especially the production of cloth. In these tentative and small-scale ways, people worked to undermine British support for Grenville's policy.

In June 1765, after receiving word Parliament had actually passed a colonial stamp act scheduled to take effect on November 1, the Massachusetts representatives, under Otis's leadership, carried Adams's call for unified colonial action to new heights. The House issued a circular letter inviting the other colonies to send delegations to a congress that would meet in New York City in October. Reflecting the tone of Adams's earlier instructions, the invitation said the congress would strive to produce "a general and united, dutiful, loyal and humble Representation of their Condition."

At the same time the House proposed an all-colony congress, the Virginia House of Burgesses, led by Patrick Henry, approved resolutions that advanced arguments resembling those Adams had fashioned a year earlier. The burgesses declared that the rights of Englishmen guaranteed in Virginia's royal charters stipulated that Virginians could only be taxed by legislators they elected. An additional resolution the burgesses adopted but quickly rescinded was also widely reported in newspapers. That resolve declared that the colonists were not bound to accept any tax unless it was levied by their representatives. Because it implied that colonists should disregard a law passed by Parliament, the statement flirted with treason.

The constitutional arguments advanced in the colonial petitions mattered. As Adams continually stressed, if Americans acquiesced in even one of Parliament's taxes, they would give the MPs a precedent to tax *any* of the colonists' possessions. In building their case against taxation, colonial assemblies often argued, as Adams did, that the restrictions on colonial trade would undermine Great Britain's economic welfare. However, although they staked out bold positions, by limiting themselves to petitioning, the colonial assemblymen advocated passive resistance. The legislators seemed to believe Parliament would eventually realize that its new colonial program harmed Britain's overall economic situation. Of course, one could hardly have expected more. The colonial assemblymen were in many instances fundamentally conservative planters and merchants, and they had been brought up in a political world steeped in the principle of petitioning for redress. Regular, orderly, and legal methods must, they believed, be followed. Adams shared that view and in the summer of 1765 supported the tactic of passive resistance. Although Adams and the colonial legislators did not exert immediate, intense pressure on Parliament to rescind the Stamp Act, others did.

By mid-1765, colonial merchants contemplated waging economic warfare by boycotting British goods until Parliament repealed its taxes. This approach would also foster an increase in colonial manufacturing, another form of economic coercion. Based on his belief that trade made the colonies valuable to Britain and also on the fact that a boycott was legal, Adams approved this course of action. Well-organized economic resistance could, he reasoned, turn prophecies about the Stamp Act producing economic hardships for Britain into reality. If British merchants and manufacturers could be enlisted against the Stamp Act, that would pressure Parliament to change its policy. But the boycott strategy, even if successful, would take time, and it could not stop the Stamp Act from taking effect.

Many Bostonians and radicals elsewhere wanted more active resistance. They took to the streets to neutralize the Stamp Act before it could be implemented. The first colonial crowd action against the Stamp Act occurred in Boston on August 14, 1765, and it targeted Andrew Oliver, the stamp distributor for Massachusetts, who was also the secretary of the colony. The plan originated with the Loyal Nine, middle-class Bostonians who came primarily from the artisan and shopkeeper ranks and who formed the nucleus of what became the city's Sons of Liberty. Although the Loyal Nine considered Adams a friend, he was not a member of the group, nor is there any clear evidence he worked directly with them in their August 14 ventures. Having first arranged for usually antagonistic working-class groups from the city's northern and southern sections to unite against the Stamp Act, the Loyal Nine fashioned effigies, potent symbols often used when people took to the streets. When daylight came on that Wednesday, it revealed an effigy of Oliver along with one of the devil peeping out of a boot. The effigies dangled from the Liberty Tree, a large old elm located in South End near the Boston Common and about one-half mile from Faneuil Hall, which became a staging area for anti-British activities. The effigy of Oliver carried the verse "A goodlier sight who e'er did see? / A Stamp-Man hanging on a tree!" Thousands viewed the display.

Throughout the day members of the Northside group, led by Henry Swift, stood guard so the effigies could not be removed. In the evening, a large crowd, headed by Ebenezer Mackintosh of the Southside group, took charge and paraded the effigies through the city. The crowd, which at times perhaps numbered three thousand, came upon the small building that reportedly would serve as Oliver's stamp distribution office. The crowd demolished it. The throng then marched in an orderly fashion to Fort Hill for a celebration, which included beheading the Oliver effigy and burning all the effigies. Boards ripped from Oliver's stamp distribution building fueled the fire. The Loyal Nine soon left the celebration. After they departed, members of the crowd, apparently under no one's direction, traveled the short distance to Oliver's home and attempted to burn his coach. In the process, they destroyed garden furniture, smashed windows, and consumed some of Oliver's wine. However, nothing was stolen.

Andrew Oliver resigned his stamp distributorship the next day. His resignation satisfied the Loyal Nine; they saw no reason for further crowd action. Nevertheless, on August 26, crowds, not led by the Loyal Nine or other middle-class persons, sought out a variety of targets, including three men associated with enforcing Britain's customs regulations. As the evening deepened, a large crowd, by all accounts made up primarily of members of the lower orders, sought out the main target: Thomas Hutchinson, the colony's wealthy lieutenant governor. He evaded those he labeled "the Ruffians" by fleeing to a neighbor's home. But Hutchinson's mansion and possessions could not run. The crowd spent most of the night and early morning ransacking and then demolishing large sections of the house. As Hutchinson recounted the event, when "the hellish crew" finished at about four in the morning, nothing remained of his house "but the bare walls and floors." Members of the crowd also stole many valuable items. That is significant. Traditionally, British and American crowds might purloin food from hoarding merchants, but they did not make off with personal property such as money or clothing. The theft of personal property and the lower-class character of the crowd suggests Hutchinson was targeted in part because he was a rich aristocrat. Governor Bernard thought so. Reflecting on the events of August 26, he voiced the fear that Boston would soon experience a war waged for the purpose of "taking away the Distinction of rich and poor."

The crowd actions of August as well as Boston's other Revolutionary crowd actions have been attributed to Samuel Adams. He has inaccurately been depicted as the man, the propagandist, the dictator who controlled "the Boston mob." That interpretation originated with Governor Bernard and loyalists, who, in addition to hating Adams, assumed ordinary people could not act for their own logical reasons. Loyalists reasoned that since Adams was closely associated with the lower orders and since the lower orders must have been manipulated to act, Adams must have been the puppeteer. Bernard talked of Boston's trained mob. Hutchinson sneered that the "mob . . . might be let loose, or kept up" depending on what its "keepers," the leaders of "the liberty party," wanted. Loyalist Peter Oliver, the stamp distributor's wealthy brother, put it more emphatically. In 1781, referring to his fellow Americans and the coming of the Revolution, he asserted: "As for the People in general, they were like the Mobility of all Countries, perfect Machines, wound up by any Hand who first might take the Winch." Oliver considered Adams particularly good at cranking the winch. His "power over weak Minds was truly surprizing"; Adams could "turn the minds of the great Vulgar" to whatever course he chose. Hutchinson and Oliver could not see that ordinary people might have their own reasons for taking action. Unfortunately that myopic view was perpetuated by many latter-day scholars who repeated the partisan claims that people joined crowds because they were manipulated by propaganda and by Samuel Adams.

Ordinary colonists did not need to be goaded into opposing British policies. Dire circumstances and their own sense of justice animated them. Many Bostonians, and others throughout the colonies, could not passively wait for Parliament to change its mind about taxing the colonists. Boston was already facing hard times, and British imperial reform exacerbated the city's difficulties. The close of the Seven Years' War in 1763 ended what one historian has accurately called Boston's artificial wartime prosperity. And while all major American cities suffered from a postwar recession, Boston hurt the most. In 1764, smallpox ravaged the city. In January 1765, in the midst of a bitterly cold winter, several leading business firms failed. John Rowe, a wealthy merchant, observed that the repeated bankruptcies caused a general consternation. Businessmen moaned about bad times and dull trade. In June a Bostonian maintained that the West Indies trade had plummeted 80 percent within the past year and that a person rarely saw cash circulating in Boston. He blamed these developments on the Sugar Act.

All this happened at a time when the city's government, the town meeting, teetered on the brink of bankruptcy. Samuel Adams's tax-collecting woes offer a useful illustration of the problems Bostonians faced. A town meeting report of May 1765 revealed that five tax collectors had not yet gathered back taxes totaling slightly more than £18,000. Adams, who perhaps not coincidentally had declined another term as a tax collector in March 1765, accounted for just over £8,000 of that deficit. By July 1765, under increasing pressure to obtain these back taxes, Adams abandoned his easygoing ways. In an effort to collect unpaid taxes, some on his books since 1759, Adams sued delinquent taxpayers, including two shoemakers, two carpenters, and "Jack a free Negro."

In such difficult times, people who had little or no economic reserve stared poverty in the face. Ordinary Bostonians, therefore, had special reason for wanting to abolish or at least neutralize the Stamp Act. That was doubly true for the city's seafarers, who confronted the additional threat of literally losing their liberty by being impressed into the British navy. It was the common people who most knew and hated the British press gangs. It was the commonality who could not afford to wait for passive measures—petitions and possible economic boycotts—to overturn Parliament's new taxing laws. Ordinary people, on whom rich aristocrats often heaped contempt, had to work or starve. They reasoned that, if they could stop the implementation of the Stamp Act, they could continue to work, to survive. These people did not have to be controlled by Samuel Adams or anyone else. They did not have to be propagandized. They had their own good reasons for taking immediate and aggressive action, for transforming the Adams-Otis rhetoric into political action.

Samuel Adams applauded the accomplishments of Boston's first anti–Stamp Act crowd. He proclaimed that August 14, 1764, should be remembered forever in America. It was the day "the People shouted; and their shout was heard to the distant end of this Continent." Adams and other Whig leaders, however, had no hand in the crowd actions of August 26, and Adams was horrified by their "truly *mobbish* Nature," which included stealing money. Boston's noted defenders of American liberties, Adams among them, thus treated the two major August crowd actions very differently. The town meeting ignored the events of August 14 but responded to the August 26 assaults by holding an emergency meeting the next day. After expressing its revulsion at the extraordinary and violent activities, the meeting urged the city's officials and citizens to do their utmost to prevent recurrences. The vote was unanimous. The *Boston Gazette,* the most radical newspaper in the colony, expressed the sharp distinctions that persons like the Loyal Nine and Adams made between what happened on the fourteenth and the twenty-sixth of August. The publishers, one a member of the Loyal Nine, claimed that virtually all Bostonians wore smiles after the events of August 14. The violence that occurred a dozen days later evoked gloom. Leading Whigs, including Adams, certainly tried to distance themselves and their city from the outrages of August 26. Although they knew Mackintosh had participated in the attack on Hutchinson's home, the leaders put out the story that "vagabond strangers," not Bostonians, perpetrated the outrage.

Adams and other popular leaders distinguished between the two August crowd actions for both philosophical and practical reasons. They believed, first of all, in the rule of law. As Adams explained later in 1765, "when our sacred rights are infringed, we feel the grievance, but we understand the nature of our happy constitution too well, and entertain too high an opinion of virtue and justice . . . to encourage any means of redressing it, but what are justifiable by the constitution." And while he heaped contempt on the *"mobbish"* events of August 26, Adams offered a revealing defense of the earlier crowd actions. Writing to an Englishman, he recounted the events of August 14 and maintained that Americans believed the Stamp Act endangered their essential, unalienable rights. He then speculated on what the English might do in the same situation. "After taking all *legal*

Steps to obtain redress *to no Purpose,* the *whole People of England* would have taken the same Steps [the Bostonians took] & *justified themselves."* Adams did not have to add that the process he described met the standard set by John Locke for how an aggrieved people might justly respond to perceived tyranny. But neither Adams nor anyone else who followed Locke would sanction the August 26 violence. All legal means of redress had not been exhausted; the August 26 crowd's violent actions smacked of class warfare.

Practical considerations also made "truly *mobbish"* crowds unacceptable. Adams wanted to travel the constitutional high road, and he hoped to elicit British sympathy for the supposedly beleaguered and debt-ridden colonists. The attacks on private property, especially the wholesale destruction and looting of property belonging to royal officials, would outrage British politicians. Their anger would in turn stiffen opposition to repealing Parliament's noxious laws. Thus, for pragmatic as well as philosophical reasons, Adams and other leaders of the popular party strove to ensure that nothing resembling the crowd actions of August 26 would occur again. They succeeded, but not because they controlled the crowd or bribed crowd leaders, as some have thought. They succeeded because the lower classes themselves saw where their interests merged with those of the middle and upper classes in defending American liberties. Moreover, the success of collective action in Boston and elsewhere reduced the need for yet more crowd actions.

The leaders of the popular movement in Massachusetts, and in other colonies as well, clearly did not head a unified group. Supporters of the popular colonial position agreed on the ends: parliamentary taxation must be resisted. They did not necessarily agree on the means. Adams and his fellow Whig leaders of the popular party, like their counterparts in other colonies, wanted to pursue only legal, constitutional avenues of opposition. They had ready answers to basic questions about methods. Should one petition for redress of grievances? Of course. Support persons bringing economic pressure to bear by boycotting British goods and by increasing colonial manufacturing? Excellent. Should one organize—or at least applaud—large nonviolent demonstrations, particularly those involving symbolic acts such as hanging stamp distributors in effigy? Yes. The leaders could argue that these activities proved that the commonality, not just elected officials, opposed Parliament's schemes. Moreover, leading Whigs realized that some crowd actions achieved desirable results. If they prevented the Stamp Act from taking effect, that might make it easier to get the act repealed. On the other hand, violent outbursts tinged with hints of class warfare—what happened in Boston on August 26—must be squelched.

The popular forces soon had reason to hope the Stamp Act would disappear. On September 9, Bostonians received the news that the Grenville administration had been replaced in July. Better yet, General Henry Seymour

Conway, one of the few MPs who vigorously opposed the Stamp Act, had become secretary of state for the Southern Department in the new ministry. Conway now had the principal administrative responsibility for the colonies. Apparently at Adams's urging, the town meeting acted quickly to take advantage of the change in administrations. On September 18, the meeting selected a committee that included Adams and whose recommendations he wrote. The committee was to contact General Conway and Colonel Isaac Barré, another MP who had denounced the Stamp Act. Barré had electrified Parliament by calling the Americans "Sons of Liberty" and by describing them as a people jealous of their liberties. Americans would, Barré predicted, vindicate their rights if they were ever violated. The recommendations Adams produced called for sending Conway and Barré formal addresses thanking each for his noble speech defending the colonies' rights. In addition, copies of these speeches should be obtained and placed "among our most precious Archives." And, as soon as possible, paintings of the two great men should be acquired and placed in Faneuil Hall "as a standing Monument to all Posterity, of the Virtue and Justice of our Benefactors, and a lasting Proof of our Gratitude." Ever the thinking politician, Adams understood the value of cultivating allies, and here he worked the art of political flattery with impressive thoroughness.

With allies across the Atlantic, Adams increased the pressure. When he again prepared the town meeting's instructions for its representatives, which were approved on September 18, 1765, Adams reiterated the basic themes of the May 1764 instructions, but with less delicacy. He now flatly declared the Stamp Act "unconstitutional." Only representatives chosen by the people could levy taxes, and "it is certain that we were in no Sense represented in the Parliament . . . when this Act of Taxation was made." Adams proclaimed that the representatives should not join in any public measures that countenanced or assisted in executing the Stamp Act. Certainly no tax funds should help put the Stamp Act into operation. By inviting the representatives to find a way to subvert an act of Parliament, Adams danced close to the line separating legal protest from treason. But his position likely pleased the bulk of the Bostonians who had joined in the recent crowd actions.

It turned out—and given how the Boston Caucus operated, Samuel may have known it—that Adams was crafting his own instructions. The death of Oxenbridge Thatcher had opened a seat in the Massachusetts House, and on September 27 the Boston Town Meeting selected Adams as one of its four representatives. Wasting no time, Adams was sworn in that day. This election, obviously a personal milestone for Adams, signaled a change in leadership for Massachusetts and, in time, for the colonies as a whole. James Otis Jr. and Adams were soon working together so closely that court party leaders often mentioned them in the same breath. But, as their 1764 writings indicated, the two men had important philosophical as well as personality differences that, over time, would cause the breakup of their partnership. Otis, a magnificent and fiery orator, could be disturbingly inconsistent on the issue of whether or not Parliament could constitutionally tax the colonies. In 1765 Otis escaped being branded as a turncoat only because he published items anonymously. By 1766 he seemed to have flip-flopped once more as he argued that America's rights were being trampled. Adams, who was no orator, balanced Otis's fire with a noted reserve. Adams also possessed a deft political sense Otis lacked. Most important, Adams never wavered in his defense of colonial rights, and his presence in the House made the representatives much less likely to defer to court party elites. Once Adams entered the House, it never again compromised with the Council as it had under Otis's leadership in late 1764 when drafting a petition against parliamentary taxation. Thomas Hutchinson, who had embarrassed Otis and the House by his skillful maneuvering to water down that petition, witnessed the profound change. Ruefully noting that the "liberty party" had made a "great advance" during Samuel Adams's first session in the House, Hutchinson attributed that movement to Adams's "influence." Governor Bernard also recognized and lamented the difference Adams made. Bernard complained that, after Adams entered the House in 1765, its addresses to him had "the Air of a Manifesto."

Adams demonstrated his influence quickly. It was evident in the way the House responded to the governor's September 25 address on the opening of the legislative session. While saying he disliked the Stamp Act, Governor Bernard defended Parliament's right to pass it. Then, alluding to the August crowd actions, he rebuked Boston for being a lawless city where the people supported mobs. Two days later, on the day Adams assumed his seat, Bernard recessed the House until October 23 on the pretense that many members had not yet reached Boston. Shutting the House down for a month proved a mistake. It gave the popular party extra time to craft an effective response. Because Otis spent much of October attending the Stamp Act Congress in New York, the task of formulating a response fell mainly on Adams. From that time forward, Adams became the principal author of the House replies, petitions, and circular letters. And, as both friend and foe attested, impressive political prose flowed from his pen. Even when others drafted documents, Adams was routinely called upon to add his own editorial flourish.

The response to the governor's address, issued when the House reconvened on October 23, mocked Bernard by reminding him that he had fled the city when the August 26 crowd actions erupted. Far from being lawless, when Bernard's flight left them to their own devices, Bostonians had "raised a spirit" among all classes that prevented any further violence. Indeed, Bostonians endeavored to use only "legal and regular" methods to defend their liberties. This helped demonstrate, as Adams put it, that Bostonians were "a people ever remarkable for their loyalty and good order;

though at present uneasy and discontented." The problem was, of course, the Stamp Act. That pernicious legislation violated both the Massachusetts Charter and the basic rights of Englishmen.

Embracing positions advanced in other colonies, Adams underscored two additional points. First, the colonists were not represented in Parliament, and, moreover, such representation would be "impracticable." Although Adams did not elaborate, the clear implication was that, since the colonists could not be represented in Parliament, they could *never* be taxed by Parliament. The second point flowed from the fact that colonists accused of violating the Stamp Act could be hauled into vice-admiralty courts, which did not use the jury system. Invoking England's most sacred guarantee of liberties, Adams contended that adjudicating these cases without a jury violated Magna Carta. Pushing even harder, Adams warned that if the king's Massachusetts subjects were not governed "according to the known stated rules of the constitution," they might, horror of horrors, "become disaffected." So, if any thoughts of independence eventually crept into American minds, the blame would rest solely on British politicians who had acted unconstitutionally. Once again Adams was putting his opponents in the wrong.

Illustrating the kind of cross-colony fertilization that occurred time and again as the resistance movement progressed, the arguments Adams employed matched well with positions the Stamp Act Congress enunciated in late October. In a statement of essential principles, the congress trumpeted the colonists' loyalty to the Crown and acknowledged "all due Subordination" to Parliament. However, the delegates held that the colonists possessed all the rights of Englishmen, which included being taxed only by their own representatives. Since Americans were not, and from their local circumstances could not be, represented in the House of Commons, Parliament could not tax them. Moreover, extending the powers of the vice-admiralty courts violated the people's "inherent and invaluable Right" to trial by jury. Just as Adams had done, the Congress warned that restrictions on colonial trade would inhibit American purchases of British manufactured goods. Thus for both constitutional and pragmatic reasons, Parliament should repeal the Stamp Act and other recent laws restricting American commerce.

Shortly after the Stamp Act Congress adjourned, the Massachusetts House prepared a similar statement. The House approved fourteen resolves that, as Hutchinson indicated, Samuel Adams composed. Although the resolves generally covered the same ground the Stamp Act Congress traversed, on two substantive issues Adams was more radical. While the Stamp Act Congress explicitly admitted Parliament's supremacy, Adams merely stated that Massachusetts had the greatest veneration for Parliament. Hutchinson noted the difference, which he found both galling and alarming. The failure to acknowledge the supremacy of Parliament did not hap-

pen accidentally. The instructions Adams crafted in May 1764 had not mentioned Parliament's supremacy. Adams also outdistanced the Stamp Act
Congress by asserting that "certain essential rights" were "founded in the
law of God and nature, and are the common rights of mankind." Well ahead
of many other popular leaders, Adams here enunciated the proposition that
the colonists' rights rested on more than the colonial charters and the
British constitution.

Having done what he could with official political pronouncements,
Adams joined other prominent Boston Whigs as they worked with the
Loyal Nine and with established crowd leaders to keep opposition to the
Stamp Act within legal bounds. By the fall of 1765, the members of the
Loyal Nine had dramatically expanded their membership and, along with
popular leaders in other colonies, embraced the name Sons of Liberty. In
an effort to ensure that nothing untoward happened in future crowd
actions, popular party leaders and the Sons of Liberty worked closely with
Ebenezer Mackintosh, the leader of the South Boston crowd, and with
Henry Swift, the leader of the Northsiders. On November 1, as church
bells pealed, normal business ground to a halt, and anti–Stamp Act effigies
were hung on the Liberty Tree. At two o'clock, the figures were cut down,
carried through the streets to the public gallows, strung up, taken down, and
then ripped apart and cast to the winds. A crowd of about three thousand,
accompanied by columns of men on horseback led by Mackintosh, witnessed the spectacle. This huge, orderly crowd included many inhabitants
from the surrounding countryside. Crowd actions, and the threat of them,
worked in Boston and throughout America. All the stamp distributors in
the mainland colonies resigned their posts or promised not to distribute
stamps. So, on November 1, 1765, when the Stamp Act officially went into
effect, no one implemented it. Since no stamps were available, colonists
could argue for carrying on business as usual, except of course for any boycotts against British goods.

The events of November 5, "Pope's Day," a day noted for anti-Catholic
crowd activities and violence, also pleased Adams and other popular-party
leaders. The Northside and Southside groups skipped their usual end-of-
the-day combat. Instead, Mackintosh and Swift, resplendently attired in
uniforms and carrying speaking trumpets supplied by the Sons of Liberty,
led their effigy-carrying forces in a united protest against the Stamp Act.
Under the leadership of Mackintosh and Swift, the normally antagonistic
North and South Boston factions first met in King Street and then
marched harmoniously to the Liberty Tree and then to Copp's Hill, where
they jointly burned their effigies. Even Hutchinson had to admit that the
demonstration seemed remarkable for the peaceful, orderly behavior of
those who paraded through the streets. Adams and other proponents of
peaceful protest had succeeded, at least for now, because the members of
the crowd were not inherently prone to violence and because they shared

the goal of defeating Parliament's new colonial policy.

The money needed to supply Mackintosh and Swift with impressive uniforms and speaking trumpets came in part from the pockets of John Hancock, a young merchant who had inherited between £70,000 and £100,000 in late 1764. From that time forward, Adams befriended Hancock and assiduously drew him into anti-British activity. As Adams put it, he wanted to make the young man's fortune work for the benefit of Boston.

The economic war against Britain also intensified in the fall of 1765. New York City merchants led the way. On October 31, 200 of them pledged to stop buying British merchandise until Parliament repealed the Stamp Act. Within a week, Philadelphia merchants followed suit. Boston did not produce a formal agreement until December 9, but 250 merchants and traders signed it. Nonimportation might help force the British to retreat, but the program raised the specter of crowd violence since it meant less shipping, and less shipping meant less work. It would take time for that potentially explosive mix to develop because many Boston merchants planned ahead. They obtained shipping papers before November 1 for vessels not scheduled to leave port for weeks. But by early December, as the supply of prepurchased shipping papers dwindled, merchants and the lower orders clamored for relief. The popular forces, the Whigs, needed to find a way to do what the crowds in Boston and other colonial cities advocated: carry on business as if the Stamp Act did not exist.

Boston's leading Whigs began pursuing that goal shortly after the city's merchants formally embraced nonimportation. On December 17, in the presence of a large crowd gathered at the Liberty Tree, Andrew Oliver reiterated his earlier abdication of the post of stamp distributor. He was compelled to swear on his oath, before a justice of the peace, that he had not ever functioned as a stamp distributor and would never attempt to do so. The Sons of Liberty, who arranged all this, obviously worked to give the proceedings a legal cast. Later that afternoon, the customhouse reopened and began conducting business without stamped papers. Except as limited by the nonimportation effort, commerce could proceed as usual. That evening, the Sons of Liberty, with Samuel Adams as one of their invited guests, celebrated this achievement. Sailors, dockworkers, and others who depended on shipping for their livelihoods had even more reason to rejoice.

Having reduced the threat of crowd action by ensuring that shipping could move without stamped papers, popular leaders turned their attention to reopening the civil courts, which had also shut down owing to the unavailability of stamped paper. On December 18, the Boston Town Meeting unanimously selected a committee headed by Samuel Adams to present a memorial to the governor and his Council. Wrapping itself in a law-and-order cloak, the meeting bemoaned the closing of the civil courts because they could not obtain stamped paper. With studied disingenuousness, the

Bostonians said they could find no just and legal reason for the closures. Proclaiming that "the Law is the great rule of Right, the Security of our Lives and Propertys, and the best Birth right of Englishmen," they called upon Governor Bernard to reopen the civil courts. Adams, continuing his practice of promoting the careers of talented young supporters of America, saw to it that cousin John was one of the lawyers selected to argue Boston's case before Bernard and his Council. His Braintree resolutions in defense of American liberties had already enhanced John's reputation, and Samuel wanted him to become active in Boston.

Everyone knew that the reason the civil courts lacked stamped paper was that crowd violence and the threat of yet more violence had kept the Stamp Act from being implemented. So Bernard and his Council, headed by Hutchinson, considered the Boston memorial hypocritical nonsense. Still, they agreed that the civil courts must function. To avoid responsibility for violating the Stamp Act, Bernard and his councilors finessed the situation. Their response, produced on December 21 and considered by the town meeting the same day, called the question of reopening the courts a legal one. Accordingly, the judges must decide if their courts could operate without stamped paper. By unanimous vote, the town meeting proclaimed this an unsatisfactory answer. Although the popular party and the court party continued skirmishing over the issue, the minor courts quickly resumed operations, and by the spring of 1766 all of the courts in Massachusetts functioned without stamped papers. Massachusetts had eviscerated the Stamp Act.

The story varied slightly from colony to colony, but the results duplicated what happened in Massachusetts: the Stamp Act was effectively nullified. One aspect of the general colonial effort is especially important for illustrating Samuel Adams's ongoing efforts to achieve a unified defense of American rights. Sons of Liberty in various colonies, not just in Massachusetts, helped spearhead anti–Stamp Act activities in 1765 and 1766. To coordinate their efforts, they established committees to correspond with one another. Samuel urged that the network of corresponding committees be maintained even after the Stamp Act had been repealed. As he envisioned it, a union of correspondents in each colony might help defeat any designing men who might again assail American rights. His suggestion did not produce results in 1766, but the idea of achieving a unified colonial approach by maintaining committees of correspondence was not a passing one. Samuel kept returning to it until it bore fruit.

The colonists' triumph on the home front did not guarantee that the Stamp Act would be repealed. The ultimate victory had to be won in Britain. So Adams used his role as an author of Massachusetts House pronouncements to promote repeal. In November and December of 1765, while working to gut the Stamp Act in the colonies, Adams wrote to the Massachusetts colonial agent and to British "friends" of America to supply them with arguments. The central themes were those Samuel had been trumpeting since May 1764: trade made the colonies valuable to Britain, and Parliament could not constitutionally tax the colonists. Britain's general control of colonial trade when coupled with the American purchase of Britain's manufactured goods, he contended, already amounted to "at least an indirect Tax."

When he turned to constitutional arguments, Adams took the offensive. Again drawing on political theory popularized by John Locke, Adams stressed that the British constitution "is founded in the Principles of Nature and Reason." It followed that the constitution endowed the government with no more power than "was originally designed for the Preservation of the unalienable Rights of Nature." By again emphasizing a natural rights position, Adams insured that the colonists could challenge parliamentary taxation even if arguments rooted in the British constitution or the Massachusetts Charter were swept aside. At the same time, Adams continued to highlight the protections and rights grounded in the charter. In terms drawn from Locke, Adams described the charter, granted by the monarchy in 1691, as a compact. Violating the compact, or contract, would break it. So if the British broke the compact, the people would be justified in forming a new government. Natural rights, the British constitution, and the Massachusetts Charter formed a powerful triumvirate to protect American rights.

Adams also urged his correspondents to challenge the claim that the colonists were represented in Parliament. This was a crucial issue because even the supporters of the Stamp Act acknowledged both that the colonists did not directly elect any MPs and that Parliament could not tax the colonists if they were unrepresented. British politicians dealt with the issue by asserting that the colonists had virtual representation. In theory, MPs represented the whole empire, and, therefore, all the people of the empire were represented. The idea of virtual representation, widely accepted in Britain, reflected the fact that MPs did not have to live in the areas they represented. Adams savaged the virtual-representation argument by pointing out that every county in England elected MPs even if individual towns did not; thus, every inch of England was *actually,* not virtually, represented in Parliament.

Because he understood the potential danger in "actual" representation, Adams was not content with merely demolishing the virtual-representation theory. He realized that Parliament might let the Americans elect a few MPs and then heap taxes on the colonists. This possibility forced Adams to spell out what made colonial representation "impractical." He considered geography a crucial factor. The tremendous distance between America and England, three thousand miles, made actual representation impossible. The situation in the colonies was, he argued, so often and continually varying that even a knowledgeable MP would soon be woefully out of touch. It was also a question of power. As Adams admitted, "we think the Colonies cannot be equally and fully represented; and if not equally then in Effect not at all." That was the key. Adams and most other colonists did not want to elect any MPs because the British would not allow the colonists enough MPs—enough actual political power—to block legislation the colonists opposed. So, as 1765 came to an end, Adams endeavored to do more than help overturn a specific tax act. He became increasingly concerned with ensuring that Parliament could *never* tax the colonists.

Parliament was not interested in colonial arguments about its right to tax. The MPs even refused to consider petitions that questioned Parliament's taxing authority. And many in Britain wanted to punish America for its violent response to the Stamp Act. But Americans were not the only ones concerned about pocketbook issues. When large numbers of British merchants and manufacturers, pinched by colonial nonimportation, began clamoring for relief, the MPs listened. Rumors that Parliament would repeal the hated Stamp Act began circulating in Boston by early January 1766. Soon thereafter, the Sons of Liberty started planning for a gala repeal celebration. By early spring, the colonists knew British merchants and manufacturing interests had urged repeal of the Stamp Act. In late April the Boston Town Meeting issued instructions designed to keep the repeal celebration orderly.

On May 16 the brigantine *Harrison* sailed into Boston harbor carrying copies of the repeal act. A huge, orderly celebration took place three days later. Special lights flickered in the city's windows; fireworks lit the night. A large decorated and transparent obelisk, prepared by the Sons of Liberty, told the story of how Americans, aided by their British friends, had protected their basic liberties and defeated the vile Stamp Act. Boston staged more elaborate festivities than most localities did, but outpourings of joy occurred throughout the colonies. The colonists' exuberance should perhaps have been muted. The same day it repealed the Stamp Act, Parliament adopted the Declaratory Act. Without actually mentioning the power to tax, the Declaratory Act proclaimed that Parliament had the right to pass legislation "to bind the colonies and people of *America* . . . in all cases whatsoever." True, the great British politician William Pitt had advanced the novel thesis that the legislative power did not include the power to tax. Indeed, he held that Parliament had every power over the colonies except the power "of taking their money out of their pockets without their consent." However, Pitt's position, which was generally ridiculed in Britain, had few adherents. The colonists might also have been lulled into a false sense of security because the Massachusetts colonial agent, knowing a declaratory act of some kind would be enacted, had expressed his belief that the act would not apply to taxation. Colonists might therefore have assumed, and many did, that Parliament had conceded that it could not tax them. Still, given the Declaratory Act, it remained unclear whether the Americans had

Paul Revere engraving "A View of the Obelisk" (1766). Courtesy, American Antiquarian Society.

defeated parliamentary taxation or merely won a battle in an ongoing political war.

Looking toward the annual May election of 1766, Samuel Adams and other leading Whigs had already begun to consolidate their legislative force in anticipation of future battles. The residents of Massachusetts's rural townships despised the Stamp Act as much as Bostonians did. To help translate that resentment into votes in the House, Adams and Otis resorted to the press. They produced various items attacking representatives willing to back Governor Bernard and his court party. Adams and Otis skewered thirty-two representatives, more than one-fourth of the House, for their alleged pro–Stamp Act, pro-British position. The results delighted Samuel. Nineteen of the thirty-two targeted House members lost their seats. The popular forces also retained their strength in Boston. At the May 6 town meeting, Adams nominated John Hancock, his wealthy protégé, for a place on the four-member Boston House delegation. The meeting voted Hancock onto the delegation and reelected Adams, Otis, and Thomas Cushing, another champion of America's rights and the son of the merchant who had long ago realized Adams was not destined to be a businessman.

The popular party soon flexed its new political muscle. On May 28 the representatives selected James Otis as Speaker of the House. Rejecting the sage advice of prominent court party politicians, Governor Bernard exercised his charter-given right to negate the House's choice for Speaker. That was not a smart move. The governor's veto merely bolstered Otis's popularity, and the members of the House named Thomas Cushing Speaker.

Bernard's ill-conceived action made it easier for the popular party to eliminate Bernard's staunchest Council supporters. The Council had traditionally been made up of rich, powerful, and generally conservative men inclined to support Britain's policies. In the early days of agitation against the new imperial policy, the Council tried, at times effectively, to check the House's aggressiveness in defending America. Nevertheless, the representatives, who together with the old Council members annually elected the new Council, had deferentially continued to help keep the persons Bernard wanted on his Council. But in May 1766, perhaps not coincidentally the first time Adams participated in the process, the House stopped deferring to the governor. Following Bernard's veto of the House's choice for Speaker, the popular party used its small but workable majority to compile a list of councilors notable for the names it did *not* contain. The list did not include Thomas Hutchinson, the lieutenant governor who served as chairman of the Council's committees; Andrew Oliver, the unlucky stamp distributor and royally appointed secretary of Massachusetts; Peter Oliver, Andrew's brother and a superior court justice; or William Townsend, the king's attorney general in Massachusetts.

Samuel Adams was particularly pleased when these royally appointed executive officials got tossed off the Council, and his pleasure did not stem merely from seeing the court party weakened. Adams had long argued for the separation of powers. He considered it dangerous to let a person hold offices in different governmental branches, and he was particularly adamant about judges not serving in the legislature. Each excluded councilor was a judge. And Hutchinson held so many and varied posts that he was simultaneously serving in Massachusetts's legislative, executive, and judicial branches of government! Anyone who believed, as Adams did, in a separation of powers had a ready philosophical justification for expelling Hutchinson, Townsend, and the two Olivers from the Council.

A livid Governor Bernard did not see it that way. He denounced the House for not reelecting the "best and most able servants, whose only crime was their fidelity to the Crown." In retaliation, he resorted to his charter-given power to veto anyone selected to serve on the Council. He refused to accept six councilors he considered too friendly to the American cause. However, nothing in the charter required the House to replace the persons the governor rejected, and, therefore, when the House balked at choosing others, Bernard had to make do with twenty-two councilors.

Bernard and Hutchinson searched for innovative ways that would allow Hutchinson to function as a member of the Council, but the House parried these maneuvers. Writing for the representatives, Adams noted that, by scheming to keep a place on the Council, Hutchinson provided "a new and additional instance of ambition and a lust of power." While Adams's own conflicts with Hutchinson stretched back to the land bank controversy, Samuel was, in 1766, not speaking merely for himself. Many in the popular party believed that the aristocratic Hutchinson, an advocate of bowing to Britain's supremacy and the acknowledged leader of the court party, ruthlessly grasped at power in Massachusetts. They were right.

Keeping Hutchinson off the Council made a real difference. James Bowdoin, a Boston merchant numbered among the supporters of American liberties, replaced him as chairman of the Council's committees. Hutchinson himself conceded that "from this time the council, in matters which concerned the controversy between the parliament and the colonies, in scarce any instance disagreed with the house." The court party had lost a vital power base.

In addition to purging the Council, the representatives elected Adams clerk of the lower house, and Governor Bernard could not negate that selection. In the late colonial era the clerkship carried a modest annual stipend of £90, which was only raised to £100 in the last year Adams held the post. Still, that salary formed an important part of the Adams family income and hence attested to the fact that Samuel made his living as a politician. (For this reason, as well as others, he was, arguably, America's first professional politician.) Being House clerk reinforced Adams's role as a principal author of House documents and gave him the power to release those documents when he considered it politically advantageous to do so.

Adams's election as clerk did not produce the immediate shock waves that accompanied the Council purge. In time, however, it helped unleash far more powerful quakes.

Samuel Adams's political status evolved dramatically in the two years from May 1764 through May 1766. When the period began, he was a leader of the Boston Caucus and a tax collector who was not very good at the job. Then, drawing heavily upon philosophical ideals and political techniques he had used during the land bank controversy, he produced the precocious Boston Town Meeting instructions of May 1764. They forcefully delineated the case against parliamentary taxation and pointed the way to a unified colonial opposition to that taxation. Elevated to membership in the Massachusetts House in September 1765, he quickly assumed a leadership role, especially as the author of documents that championed American liberties. By May 1766, with the House clerkship in hand, Adams was, all agreed, a major force in the popular party. More than that, friend and foe alike viewed him as the popular party's most skillful politician. He lacked oratorical skills, but he wrote with power and clarity. His determination to safeguard the colonists' constitutional liberties was unmatched. And while he opposed "*mobbish*" crowds, he did not disdain those in the lower ranks of society. He mingled with them and was especially sensitive to their concerns. His opponents might derisively refer to him as "Samuel the Publican," but he understood that more than leaders were involved and that it was the ordinary people he mingled with who "shouted."

Parliament's efforts to tax the colonists helped catapult Samuel Adams to political importance in Massachusetts, not just in Boston. In the spring of 1766, it was not at all clear whether Parliament, having gotten a bloody nose from its Stamp Act, would renew its effort to tax the colonies. But if Parliament, supported by the Massachusetts court party, did try again, Samuel Adams and the popular party of Massachusetts were better positioned than ever before to resist any assault on American rights.

3

The Lurking Serpent

*M*assachusetts court party leaders often groused about Whigs seeking power for selfish ends. Envy, especially of Thomas Hutchinson, and thirst for political office supposedly drove the leading Whigs. Boston's popular party leaders, and many of their colleagues from outside the city, did despise Hutchinson. And, although he corralled an amazing number of political posts for himself, some of the antagonism he sparked arose from jealousy or a thirst for prominence. James Otis Jr. and his father had been politically conservative before 1761, and both became bitter when Thomas Hutchinson, rather than the senior Otis, gained the appointment as chief justice of Massachusetts in late 1760. Moreover, even after he became a leader of the popular party, James Otis Jr. seemed willing, at times, to support the royal government in exchange for political preference. Jealousy undeniably tinged the animus John Adams expressed toward Hutchinson.

Although some leading Whigs envied Hutchinson, court party analysts should have remembered points Hutchinson himself admitted: ordinary people also hated him, and their hatred stretched back decades. As he recounted his opposition to paper-money schemes such as the land bank, Hutchinson boasted he pushed a hard-money bill through the House in 1749. He also observed that his victory against paper money cost him more than a seat in the House; it left many of the city's inhabitants furious with him. They threatened him with "destruction," and when his house accidentally caught fire, Bostonians cried, "Let it burn." People of all ranks justifiably thought that the court party headed by Hutchinson composed an arrogant aristocracy. The great majority of Bostonians had ample reason to think that members of the court party habitually sacrificed the people's interests and rights for their own advancement. If one believed in protecting basic freedoms, if one believed in anything remotely approaching the ideal of social equality, one logically distrusted Hutchinson and his aristocratic crew. Samuel Adams did. From the time he published his first political analysis, Adams did more than stand ready to oppose British threats to the people's fundamental rights. He also stood

43

against the local aristocratic nabobs who did the royal governor's bidding and who viewed the poorer citizens with contempt.

The aggressive political moves, such as purging the Governor's Council, that the popular party undertook beginning in May of 1766 thus stemmed from much more than petty jealousy or lust for political office. The Whigs' actions reflected the lingering fear that Britain, aided by its court party allies, might again try to subvert American liberties. Assessing the situation in late 1766, Adams acknowledged that the British government did not pose an imminent danger to American freedoms. Nevertheless he told a prominent South Carolina Son of Liberty that every colony should be awake and ready to counter a surreptitious assault on the people's rights. Having likened the threat of the Stamp Act to something as obvious as confronting a giant sea monster, Samuel warned against the less visible threat of "the lurking Serpent" that, lying concealed and unnoticed by the unwary passerby, suddenly "darts its fatal Venom."

In June 1766, after ousting Governor Bernard's favorites from the Council, the Massachusetts House implemented further measures to guard against the lurking serpent. Urged on by Adams, the representatives authorized a physical change that was both symbolic and useful to the popular party. The members of the House, the acknowledged people's branch of the General Court, approved building a gallery so citizens could observe their representatives' deliberations. Until that time, roll calls were not routinely taken, and so constituents might not know how their representatives voted. Now they would. From Adams's perspective, a gallery offered another benefit. If large numbers of Sons of Liberty and other Whigs packed the gallery, they might influence the House votes.

The representatives took another significant step in November 1766 when they created the position of colonial agent in London for the Massachusetts House of Representatives. Otis and Adams distrusted Richard Jackson, the MP who had replaced Mauduit as the colony's agent. Jackson seemed too friendly with Bernard and Hutchinson. So Adams and Otis convinced the representatives that Dennys De Berdt, who had represented the House on an ad hoc basis, should become their agent. After De Berdt was appointed, Adams used his capacity as House clerk to change the lines of communication. He halted the practice of routinely letting the Council examine letters sent to an agent. Making that alteration kept sensitive political information out of court party hands and allowed Adams freer rein to issue instructions to De Berdt when the House was not in session.

Again exploiting his role as House clerk, a position that made him responsible for all House papers and for the official journal of House actions, Adams introduced a procedural change that increased his and the popular party's power. Until Adams became clerk, addresses the House sent to the governor routinely appeared in the newspapers shortly after he received them. However, petitions and other documents sent to Parliament,

British government officials, or the monarch were withheld from publication until they could reach England. Adams abandoned that tradition. If he thought it would benefit the colony's position, Samuel released items for publication as soon as the representatives approved them. He knew that once the petition or letter appeared in Massachusetts papers, it would be reprinted throughout the colonies. The House clerkship was not a bully pulpit, but, through political innovation, Adams came close to making it one. In these, as with so many of the other innovations he developed and exploited, Adams moved toward the modern political system of drawing the people into the political process while simultaneously developing methods, especially the use of the available media, to spread his political message.

Adams steadfastly emphasized a continental approach as he labored to protect American freedoms. From the start of the time of troubles with Britain, he stressed the importance of the colonies working in unison. He broached the idea yet again in a December 1766 letter to Christopher Gadsen, a leader of South Carolina's Sons of Liberty. Samuel said he wished merchants from all the colonies would organize and communicate with each other. That kind of "Union" might help alert the people to subtle efforts to tax them. To illustrate the danger, Adams offered the example of Parliament's 1765 Quartering Act, which ordered the colonists to pay some of the costs of maintaining British troops posted in their colony. This legislation, he argued, taxed the colonies as effectively as the Stamp Act. Samuel then raised an issue to which he returned with increasing intensity over time. Observing that some British politicians contemplated stationing troops in America's populated areas, he spoke of the danger of a standing army, especially in peacetime. It constituted more than a disturbance; it was "in every respect dangerous to civil Community." Writing to De Berdt, Adams proclaimed standing armies were *always* dangerous to virtue and liberty.

Adams could not shake the fear that the British might again pursue measures "calculated to enslave" America. Over time, many Americans, including Adams, made the theme of Britain turning the American colonists into slaves a central part of their rhetoric. But that powerful imagery ran afoul of a bothersome fact: slavery was legal in every British colony in America. So colonists who moaned about being reduced to political slavery opened themselves to the charge of hypocrisy. Samuel Adams could not be numbered among them. One of his relatives recounted how Samuel responded in the mid-1760s when his wife received a young black female slave named Surry as a present. He said that no slave could live in his house; if Surry came, she must be free. Although nothing in the records indicates what Elizabeth Adams thought about the situation, it seems likely she agreed with Samuel. In any case, Surry entered the Adams home as a free woman, and she lived as a servant in the Adams family for decades.

Samuel, who strove for political consistency, did more than ensure that his own family avoided the taint of slavery. He endeavored to see that

Massachusetts could not be accused of inconsistency on the question of liberty and slavery. In May 1766, under the caucus system Adams helped mold, the Boston Town Meeting openly confronted the issue of American freedom and slavery. Immediately after informing its representatives that they must "be very watchful over our Just rights, liberties and privileges," the meeting instructed the representatives to seek a ban on the importation and sale of slaves and to push for the abolition of slavery in the colony. The next month, the House put Boston's representatives on a committee to prepare a bill outlawing the importation of slaves. These efforts did not result in legislation until 1771, when the General Court finally passed an anti-importation law. The governor, however, vetoed the bill and also thwarted a similar attempt in 1774. Although unsuccessful in his efforts to undermine slavery, Adams was one of the American Whigs who realized the inconsistency of denouncing the British for allegedly trying to reduce the Americans to slavery while that odious system flourished in America. An important indication of how blacks perceived Adams's thrusts against slavery comes from the fact that, when a group of Massachusetts slaves petitioned for freedom in 1773 and pressed the petition in early 1774, they asked Adams to intercede on their behalf and he did.

Despite Adams's suspicions about British intentions, a relative political calm settled over Massachusetts once the initial fireworks set off by the Council purge of May 1766 subsided. Major differences persisted, but the governor and the members of the House attempted to fashion reasonable compromises as they worked through a thorny political agenda. One vexing and potentially explosive problem concerned compensating victims of the Stamp Act crowds. In June, operating under directions from the home government, Governor Bernard began pressuring the House to pay compensation. Since crowd actions had erupted in various parts of Massachusetts, many people would receive help, but the detested Hutchinson would benefit the most. And, while the British government had merely recommended that the colonial legislatures fund recompense, Bernard created an additional problem by labeling compensation a "requisition." If the representatives accepted that language, they would concede that the colonists could be taxed by order of the British government. A further complication arose because individuals still languished in jails for participating in the crowd actions. These intertwining issues produced festering disagreements until Joseph Hawley, a bright young lawyer from Northhampton who shared Adams's political views and friendship, fashioned a compromise. Rejecting the term "requisition," the House declared it would, of its own volition, support a compensation measure in a bill that would offer a full pardon and amnesty to any crowd members for "all burglaries, felonies, rescues, and breaches of the peace whatsoever." Both sides knew that only the monarch could issue such a pardon, but both wanted the matter settled. So Bernard accepted the compromise and signed the legislation in January

1767. The governor, no doubt, expected that the Privy Council would disallow the bill once it reached England. That is what happened, but by then Hutchinson and the other victims of the crowds had been compensated and the imprisoned "rioters" had been freed.

As the compromise linking amnesty with compensation was being hammered out in late 1766, Adams discovered an ingenious way to subvert the Quartering Act that he had described as taxation in disguise. Adams and the House attacked the legislation indirectly; they did it by helping the British army. When severe weather forced ships into Boston harbor in December, about seventy British soldiers suddenly needed temporary maintenance. The Quartering Act obliged Massachusetts to aid the soldiers. Since the House was not in session when this occurred, the governor and his Council authorized using public funds to maintain the troops. After reconvening, the House ultimately approved spending money to assist the soldiers, but it did so without mentioning the Quartering Act. As Adams put it, a sense of humanity coupled with the people's strong regard for their king had prompted the representatives to provide aid of their own free accord. Using that explanation, Adams, and the House, underscored a fundamental principle: only the citizens' elected representatives could determine how the public money would be spent. It was their freely given gift. It could not be requisitioned; it could not be wrenched from the people by an act of Parliament; it could only be given by the duly elected representatives.

In the year following the repeal of the Stamp Act, none of these issues generated anything like the conflict the Stamp Act had produced. Reflecting on this period, members of the House and Governor Bernard proclaimed it a relatively tranquil time brought on, in part, by a mutual desire to work together as harmoniously as possible. These efforts calmed the churning political waters, but the calm proved deceptive. As 1766 gave way to 1767, both the popular and court parties became increasingly convinced that the other party pursued a horrific agenda. The popular party suspected that the British, aided and abetted by arrogant Massachusetts aristocrats, would attack America's liberties. The court party feared that their enemies wanted independence and would manipulate lower-class rowdies to achieve it. Because each side believed it must control the legislature to thwart the other side's evil schemes, each group considered the May 1767 election crucial.

The changes Adams and the popular party had introduced into the House—installing a gallery and Samuel's policy of quickly releasing House documents—were designed to help the popular party win elections. To increase its chances for victory, the party also initiated the practice of commemorating events associated with the recent defense of American freedoms. The anniversary of the repeal of the Stamp Act fell conveniently close to the annual May election, and Boston Whigs took advantage of the opportunity. On the afternoon of March 18, large numbers of people gathered at Faneuil Hall, which was lit up to signal the occasion's importance. There at the home of the Boston Town Meeting, people drank a variety of pro-American toasts. The Liberty Tree was also illuminated, as were the residences of various Whigs. John Rowe, who participated in the festivities, wrote in his diary that "I never saw more Joy than on this occasion." Celebrating March 18 became an instant tradition, and so did August 14 festivities that commemorated the first Boston crowd action against the Stamp Act.

Although the celebrations inaugurated in 1767 became more elaborate over time, the assessment John Adams offered of the August 14, 1769, event probably applies to the earlier 1767 activities as well. John credited the duo of Samuel Adams and James Otis with political shrewdness in promoting such festivals. John said the gatherings touched the minds of the people and "impregnate[d] them with the sentiments of Liberty." He also frankly admitted that the events were designed to serve the more immediate political goal of making the people fonder of their leaders "in the Cause" and more "adverse and bitter" toward all who opposed the cause. John might have overestimated the influence political festivals exerted, but he accurately described what Samuel and other Whig leaders hoped to accomplish. The celebrations added yet another political weapon to the Whig arsenal.

Governor Bernard, who desperately wanted his firmest supporters returned to the Council, also poured extra effort into winning the 1767 election. He placed his hopes mainly on preferment, the dispensing of political posts and favors. By linking a person's self-interest to the government, preferment gave the beneficiary a powerful motive to support the government. Bernard took to personally supervising the dispensing of even minor political favors. Political considerations always played some part in appointments, but Bernard now used patronage and other political rewards in such a partisan way that his brazenness embarrassed some of his supporters. Judge John Cushing, a court party man, lamented how Bernard went about gathering votes. In exchange for supporting his candidates, Bernard was putting "Scandalous and unfit persons" into office, throwing commissions at people, and promising almost everybody some kind of preferment.

Bernard's tactics failed. The May 1767 election did not alter the balance of power. The popular party kept control of the House, and the representatives again refused to vote for Hutchinson and other court party politicians Bernard wanted on his Council. Adams retained his post as clerk of the House. Samuel was delighted with these victories, but pleasure soon gave way to anxiety when Parliament took steps that revealed that the lurking serpent had indeed begun darting "its fatal Venom."

In the summer of 1767, Charles Townshend, one of the most brilliant debaters in Parliament, pushed the MPs to make the Americans acknowledge the supremacy of Parliament. As chancellor of the exchequer, the chief financial minister in the British government, Townshend developed a plan ostensibly to raise revenue from the American colonies. He believed, and Adams agreed, that any program designed to garner revenue constituted a tax. However, during the Stamp Act troubles, Benjamin Franklin, a colonial spokesman then in England, had suggested that the colonists distinguished between internal and external taxes. According to this view, the colonists would oppose any direct *internal* taxes, such as the Stamp Act; *external* taxes might, however, be acceptable. Although Townshend considered this reasoning absurd, he seized upon the alleged distinction between internal and external taxes. In formulating his plan, he even avoided the word "tax." Townshend proposed that Parliament levy duties on tea, glass, paper, printing materials ("red and white lead, and painters' colours") shipped to America. These "external" duties would be collected in the colonies.

Townshend's complex proposals revealed the aptness of Samuel's imagery of the lurking serpent and the unwary passerby. Although labeled a revenue measure, the Townshend plan imposed relatively low duties and would only raise about £37,000 per year. When combined with other changes in trade regulations, the British government's annual income would actually *drop* by about £23,000. Townshend obviously was not hunting immediate revenue. He was stealthily pursuing constitutional leverage. He wanted to establish a precedent for future and much higher levels of taxation. As Adams had warned, if the colonists once paid even small duties, they could, in time, be compelled to carry a heavy tax burden. Townshend also struck at the power of the purse that colonial legislatures utilized to hamstring royal governors and undermine judicial enforcement of the trade laws. Townshend's plan earmarked the new duties to pay the salaries of royally appointed government officials, including colonial judges. Townshend had good reason to believe he could inflict his venomous thrust on unwary colonials. John Huske, one of the few American-born MPs, praised the Townshend plan. Even more important, the colonial agents, a group that had challenged passage of the Stamp Act, did not articulate complaints about what were quickly dubbed the Townshend duties.

The chancellor of the exchequer was also determined to make the colonists obey Britain's trade laws. To achieve that goal, Townshend introduced legislation creating the American Board of Custom Commissioners. He anticipated that stationing this board in America would produce better enforcement of the existing trade regulations. Tighter control would diminish, if not eradicate, American smuggling. British officials considered locating the new board in Philadelphia, New York City, or Boston. Although the reason for the final choice was not recorded, it is hardly surprising that the British decided to put the board in Boston. In 1767 Boston was a major smuggling port. Probably more significant, the English already deemed Boston the center of colonial opposition. Indeed, the city was well on the way to earning the title Peter Oliver gave it: "The Metropolis of Sedition."

Parliament passed the Townshend duties in June 1767. At the same time, it authorized the American Board of Custom Commissioners, which began functioning in November. By enacting the Townshend duties, Parliament created a constitutional gauntlet for all the colonies to run. And by placing the board of custom commissioners in Boston, the British signaled their intention to punish the city for its role as a smuggling center and as a breeding ground of opposition to Britain's new imperial policy.

The colonial legislatures were not in session when news of the Townshend duties reached America. In Massachusetts, Adams and the other Boston representatives, all members of the popular party, urged Governor Bernard to convene the General Court. Bernard refused, but Adams and his fellow Whigs had another political forum at their disposal. The Boston Town Meeting swung into action on October 28. It also pressed the governor to call the legislature into session and, without once directly mentioning them, declared war on the Townshend duties. Proclaiming that Massachusetts faced poverty and economic ruin, the meeting laid out a plan to promote industry, economy, and manufacturing. The town meeting challenged the Townshend duties by agreeing to do its utmost to encourage the domestic manufacture of glass and paper.

Even more important, adopting the language of Parliament's navigation acts, the meeting compiled an extensive list of over fifty enumerated items that would not be imported after December 31. The town meeting asked Bostonians to sign an agreement supporting nonimportation and also sent copies of the document to all Massachusetts towns as well as to the major cities and towns throughout the continent. Boston was trying to resurrect the nonimportation weapon that had helped destroy the Stamp Act.

Boston's actions outraged the British. Writing from England in late December, Benjamin Franklin reported that Boston's resolutions "made a great noise here" and that "the newspapers are in full cry against America." A commentary that appeared in a London newspaper in early 1768 gives a sense of the way many Britons had come to view Bostonians. The author mused on the fact that Barlow Trecothick, a Boston-born MP, was up for reelection. "I think we might now, with equal propriety," the author sarcastically opined, "seek a representative from among the French or Spaniards, as from Boston, for neither of these countries have, as yet, outdone the Bostonians in malicious combinations against our existence."

By February of 1768 many towns in Massachusetts, Rhode Island, and Connecticut had embraced Boston's nonimportation plan, but Philadelphia and New York had not. Then in March about one hundred Boston merchants formally pledged to stop importing virtually all European goods for a year or until Parliament repealed the Townshend duties. As Adams had urged, committees of correspondence kept merchants in the individual colonies informed of these developments. New York City agreed to the

Boston proposal, but Philadelphia's merchants held back. Without Philadelphia, colonial nonimportation could not succeed. So, despite the efforts of the Boston Town Meeting and many Boston merchants, the colonists still had not created an effective boycott by the spring of 1768.

America's less-than-solid support for nonimportation could not be blamed on a failure to grasp the significance of the Townshend duties. Beginning in early December 1767 and continuing through mid-February of 1768, John Dickinson's extraordinarily popular *Letters from a Farmer in Pennsylvania* forcefully laid out the issues. While conceding that Parliament could regulate both the colonial trade and manufacturing, Dickinson insisted that *any* bill enacted by Parliament solely for the purpose of raising revenue was unconstitutional. Therefore, he said, even small taxes, such as the Townshend duties, set a dangerous precedent. As Dickinson phrased it, if Parliament could levy a tax of one penny, it could levy a tax of millions. Adams, of course, had made all these points before but not in widely reprinted essays.

Well aware that the Pennsylvania legislature would not vigorously challenge the Townshend duties, Dickinson sought help from Massachusetts. Writing to James Otis, he said that he expected Massachusetts would again take the lead in "the Cause of American Freedom." "The Farmer," as Dickinson came to be known, was not disappointed. On January 20, 1768, the Massachusetts House approved what it called a humble petition to the king. The petition, which Adams had a major hand in crafting, endorsed many of Dickinson's arguments and incorporated language Adams had earlier employed. After expressing loyalty to the king, the representatives recounted how their ancestors had invested their own money to create and develop the colony. Massachusetts, according to the assemblymen, had cost the mother country little, and yet Britain reaped enormous profits from the colony's trade and from supplying Massachusetts with manufactured goods. Then came the essential philosophical arguments. First, based on "the fundamental rights of nature and the constitution," the people of Massachusetts could be taxed *only* by their own elected representatives. Second, local circumstances made it "utterly impracticable" for the people of Massachusetts to be represented in Parliament. The petitioners' logic suggested that anything Parliament did solely to raise revenue in the colonies constituted a tax and was therefore unconstitutional. Adams championed that position. He could not, however, convince a majority of the representatives to say it openly. The petition merely lamented that the people would not truly be free subjects if those revenue acts remained in force. The representatives closed by imploring the king to help his loyal but beleaguered Massachusetts subjects.

Soon after approving the petition to the king, the representatives took action that eventually became both extraordinarily contentious and a significant milestone on the road to revolution. It began when Whig leaders sought to have copies of the House's petition forwarded to the other American assemblies along with a circular letter urging those colonies to consider taking similar action. When this proposal was first debated and voted upon, the House defeated it. But Otis and Adams, having already demonstrated that they shared Dickinson's belief in the value of unifying colonial efforts, campaigned for a reconsideration. They succeeded. On February 11, the House approved the circular letter and also expunged the first vote from the House records. The circular letter, authored by Adams, emphasized the ideal of unified colonial action. When faced with issues vital to all the colonies, their individual assemblies "should harmonize with each other." If the other assemblies agreed, they too would petition the king. The circular letter summarized many points included in the petition; but, using language he had employed before, Adams expanded upon crucial issues. It would, he observed, *never* be possible for the colonists to have representatives in Parliament, in part because the colonists would not be equally represented. And while the petition rested the representatives' claims on the charter and the rights of Englishmen, Adams also placed great weight on natural rights. He declared that "it is an essential unalterable right in nature" that a person's property "cannot be taken from him without his consent." Since this was a natural right, more than their charter or even the British constitution protected the people. And while the House petition waffled on the question of the constitutionality of the Townshend duties, Adams did not. The circular letter stated that acts Parliament passed solely for raising revenue in America were "infringements" of the people's "natural and constitutional rights."

The circular letter also addressed issues that the petition passed over in silence. After taking brief swipes at the Quartering Act and the American Board of Customs Commissioners, Adams directly challenged how the Townshend duties would be spent. He stressed that the people's freedom might be subverted if the Crown both appointed the governor and forced the colonists to pay him whatever the monarch might determine. The integrity of the American judicial system could also be undermined. The danger stemmed from the fact that the American judges were appointed and dismissed at the monarch's pleasure. If judges also received their pay from the British, they would be totally independent of the colonial legislatures. Adams thus averred that the Townshend duties endangered many of America's essential freedoms.

In the petition to the king, the circular letter, and messages to their London agent, the representatives carefully stressed their loyalty to king and country. They trumpeted the fact that, contrary to what some malicious people said, the colonies did not want independence. Adams, speaking for the House, told colonial agent De Berdt that the colonists did not harbor even a distant thought of independence. He insisted that, if offered independence, the colonists would refuse it. Such protestations of loyalty only sugarcoated the bitter message: the Townshend duties must go.

By early 1768 the popularity of Dickinson's *Letters* and the Massachusetts attack upon the Townshend duties suggested that most colonists agreed with what Townshend had uttered privately: a tax was a tax. Maintaining that an internal tax differed from an external tax was absurd. Calling a tax a duty or a requisition could not disguise the truth. Equally important, most colonial leaders contended that those taxes were unconstitutional because they were levied on an unrepresented people. Still, as the differences between the Massachusetts petition to the king and the Massachusetts circular letter demonstrated, translating philosophical ideals into effective political action proved difficult. At a crucial juncture, the petition to the king backed away from a frontal assault on the Townshend duties. It took two attempts and political maneuvering by Adams and Otis to win approval for Adams's hard-hitting circular letter.

The colony-wide May election arrived before Massachusetts learned how the British would respond to the House's petition. Adams entered the 1768 election campaign by taking up his favorite weapon, the pen. He wrote a series of three letters, signed "A Puritan," which appeared in the *Boston Gazette* in April. While ostensibly assessing the degree of "Popery" that existed in various Massachusetts towns, Adams actually commented on the extent to which certain individuals and geographic areas did or did not support American liberties. He promoted the idea that only committed advocates of American rights, only Whigs, should be elected to the House.

In Boston, Adams's continuing problem with uncollected taxes gave the court party a special opportunity to attack him. The city's deepening economic woes had led to a lawsuit that eventually resulted in a £1,463 judgment against Adams. He had to pay that huge sum by March 1768 or face possible imprisonment. Samuel began making payments but still owed what he described as a large balance when the deadline arrived. He petitioned the Boston Town Meeting for a six-month delay so he could garner the long overdue taxes. Adams described how, in the early 1760s, hard times in Boston had made collecting taxes so difficult that he used the tax moneys obtained in one year to pay the previous year's requisition. The meeting approved his request, but his irregular methods opened him to a charge of gross mismanagement bordering on criminality. Members of the court party refused to let the matter rest. They demanded and got another town meeting to vote on reconsidering the Adams petition. A lengthy, heated debate erupted at that second meeting. Although they could make Adams squirm and perhaps even humiliate him, the court party people lost. The meeting overwhelmingly reaffirmed its decision to give Adams a six-month extension. Nevertheless, a six-month reprieve could not have saved Samuel; it took a subscription of over £1,000 raised by friends to keep him from financial ruin. He managed to escape further responsibility in 1769 when the town meeting transferred the task of gathering the remaining uncollected taxes to another collector. In 1772, with more than £1,100 of those taxes still outstanding, the town meeting finally ended Samuel's agony by acknowledging that the taxes would most likely never be collected and by deciding that nothing more could be done.

Bostonians, and not just members of the court party, grumbled about Adams being treated so leniently. Still, the tax collection issue, embarrassing as it was, did not diminish his popularity. In the May 1768 election, the town meeting once again reelected him, along with Otis, Cushing, and Hancock, to the House. The returns from the rest of Massachusetts indicated that a majority of the House would once again support the popular party. As they had done the two previous years, the representatives again refused to seat Hutchinson and other favorites of Governor Bernard on the Council. But this time the contest was close. Bernard complained, and probably justifiably so, that Hutchinson suffered defeat only because Adams and Otis, the men Bernard considered the "chief heads" of the opposition, ambushed Hutchinson on the second round of voting. They did it by announcing that the British government had granted Hutchinson a pension of £200 a year. They also pointed out that, because of the Townshend duties, the colonists would pay that pension. Making those points did the job. Hutchinson's support withered, and he lost any chance of again sitting on the Council. Nevertheless, the closeness of this election gave the court party hope that it might regain the ascendancy. Much would depend on how the British responded to the House's challenge to the Townshend duties.

A copy of the Massachusetts circular letter had reached England in April 1768. Parliament was not in session, but the king and his ministers acted quickly. Fearing that the circular letter might produce another colonial congress—this one aimed at the Townshend duties—Lord Hillsborough, the secretary of state for the colonies, immediately wrote to Governor Bernard and instructed him to tell the House that the circular letter must be rescinded. Bernard presented the demand to the House on June 21. Two days later, the representatives revisited ground they had traversed in mid-February. Accusing Bernard of misrepresenting their actions to the Crown, the representatives asked the governor to give them copies of his correspondence with the home government. That outrageous request, which Adams championed, constituted a clever political ploy. If Bernard refused, the charges against him would gain credence. If he supplied the letters, Adams and others would use them as bludgeons against him. Once having fashioned this useful tactic, Adams resorted to it time and again in the ensuing years.

Bernard responded the next day. He warned the representatives that he would dissolve the House unless it revoked the offending resolution. Moreover, he would not again call a House into session until the king authorized it. On the question of forwarding copies of his letters, he said his correspondence would be made public only when he chose to do so and then only for his own reasons. Bernard increased the pressure on June 26 by informing the representatives that, if they delayed much longer, he would consider it a refusal to rescind. Three days later, the representatives asked for a recess so they could consult with their constituents and receive instructions. Bernard refused. The House now had only two options. It could fight and be dissolved, or it could surrender.

On Tuesday, June 30, the representatives met to determine their action. They began by having the House gallery cleared and taking measures to ensure that they would not be interrupted. Faced with the expressed displeasure of the king and with Bernard's bullying threats, the members chose to fight. By a roll-call vote of 92 to 17, they refused to rescind; agreeing to revoke would, they argued, "have left us but a vain Semblance of Liberty." They then sent Bernard a lengthy address authored principally by Adams. It justified their former deeds as reasonable endeavors rooted in the right to petition. Moreover, the representatives' efforts had actually helped foster "Ease and Quiet" among the people, who now peacefully awaited the king's response to their humble petition. Once again employing Lockean terms, the representatives described themselves as "preserving Life, Liberty, and Property."

Taking the offensive, the House appointed a committee, headed by Samuel Adams, to ask the king to remove Governor Bernard. It seems likely that Adams had already drafted a petition or portions of it because he presented it to the House later that day. This quick action lends weight to Governor Bernard's exasperated claim that whenever Adams was placed on a committee, he "pulled out a set of resolves, ready cut & dryed." The lengthy pronouncement resembled a bill of indictment more than an ordinary petition. It charged Governor Bernard with having "an arbitrary Disposition" and spelled out the particulars in fourteen paragraphs. Most were short, and most opened with "He has" followed by a recounting of Bernard's failings and evil deeds. The savagery of parts of the attack may have given some representatives pause. The House deferred action, ostensibly so the committee could supply evidence to support all the charges leveled against the governor. The committee did not get the chance. Bernard prorogued the House that day and dissolved it the next. The House was not convened again until after the next general election.

Samuel Adams played a central role in the battles that erupted over the Massachusetts circular letter. He served on every important committee the House appointed to compose petitions or other position statements. But, while other leading members of the popular party, including James Otis, were placed on various delegations that carried messages to Governor Bernard, Samuel never once served on such a committee. At first glance, that seems odd. Samuel had a penchant for being moderate when moderation might help achieve his goal. And everyone agreed he could be charming, even if Peter Oliver depicted him as having chameleon-like charm. The reason that Samuel was always omitted from these committees can perhaps be traced to this illuminating fact: the representatives knew that the governor detested Adams more than any other member of the popular party. Bernard considered him, and rightly so, more intractable, more dangerous than Otis. Otis swung back and forth on the question of Parliament's authority to enact whatever legislation it chose regarding the colonies. Adams, who insisted that Parliament's power had boundaries *and* that Parliament could not overrun them, held fast to the ideas he had enunciated as early as the 1740s. The people must know their constitutional rights and steadfastly maintain them. Others might waver; Samuel Adams would not.

When confronted with challenges to the new colonial policy, British politicians followed a divide-and-conquer strategy. They aimed to isolate a troublesome colony, or even a city like Boston, and by punishing its inhabitants intimidate colonists elsewhere. Dissolving a house of representatives would, the theory went, bring the Americans to heel. Just the opposite happened. When other colonies learned that the Massachusetts House had been dissolved, expressions of sympathy and support for the glorious ninety-two who voted against rescinding streamed into Massachusetts.

As the increasingly acrimonious struggle against the Townshend duties unfolded, Massachusetts and especially Boston also had to deal with the American Board of Custom Commissioners, the second half of Townshend's plan to bring the colonists under tighter control. By chance, three of the five members of the board arrived in Boston on November 5, the day antipope crowds took over the streets. When the three men landed in 1767, they encountered a crowd of perhaps a thousand carrying twenty effigies bearing the labels "Liberty & Property & no Commissioners." The nonviolent crowd did no more than escort the customs commissioners to their quarters. Although they landed without violence, it took little time for the commissioners, as Adams observed, to "alarm the People." Most merchants and seafarers disliked the British Navigation Acts, but the customs commissioners did more than enforce trade regulations. The board created its own coast-guard patrol, and the crews often got their pay from their seizures. Worse yet, customs commissioners developed a system one historian dubbed "customs racketeering." By altering how they applied rules or by enforcing obscure regulations, customs officials could confiscate property even if owners tried to comply with the law. Aggrieved colonists could do little about the injustices. Because the trade laws protected them, commissioners or their agents could practice customs racketeering with virtual impunity. Under the laws, if one could show probable cause for seizing goods, a person found innocent of the alleged violation still had to pay the court costs. And to the chagrin of its innocent victims, the admiralty courts that tried the cases typically decided that probable cause had existed.

Customs racketeers preferred targeting less powerful merchants or owners of small vessels who could not afford the costs of mounting a legal defense. Even common seamen fell victim to customs racketeering. Long-established tradition allowed sailors to carry small amounts of trade goods in their sea chests. But using the technicality that no such items could be transported without proper papers, by 1768, customs agents were confiscating sea chests containing trade goods. Not surprisingly, anticommissioner hostility intensified. The customs commissioners responded by repeatedly asking for military protection. Writing to colonial agent De Berdt on May 14, Adams summed up how most Bostonians had come to view the customs board. The people, he said, generally hated the commissioners as much as they had hated the Stamp Act distributors. If Samuel had known what would happen three days later, he would have been even harsher in his condemnation.

The commissioners' repeated calls for military support eventually worked. HMS *Romney,* a fifty-gun warship, dropped anchor in Boston harbor on May 17, 1768. This display of military force—the first aimed directly at Boston—made the situation more volatile, and that volatility was further heightened because the *Romney* arrived shorthanded. To remedy his manpower shortage, Captain John Corner had men from inbound vessels pressed into service aboard the *Romney.* Boston crowds had often challenged impressment, and they did so again. The anti-impressment crowds of 1768, like those before them, were composed primarily of the kinds of individuals most likely to be impressed: seafarers and young men from the lower classes. No one needed to inform them of the immediate threat to their freedom. It was not necessary for Samuel Adams, or anyone else, to instruct them. And there is no evidence Adams tried to direct their actions.

The common people's anger came to a head on June 10 when commissioners used a customs racketeering technicality to seize John Hancock's merchant ship the *Liberty.* Although he possessed a well-deserved reputation for smuggling, for political reasons Hancock had curtailed his illegal activities. The commissioners did not, however, target him for his notorious smuggling operations; rather, they seized the *Liberty* because Hancock had spoken contemptuously of customs commissioners and because he was a highly visible member of the popular party. Numerous Bostonians supported Hancock. He was, after all, a well-liked leader who employed many people in his extensive business activities. But more than support for Hancock was involved. Customs racketeering and impressment were at the root of popular enmity. Indeed, on June 9 before the commissioners confiscated the *Liberty,* a crowd armed with stones forced the release of a man who had just been pressed. Impressment was, in fact, a central issue in the *Liberty* incident. When British sailors and marines came to tow the *Liberty* to the *Romney,* they were confronted by what the *Boston News-Letter* called an ever increasing crowd that included many sailors and "vagrant[s]," just the kind of individuals press gangs often seized. The crowd showered the British with stones until they rowed out of rock-throwing range. Elements of the crowd also assaulted and bloodied the two commissioners who had ordered the seizure of the *Liberty*. Later the crowd snatched a pleasure boat belonging to a commissioner, dragged it onto a commons area, and burned it. Belying the image the term "mob" now conjures up, after holding a discussion on what to do next, the participants voted to disperse and did so without further incident. Within the next two days, fearing for their lives, four of the five customs commissioners together with their families and various customs personnel—a total of sixty-seven people—fled to the *Romney* for protection. It is significant that commissioner John Temple, who often disagreed with the policies his fellow board members pursued, saw no need to flee and was not molested.

In an effort to dampen the people's anger, the commissioners, relying on a negotiator, acquiesced in Hancock's suggestion that he post a bond and have his ship returned pending the outcome of a trial. However, Adams, Otis, and others convinced Hancock to cancel the arrangement. That meant the *Liberty* incident would remain a newsworthy example of British oppression as long as the court case lasted, and that would likely be a long time indeed.

In the months that followed, Adams and the popular party adopted the tactic of downplaying the level of violence that had accompanied crowd actions in Boston. As in the case of the Stamp Act crowds, spokesmen wanted to convey the impression that Bostonians embraced only legal and reasonable means of resisting oppression. Although violent crowds were anathema to Whig leaders like Adams, they firmly believed large, peaceful demonstrations helped support the cause. They were delighted when the town meeting of June 14 that met as a consequence of the *Liberty* incident resembled a huge, peaceful demonstration. Faneuil Hall, which could hold between twelve hundred and thirteen hundred, proved much too small to accommodate the meeting, so it adjourned to the Old South Church, which had room for almost six thousand. Claiming that the critical state of affairs forced them to act, the citizens petitioned Governor Bernard. They offered a toughly worded defense of Massachusetts's opposition to the Townshend duties and also denounced the actions of both the customs commissioners and the navy. The fact was, the petitioners said, Boston found itself "invaded with an armed force, Seizing, impressing . . . our fellow Subjects contrary to express Acts of Parliament." Demanding redress, the meeting called upon the governor to ensure that the customs commissioners never resumed their posts. In addition, he should order the *Romney* out of the harbor—at least until the king and government officials in Great Britain had time to respond to the people's pleas for relief.

The Boston Town Meeting appointed a committee to prepare a formal statement on the evils of introducing an armed force into the city. As usual, Adams exerted a strong influence. He headed the committee, which included Dr. Joseph Warren and Dr. Benjamin Church, young men Adams had cultivated and put forward as talented defenders of American liberties. They transferred their report to another committee that was charged with drafting instructions for the Boston representatives. The instructions, adopted on June 17, reviewed the people's many grievances, including being overrun by swarms of government officials. The threat of military occupation merited particularly sharp criticism; in addition, a lengthy section denounced impressment and offered evidence that it was illegal. The Boston representatives should, the instructions directed, consider asking the House to pass a resolution branding anyone who called for stationing troops in Boston an enemy to both the city and the colony. The town meeting's actions did not spark a major confrontation, most probably because they were soon overshadowed by the question of rescinding the Massachusetts circular letter.

Governor Bernard understood the explosiveness of impressment, and he tried to defuse the issue. After reminding the town meeting that he could not order the *Romney* out of the harbor, the governor promised to do his best to halt impressment. At Bernard's urging, Captain Corner publicly said he would not impress any Massachusetts seamen. The governor believed his actions "have given me a little popularity," but he also glumly prophesied it would not last a week. He was right. On June 21, Bernard asked the representatives to comply with the king's demand that they rescind the Massachusetts circular letter. The ensuing fight turned his momentary popularity into a call for his dismissal.

By voting against rescinding the circular letter, the Massachusetts representatives signaled their determination to keep up the fight against the Townshend duties. Boston merchants soon sent a similar signal by escalating resistance to the duties. According to Hutchinson, Adams and Otis helped influence the merchants to stiffen their nonimportation resolve even though other cities, especially Philadelphia, had refused to join the effort. On August 1, the great majority of Boston merchants entered into a formal agreement to stop virtually all importation from Great Britain for one year commencing in January. They would boycott all items subject to the Townshend duties until Parliament abolished them. The merchants' committee of correspondence, a technique Adams promoted, would keep their counterparts throughout America informed about Boston's determined stance.

By the summer of 1768, in the aftermath of the *Liberty* incident and the fight over rescinding the circular letter, Governor Bernard and Samuel Adams agreed on one thing: to restore political peace in Massachusetts, Bernard must be replaced. Adams ventured that argument in a letter to agent De Berdt that, as usual, gave him arguments to further Massachusetts's cause in England. Bernard advanced the point as part of a campaign to secure a transfer to a more agreeable, more profitable locale. In July he sent the British government letter after letter recounting his heroic defense of the king's government against an increasingly formidable opposition. Bernard argued that only a show of military force could save the day against the demagogues who aimed to overthrow the British Empire and who for three years had used a trained mob to pursue their goal. Of course, Bostonians did not want soldiers sent to their city. In fact, as Bernard ruefully observed, antisoldier feeling ran so deep that his own Council had unanimously opposed requesting troops. Nevertheless, he stressed that Britain had only two choices: allow the situation to continue, in which case the king's government would be reduced to impotence; or use military force to stop the demagogues and their minions. He recommended sending troops. The customs commissioners, who had shifted their residence from the *Romney* to Castle William, a fort on an island in Boston harbor, also averred that only regular troops could restore law and order to Boston. The home government, which had reached the same conclusion in early June and ordered that two regiments be sent to Boston, responded by directing that an additional two regiments be dispatched, as Bernard phrased it, "to awe the Town."

The British beefed up their naval presence in Boston in the early summer of 1768, and by August rumors circulated that regular army troops would be coming. Adams discussed the possibility in a newspaper essay published on August 8. He began by trying to discredit the view that the people of Massachusetts were a mobbish lot. To prove this, he asserted that the *Liberty* crowd did no more than break a few panes of glass before being convinced to disperse peacefully. Following his traditional pattern, this defense turned into an attack. Having downplayed the level of violence in an obviously misleading way, Adams accentuated the many grievances that had generated even this supposedly limited violence in peace-loving Boston. The unjustified confiscation of the *Liberty* had been achieved "by aid of military power, a power ever dreaded by all lovers of the peace and good order." Who could blame the people for boldly asserting their freedoms when their rights were infringed, when their property was endangered, when a naval force executed unconstitutional acts before their eyes, and when they were daily threatened with military occupation? Worse yet, all of this happened while their legislature was dissolved. Such grievances justified popular protest. Indeed, if the people did not complain, and loudly, they would be made "the slaves of dirty tools of arbitrary power." As his pen name—"Determinatus"—suggested, an aggrieved people must defend their rights with determination or lose them.

Confronted with the threat that British regulars might soon arrive, the popular party worked to bolster local resolve and morale. One tactic involved making the August 14 celebration, what John Rowe called the anniversary day of the Sons of Liberty, more elaborate than ever before. The 1768 festivities, promoted by Adams and Otis, began at dawn at the Liberty Tree. Musical performances commenced at noon and concluded with the singing of the American Song of Liberty and the firing of cannon. As the *Gazette* reported it, shouts of joy arose from a huge audience "fraught with a noble ardor in the cause of freedom." Then toasts, including one to "The glorious Ninety-two," filled the air. After French horns sounded, the cannon roared again—"completing the number NINETY-TWO"—and the celebrants dispersed. Throughout these festivities, and throughout the struggle against British efforts to tax them, the supporters of American liberty linked their struggles to others famed for defending the people's rights. Thus, they toasted John Wilkes, the dissident British MP renowned at home and in America as a fighter for freedom who suffered imprisonment for his beliefs. The Bostonians also drank to Pascal Paoli, the Corsican who led his people's fight for freedom first from the Genoese and later from the French.

All this pageantry with its symbolism of defending freedom could not obscure a bald reality. The colonial resistance to the Townshend duties did not come close to equaling the resistance the Stamp Act had unleashed. The Massachusetts circular letter did not propose convening another intercolonial conference equivalent to the Stamp Act Congress. The many crowd actions that prevented the implementation of the Stamp Act were not repeated against the Townshend duties. And even after the customs commissioners retreated to Castle William, Bostonians continued paying the required shipping duties. Despite the efforts of Adams and Otis, the Boston Town Meeting, and many Boston merchants, the economic warfare waged against the Townshend duties in 1768 hardly resembled that conducted against the Stamp Act. The colonists had organized a massive and general nonimportation effort against the Stamp Act. Unified action against the Townshend duties failed to materialize. By late summer 1768 many areas, including the vital city of Philadelphia, eschewed nonimportation. As a consequence, the kind of massive pressure British merchants and manufacturers quickly exerted against the Stamp Act simply was not brought to bear against the Townshend duties.

Although the colonies as a whole did not challenge the Townshend duties as forcefully as they had the Stamp Act, letters that the royally appointed politicians and officials dispatched to England made it appear as if the people of Massachusetts, or at least of Boston, stood perilously close to outright rebellion. That was a wild exaggeration, as Adams and other Whigs strained to prove. But it was too late. Each side had come to believe that the very essence of the British constitution was at issue. And the British government had had enough of Boston's sedition. In addition to dispatching troops to Boston, it ordered that investigations be undertaken to determine if the leaders of the popular party could be indicted for treason. Affidavits were obtained against Samuel Adams and others, including his protégés Dr. Warren and Dr. Church. Although no formal charges were filed, the Whigs still had to confront the harsh reality that the British government had ordered four infantry regiments and a fleet to Boston.

Bostonians received the bad news but not the complete details in early

September 1768. Angered by an unknown essayist's suggestion that the citizens would fight if regulars arrived to reduce the people to "slavery," Governor Bernard let it be known on September 8 that soldiers were indeed coming to Massachusetts. A petition to hold a town meeting quickly circulated, and on September 10, Adams, Otis, and Warren reportedly prepared resolves for adoption. When the citizens convened on September 12, they sent a committee to Bernard to discover the source of his information and to request that he call the Massachusetts House of Representatives back into session. The meeting also created a large committee charged with assessing the situation and recommending a course of action. The committee naturally included all of Boston's representatives as well as many other noted Whigs.

When the town meeting reconvened the next day, the citizens learned Bernard's response. His anticipation that troops would soon arrive came, he said, from private information; he had not received official word. As for reconvening the House, he could not do that because the king had that issue under consideration. The town meeting responded by unanimously adopting a "Declaration and Resolves." While pledging unwavering loyalty and support for the king, the meeting said that only the Massachusetts legislators could authorize spending the citizens' money. Any attempt to tax the people or to station an army in peacetime without the people's approval constituted "an infringement of their natural, constitutional and Charter Rights." Employing the army to enforce laws passed without the people's consent would compound the offense.

The town meeting then undertook a series of defiant and symbolic actions. To promote opposition to the Townshend duties, it praised New York City merchants for adopting a strong nonimportation stance. Hiding behind the obviously spurious claim that war might soon break out with France, the meeting ordered strict compliance with a law that required all householders to keep a musket and ammunition handy. Having hinted that they might fight, the citizens invoked God's protection. The selectmen were instructed to visit the ministers and arrange for a day of fasting and prayer. More important, given Governor Bernard's refusal to call the assembly into session, the meeting attempted to come as close as possible to issuing that call itself. By express messengers, it invited all Massachusetts towns to send representatives to a convention scheduled to begin on September 22 at Faneuil Hall. Boston selected its House delegation—Samuel Adams, James Otis Jr., Thomas Cushing, and John Hancock—to represent the city at this convention. Since a similar kind of convention had helped transform England's government during the Glorious Revolution of 1688–1689, the town meeting's actions were provocative. Underscoring the importance of all it had done, the meeting ordered that its votes and proceedings be published in all the newspapers. This, in effect, meant that the news of its actions would get printed throughout America.

The town meeting's effort to re-create something like the Massachusetts House proved impressively successful. Ninety-eight towns and eight districts dispatched representatives to the convention. Thomas Cushing, the Speaker of the House, was elected moderator; Adams, the House clerk, became the clerk of the convention. For some unexplained reason, Otis missed the first half of the brief convention. The delegates began by petitioning Governor Bernard. They reiterated the request, already articulated by Boston's representatives and the town meeting, that the legislature be reconvened. The governor, who considered the convention an illegal gathering, refused to receive the petition. He did, however, return a threatening message demanding that the delegates disperse instantly. The delegates did not comply, nor did they stop imitating the House in yet another way. Just as the House might do, the convention authorized sending a letter to De Berdt, the House's agent in London. To publicize the convention in America, Adams submitted a copy of this lengthy letter to a Boston newspaper. Published on September 27, it repeated arguments advanced by the Massachusetts House, by the Boston Town Meeting, and, of course, by Adams himself. For example, the letter stressed that, despite the malicious comments articulated by "interested and designing men," the Massachusetts people, who contributed so much to Britain's wealth, were not given to mobbish violence. Instead, they protested reasonably, legally, and respectfully against Parliament's recent acts and against the prospect that a standing army, which threatened their natural rights as well as their charter and constitutional rights, would soon be stationed in their midst.

Although the delegates defied Bernard by continuing to meet, the convention, much to Adams's chagrin, did not produce radical results. The delegates had good reason to stress, as they repeatedly did, that they had assembled to promote peace and good order, not to usurp governmental powers. The delegates did little more than reaffirm support for the petition the House had sent to the king. Bernard gloated that his threatening message had sapped the delegates' courage. As he recounted it, his challenge to the legitimacy of the convention rendered the late-arriving Otis "perfectly tame" and explained why the more radical Samuel Adams failed in his attempts to cajole the delegates into adopting the harsh language often used in the House.

Bernard may have puffed up his role in blocking more radical action by the convention, but he was right about a difference between Otis and Adams. There was a growing rift between the two popular party leaders. Otis headed the conservative wing of the party, which had a very hard time even imagining the colonies might become independent; Adams led the more radical wing, which did not shrink from doing whatever was required to protect American rights. Adams's political philosophy—the people must know their rights and ardently defend them against any assailant—had been formed long before the troubles with Britain began. And while Adams the pragmatic politician would adjust to the realities of the current political scene, he refused to betray his political ideals.

By the time the convention broke up on September 29, British transports carrying more than two regiments of soldiers rode at anchor in Boston harbor amid eight warships and three armed schooners. For Samuel Adams this military presence constituted much more than another in a growing list of grievances against Britain. Since the time of troubles with Britain began, he had repeatedly expressed the hope that the mother country would abandon her new and unconstitutional imperial policy. And, as a pragmatic politician, he counted on more than arguments about natural, charter, and constitutional rights to convince the British. He had constantly reminded the British of how greatly the mother country profited from controlling American trade and from selling British manufactured goods in the colonies. He seemed to believe that the British would eventually realize that jettisoning the new imperial policy would serve their own self-interest. However, by the fall of 1768 it appeared the British could no longer be reasoned with. The mother country had forsaken reason in favor of naked military power. The serpent was darting its fatal venom.

Long before the relationship between Britain and its colonies turned sour in the 1760s, Samuel Adams had asserted that a free people must know their constitutional rights and guard them jealously. And well before soldiers marched into Boston, Adams had often warned about the special dangers a standing army posed for a free people. So the thought of British regiments descending on Boston naturally horrified him. Indeed, if the reports of his contemporaries are correct, the arrival of a British army of occupation marked a transforming moment for Samuel Adams and, in time, for the British Empire.

4

The Politics of Principle

*O*n Friday, October 1, 1768, British warships crowded Boston harbor. Sailors stood ready to fire broadsides at the city. Shortly after noon, British regulars, smartly attired in bright scarlet coats, began landing on the Long Wharf. Once ashore, the Fourteenth and Twenty-ninth Regiments, along with elements of the Fifty-ninth Regiment and accompanying artillery, paraded through the heart of the town until they reached Boston Common. The soldiers, more than seven hundred strong, marched to the beat of drums and the sound of fifes. Their muskets were charged, their bayonets fixed. None of Boston's sixteen thousand inhabitants challenged them. In an afternoon, Boston had become an occupied city. The occupying force grew quickly. Two more regiments, the Sixty-fourth and the Sixty-fifth, began arriving in November.

For Samuel Adams, the hope of reconciliation evaporated once British regulars transformed Boston into a garrisoned city. His cousin John remembered it was about the time of the occupation that Samuel decided America must become independent. Peter Oliver agreed with John Adams's assessment. Claiming his information originated with James Warren, a leading Whig, Oliver asserted the question of American independence "was settled in *Boston,* in 1768, by *Adams* & his Junto." William Gordon, who was in Boston as the Revolutionary movement unfolded and who knew Adams, reported that as late as 1774 few in the colony sought independence, but "at the head of these we must place Mr. Samuel Adams, who has long since said in small confidential companies—'the country shall be independent, and we will be satisfied with nothing short of it.'" In 1775, Samuel himself confided to a friend that the arrival of troops in 1768 had convinced him Britain had left Americans no middle ground between tamely abandoning their rights and pursuing independence.

Whether or not Samuel Adams committed himself irrevocably to independence in 1768 or sometime later, his contemporaries—Whigs and Tories alike—emphasized that he was the first popular leader to conclude that America must be independent. And it is clear that, faced with the choice of surrendering constitutional rights or following the path of resistance to a

Paul Revere engraving "A View of . . . Brittish Ships of War: Landing Their Troops! 1768" (1770). Courtesy, American Antiquarian Society.

revolution for independence, Samuel would tread the revolutionary path. However, as a politician, he knew it would take time and effort for his radical position to gain acceptance. And enunciating a belief few politicians of the day shared, he maintained that the thoughts of ordinary people mattered. He argued, in fact, that the only way to expect success in momentous political struggles was by supporting what the citizenry—the ordinary people—considered a just cause. That is why Samuel had labored so diligently to convince his fellow colonists of the dangers inherent in Britain's new imperial policy. When the arrival of troops posed a new threat to American liberties, Adams wrote prodigiously, especially for newspapers, encouraging opposition to the military occupation. By using newspapers instead of pamphlets, Adams responded quickly to the changing political scene while also promoting his cardinal political ideals.

Adams presented a multifaceted attack against standing armies. It made no sense, he reasoned, to garrison Boston since the orderly and pacific inhabitants were enjoying what he repeatedly called a period of "profound peace." Moreover, putting troops in Boston, or any American town, violated England's own Bill of Rights. Using military power to enforce unconstitutional laws compounded the perniciousness. Britain's decision to place a standing army in Boston was, therefore, unjust and unconstitutional; worse yet, it could annihilate the people's rights. Alluding to Governor Bernard and his supporters while conjuring up images of an evil future monarch, Adams warned of wicked men scheming to use military force "to awe the civil authority" and establish "arbitrary and despotic power" over Americans. The danger ran even deeper because the "military power is forever *dangerous* to civil rights." Although the British constitution had established the principle of military subordination to civilian control, soldiers thought differently than civilians. Because soldiers obeyed all orders, even unlawful ones, they might "sooner or later begin to look upon themselves as the LORDS and not the SERVANTS of the people." Soldiers might make their own laws "and enforce them by the *power of the sword!*"

Adams and his radical colleagues employed various tactics to discomfort the soldiers and the authorities who asked for them. Ironically, one again involved the Quartering Act, which required the colonial governments to provide accommodations for soldiers only if they could not be placed in existing barracks. Castle William, located on an island about three miles out in Boston harbor, could house the soldiers. Of course, billeting the troops there would hinder their ability to control the city. Therefore, Governor Bernard and Lieutenant Colonel William Dalrymple, the temporary British commander, pressed the Council to provide troop accommodations in Boston proper. Noting that Castle William had abundant room for the troops, the councilors refused with the smug observation that they could not even contemplate violating a law passed by Parliament. On October 1, Dalrymple attempted to secure quarters in the city by demanding that the occupants of the manufacturing house, a colony-owned building, vacate in two hours. The tenants, having already barred the doors and windows, sat tight. The beleaguered Dalrymple next tried to intimidate the selectmen into supplying quarters for his men. Repeating the Council's arguments, the selectmen refused. Dalrymple finally backed down. He had the Twenty-ninth pitch tents on the common and asked that the other troops, who lacked tents, be temporarily housed in the courthouse and in Faneuil Hall. The city officials agreed because they realized that approving these temporary arrangements made them appear generous and compassionate even as they opposed the standing army. By late October, after further complications, including an unsuccessful attempt to dislodge the occupants of the manufacturing house by force, Dalrymple began renting buildings in various parts of the city to serve as quarters for his troops.

As Adams had predicted, the soldiers caused more difficulties and tumults than they stopped. Dalrymple himself quickly faced a special problem. His troops deserted at an alarming rate. In just two weeks, desertions cut the British troop strength by a shocking 10 percent. To shut off this loss of men, Dalrymple placed guards throughout the town. The sentries followed the established military practice of challenging—that is, demanding acknowledgment from passersby. Those challenged, civilians as well as soldiers, were expected to respond with the shout "Friend." Bostonians justifiably resented this practice. In addition, soldiers typically ignored the city's tradition of respecting the Sabbath. The presence of troops also significantly increased the number of prostitutes in the city. And, to keep rent costs down, Dalrymple housed many of his soldiers near the homes and workplaces of less affluent Bostonians. That proximity increased the friction between the lower orders and the British regulars.

The presence of soldiers and the many problems they caused provided Adams and his fellow Whigs with ample material to fashion propaganda. They did it by creating a kind of news service that provided a day-by-day description and commentary on the effect of the regulars in Boston. The first installment appeared in the October 13 *New-York Journal* and covered the period from September 28 through October 2. At the end of this chronicle, the authors claimed what they had reported was "strictly fact," and they urged all newspaper publishers to reprint it "for the general satisfaction." This statement, and commentary interspersed within the chronicle, appeared in italics to distinguish analysis from the reporting of events. Each week for more than a year, the *New-York Journal* carried an installment of this "Journal of Occurrences." This was an innovation in an era when publishers filled their newspapers with government pronouncements along with material gleaned from other newspapers and items, especially letters and essays, supplied by private individuals. Publishers did not function as reporters, nor did they employ what today would be called reporters. So no one in America had ever published day-by-day reports of events, much less combined them with editorial comment set off in special type. Given its news value and innovative style, the "Journal of Occurrences" was widely reprinted. Having concocted this powerful public relations tool, Adams and the other "Journal" authors used it to illustrate a theme Samuel emphasized in other essays: standing armies threatened a people's basic liberties.

The "Journal of Occurrences" focused on the many grievances that grew out of the military presence in Boston and, by implication, in any colonial town. While conceding that troops might be beneficial on the frontier, stationing them in a peaceful urban area amounted to a colossal waste of money. Worse yet, it was a provocative act creating a volatile situation because the soldiers abused people and subverted the civil authority. Many soldiers lacked morals; many were criminals. The theme of criminality, buttressed by examples drawn from New York as well as Boston, highlighted the soldiers' depravity. Accounts of rapes and attempted rapes appeared with regularity. The "Occurrences" also contained numerous entries about impressment, yet another threat to American liberty.

Adams and his friends did not overlook the customs commissioners. Developing themes Adams had already trumpeted in newspaper essays, entry after entry in the "Occurrences" accused the scheming commissioners of misrepresenting the situation in Boston so regulars would be stationed there. And why did the commissioners want the soldiers? So they and their ever increasing herds of unscrupulous officials could manipulate the revenue laws to enrich themselves.

Even before the troops arrived, Adams had depicted the customs commissioners as greedy weasels. Reinforcing the "Occurrences" exposés, he again savaged the commissioners in a series of newspaper essays published in late 1768 and early 1769. Adams conceded that the commissioners employed a few honorable men. He also stressed that his critique did not apply to the one customs board member, obviously John Temple, who had attempted to thwart the other commissioners' plans. Having shown at least a modicum of fairness and balance, Adams ripped into the offending commissioners. They had, he charged, been biased against Boston even before they reached America. They treated the people insolently. They spent their time in politics and cabals, not in the king's service. They created swarms of officeholders. They maliciously misrepresented the peaceful and lawful conduct of Boston so troops would be stationed in the city. And they did all this in a venal quest for plunder.

As he assailed the commissioners and the new, intolerable horror caused by a standing army, Adams never lost sight of the fundamental grievance. In his view, the evils he catalogued ultimately sprang from Britain's unconstitutional effort to raise revenue from an unrepresented people. As a result, in late 1768 and early 1769, Samuel relentlessly attacked the Townshend duties. Given how effectively economic warfare had worked against the Stamp Act, it seemed logical to employ the same tactic. By refusing to import British goods, the British merchants, manufacturers, and their employees could, it seemed, be pressured into lobbying Parliament to repeal the duties. On the basis of this theory, Adams and Otis had helped Boston take the lead in developing nonimportation against the Townshend duties, and New York City merchants had responded by adopting an even stronger form of nonimportation. By March 1769 when Philadelphia's mercantile community finally joined the movement, all of America's important commercial centers were closed to British imports.

Because it had been dissolved in June 1768, the Massachusetts House could not even applaud the increasingly vigorous economic war being conducted against parliamentary taxation, much less actively oppose the introduction of a standing army. However, the Massachusetts Charter required that representatives be elected each May. So, as May 1769 approached, the popular and court parties renewed their election battles. Part of the campaign Adams and his colleagues waged involved linking Governor Bernard to the military occupation of Boston. That strategy received an unintended boost from Bernard himself. William Bollan, the Council's agent in England, managed to obtain letters that the governor had written to the home government. They depicted Boston as the home of lawless anti-British zealots. Learning about the letters, the town meeting, adopting a technique Adams and the House had used, petitioned the king and requested that the governor's official correspondence be made public. At the meeting's direction, Adams composed a letter to agent De Berdt to accompany the petition. After claiming that some of the king's principal appointees had misrepresented the situation in Boston, Adams developed a new line of argument in support of obtaining Bernard's letters. He linked their release to the established right to know the evidence presented by one's accuser and added that releasing the letters was even more imperative when, as in this case, the accuser was not a disinterested person.

Two weeks later, Adams used Bernard's alleged misrepresentations of Boston both to question criticism voiced by General Thomas Gage, the commander-in-chief of the British army in America, and to undermine the court party's credibility. Writing as "A Bostonian," Adams suggested that Gage's negative attitude toward Boston probably stemmed from biased information supplied by Governor Bernard "and his *few adherents* in the province." Once again emphasizing a fundamental right, Adams pointed out that Boston had to be considered innocent until evidence proved otherwise.

In the late spring of 1769, Bostonians learned that Bernard would be made a baronet and would probably soon be replaced as governor. That combination made him an especially inviting target for political invective. Just before the annual election, Adams penned a classic piece of political sarcasm that turned the honor of becoming a baronet against Bernard. Writing as "A Tory," Adams mockingly congratulated Bernard for having troops sent to Boston and for quartering them in the town. These achievements, the imaginary Tory opined, showed how much the governor loved the people's rights. Of course, it was a pity the worthy governor did not have a pension to support his new title. However, a well-chosen assembly could remedy the problem. And if that did not happen, why, a tax on the improved lands of the colonies would do the job of supporting Bernard and his friends. "A Tory" closed by calling himself "the most *servile* of all *your* Tools." Although he did not use these words, Samuel's venture into fiction almost shouted: to protect your rights, vote the popular party, vote Whig.

Whig leaders also cleverly asserted that the standing army threatened the integrity of the election process itself. On May 5, 1769, the Boston Town Meeting issued a "Declaration of the People's Rights and Freedom of Election," which Adams had prepared before the gathering occurred. The declaration ordered the selectmen to call on the British commander, General Alexander Mackay, "to claim in Behalf of the Town the full Right of British Freeholders & Subjects . . . founded in the Principles of the British Constitution." The meeting wanted the troops moved out of the city when the election of representatives took place. General Mackay, who had just arrived and who hoped to reduce the friction between soldiers and civilians, replied that he could not comply with the meeting's request. He did, however, offer to confine the soldiers to their barracks on election day. The meeting seized upon this concession as an acknowledgment of the legitimacy of its request. The citizens voted to hold the election but only after "declaring their clear and full Sense, that the presence of an armed force in the Town, during an Election of so great Importance, is a gross Infringement of their constitutional Rights." The town meeting also proclaimed that holding the election could not be considered as a precedent or as a voluntary movement away from "the incontestable rights of British Subjects & freeholders." That point had the Adams touch.

Boston's voters resoundingly reelected Adams, Otis, Cushing, and Hancock. Each man received more than 98 percent of the votes cast. Whigs did well throughout the colony, so a political replay occurred when the legislature convened on May 31, 1769. Once again Cushing became Speaker of the House. Adams continued as clerk. Once again the name of Thomas Hutchinson did not appear on the list of Council members. Governor Bernard vented his anger by negating eleven of the twenty-eight names submitted for membership on the Council. Responding in its now typical way, the House refused to name replacements for the vetoed councilors.

The acrimony between the representatives and the governor never diminished. In missives drafted principally by Adams, the representatives peppered Bernard with strident defenses of the people's rights. In addition to denouncing the military occupation in general, the legislators expressed righteous indignation over the fact that a military guard stood by their door and British cannons were pointed at the statehouse. Calling this an insult to the legislature's right to function freely, the representatives exhorted the

governor to order both the sea and land forces out of Boston for the duration of the legislative session. When Bernard replied, as he always did, that
he lacked the power to remove military forces, the representatives responded with evidence that he did have the authority. Echoing one of Adams's
choice themes, the House also retorted that if the governor could not order
the removal of the troops, then the military power, always dangerous to civil
liberties, had become an absolute power. Although the representatives
declared they would remain in session because the charter required it, they
announced that they would not conduct normal legislative business until
the pernicious assaults on the dignity and rights of the legislature stopped.

Bernard fought back. On June 15, after labeling the representatives' non-
activity a waste of the people's money, he said he would remedy the House's
aversion to troops by ordering the representatives to meet in Cambridge
across the Charles River. Bernard's tactics opened him to a searing counter-
attack. The representatives, having been forced to convene in Cambridge,
escalated their rhetoric. Placing a standing army in the province during
peacetime unchecked by civilian authority constituted "a dangerous innovation"; planting soldiers with cannon in front of the statehouse while the
assembly met constituted "the most pointed insult ever offered a free people, and its whole Legislature." The fact that the cannons were hauled away
the day after the legislature moved to Cambridge heightened the insult. The
assemblymen had, they proclaimed, refused to follow the normal routine
because doing so would undermine the dignity and freedom of the legislature. And while Bernard might consider those things unimportant, the representatives believed otherwise. Their time had been well spent, and their
constituents would agree since "no time can better be employed, than in the
preservation of the rights derived from the British constitution. . . . No trea-
sure can be better expended, than in securing that true old English liberty."
The assemblymen also emphasized that, since they continued to meet out of
necessity, their actions could not be construed as a surrender of the people's
and the legislature's "constitutional rights, liberties, and privileges."

Governor Bernard, who said that every dip of Adams's pen "stung like an
horned Snake," clearly was losing the word battle with Adams and the rest
of the Massachusetts House. And although it was well known that Bernard
would soon travel to England and probably never return, the representatives
took no chances. On June 27, they petitioned the king to remove Bernard
from the governorship *forever*. The petition was based on the document the
House had considered just before being dissolved a year earlier and used
some of that first petition's language. With the new grievance of military
occupation, the harsh tone of the June 1768 indictment gave way in June
1769 to undisguised, sarcastic viciousness. The fate of the two petitions, both
of which Adams probably composed, indicated how far Bernard's position
had eroded. When presented with the June 1768 petition, the House had
deferred action. Now a year later, in a very full House of 109 members, the

more acerbic anti-Bernard petition received unanimous approval.

Right after petitioning for Bernard's ouster, the House adopted a lengthy set of resolves prepared by a large committee that, as usual, included Samuel Adams. The representatives stressed that they were defending the people's most basic natural and constitutional rights against unwarranted, unconstitutional attacks. The resolves offered a lengthy list of grievances that Massachusetts, and the colonies in general, had against Britain's imperial policy. The evils of the customs commissioners and their multiplying minions, of a standing army, of taxation without representation, of extending the power of the admiralty courts, and of threatening to take people out of Massachusetts to face trial were all recounted. Bernard merited special condemnation for supposedly misrepresenting Boston and Massachusetts as being riot torn and virtually ungovernable. He was also lambasted for suggesting, as he did in the private letters agent Bollan had obtained, that the Massachusetts Charter should be revised so the Council would be appointed, not elected.

By early July 1769, the members of the House and Bernard found it virtually impossible to maintain even a pretense of civility. The arrival of news from Virginia exacerbated the situation. In mid-May, in part to support Massachusetts and Boston, the Virginia House of Burgesses had adopted strongly worded resolves defending the American Whig positions on taxation, the right to petition for redress, and the right to be tried where an alleged crime occurred. Virginia's resolves took on great significance because the burgesses sent copies to all the colonial assemblies and asked for their concurrence. The Massachusetts representatives responded on July 8 and, reflecting the ideal of the colonies working in unison, adopted resolves incorporating the essence, and often the wording, of the Virginia resolves. The assemblymen added many other sections that repeated their earlier, especially their anti-Bernard, pronouncements.

Bernard did not shrink from the challenge. He escalated the conflict by telling the legislators that Parliament required them to underwrite the maintenance of the troops stationed in Boston. He might have guessed the response. On July 15 the representatives declared that supplying the funds would obliterate the legislature's and the people's rights. Because of the obligations they owed their constituents, the representatives could never comply with the governor's request. Bernard had had enough of Adams, Otis, and the rest of the popular party. Proclaiming that the House's actions constituted an "invasion of the rights of the imperial sovereignty," Bernard immediately suspended the General Court and postponed a further meeting until early 1770.

While the legislature and governor engaged in increasingly acrimonious confrontation, the civilians and soldiers coexisted uneasily. To discredit the idea that troops were needed to maintain peace, Bostonians strove to maintain tranquillity. The British generals in command from November 1768 through mid-August 1769 matched the civilian effort at self-control. Recognizing the explosive, no-win nature of the situation, the British commanders requested transfers for themselves and endeavored to keep things quiet until those transfers arrived. In addition, for all the problems the soldiers created, their presence pumped money into Boston's economy.

The relative quiet that existed in the city made it easier for the British government to implement a plan to reduce tensions by withdrawing troops from Boston. In addition, the British needed more soldiers in Ireland. The decision of how many, if any, regulars should stay in Boston fell to General Gage. He quickly arranged for the removal of two regiments. The Sixty-fifth shipped out on June 25; the Sixty-fourth and the artillery followed in July.

By early August, Boston's Whigs had good reason to rejoice. Bernard sailed on August 1, never to return. Perhaps because Bostonians thought the remaining soldiers would soon vanish, the last entry in the "Journal of Occurrences" was for August 1, 1769, and recounted the joyous exuberance that accompanied Bernard's departure. On August 3, the Reverend Samuel Cooper, a leading Boston Whig, observed that the greater part of the military had departed, "and it is said the remainder will not tarry long among us." Nevertheless, two regiments remained, and, as Adams realized, so did the difficult task of defeating any parliamentary taxation. Partial victories were just that, partial. So Adams and Otis continued their practice of using special anniversary days to champion colonial resistance. The anniversary of the people's Stamp Act resistance of August 14 featured impressive celebrations designed to cultivate what John Adams described as the sensations of freedom. The emphasis the festivities placed on supporting America helped produce a significant change in the meaning of a powerful term, "patriot." Now when the leaders of the popular forces talked of "patriots" and of "patriotism," they were speaking of loyalty to America, not to Great Britain or to the British Empire. Being a patriot had come to mean supporting American rights.

Despite the Whigs' efforts, as the summer of 1769 drew to a close, support for nonimportation waned. In late August, writing as "Populus," Adams tried to halt the slide. Asserting that America's "Salvation" was at stake, Adams implored merchants to continue backing nonimportation. And, following his usual strategy, he went on the offensive. Drawing upon the dislike of Governor Bernard, Adams observed that the governor knew nonimportation could scuttle the taxes that would provide him with a pension. As Adams presented it, that fact helped explain the actions of John Mein, a merchant and the publisher of the *Boston Chronicle,* the newspaper voice of the court party. Mein had been printing shipping records that purportedly revealed how various Boston Whig merchants violated the nonimportation agreement. After challenging some of Mein's evidence and implying that the publisher was doing the bidding of Bernard and his cronies, Adams warned Mein about putting himself in opposition to "an awakened, an enlightened and a Determined Continent." In a parting shot, Adams chastised Thomas Hutchinson's two merchant sons for not supporting nonimportation.

Everyone considered nonimportation crucial. It was the only effective weapon the colonists had fashioned to fight parliamentary taxation. And, as Adams knew all too well, pumping up support for the existing nonimportation effort was merely a stopgap measure. The nonimportation agreement obligated America's merchants only through January 1, 1770. Equally important from Adams's perspective, because it only targeted the Townshend duties, the agreement was too limited. Believing the colonists must be consistent in defending their basic rights, Adams and Otis wanted nonimportation sustained until Parliament rescinded *all* the laws that taxed Americans. That meant waging economic war until Parliament repealed the Sugar Act as well as the Townshend duties. But the Sugar Act duties, which were neither highly visible nor particularly burdensome, had recently been lowered. As a result, concerns about consistently defending principle melted away; few Americans seemed willing to suffer the hardships of nonimportation to attack the Sugar Act.

The British government hoped to take advantage of the fact that most Americans, like many people in Great Britain, developed a convenient amnesia about constitutional principles when they bumped against immediate economic self-interest. In May 1769, the government sent a circular letter to the colonies that, while reiterating the British view of the supremacy of Parliament, indicated that the administration had no plans to levy further taxes on Americans. Moreover, when Parliament next convened, the administration expected to eliminate the Townshend duties on glass, paper, and painting materials as being "contrary to the true principles of Commerce." Realizing that the British aimed to undermine nonimportation, Adams and Otis exhorted Boston's merchants to press for total victory before the British acted. On September 2, 1769, the merchants' correspondence committee sent a letter to Philadelphia's merchants asking them to continue nonimportation until Parliament repealed all its revenue acts, including the Sugar Act.

As Boston's merchant committee waited for a response, James Otis was effectively removed from the political scene. Angered by a report that customs commissioners had labeled him an enemy of the king, Otis, accompanied by Adams, met with the commissioners on September 1. The participants kept the reason for the meeting secret, but, if it was designed to fashion a compromise, it failed. Then, on September 4, Otis published an extraordinary essay under his own name. Denouncing John Robinson and three other commissioners, Otis said he had asked for personal satisfaction but had not received a proper answer. In short, he had demanded a gentleman's satisfaction—a duel. When Otis strolled into the British Coffee House the next evening, he and Robinson fought. The press carried conflicting versions of what happened. Adams entered the fray as "An Impartialist" and was anything but impartial. He implied that Robinson had participated in a prearranged plan to assassinate Otis. And no one could deny that Otis received a vicious blow on the head that probably hastened his already discernible descent into mental instability. After the fight, Otis oscillated between periods of lucidity and bouts of irrational behavior.

Even before the coffeehouse brawl, Otis's popularity had been declining. Samuel Adams had, in fact, supplanted him as the leading Whig in Massachusetts. But Otis's efforts would be sorely missed in the nonimportation effort. As acting governor Hutchinson attested, the team of Adams and Otis had been instrumental in convincing Boston's merchants to support nonimportation. Now, Otis could no longer play his usual animating role. Undaunted, Adams pressed on. A town meeting was scheduled for October 4 to examine the issues of nonimportation and its natural twin, support for American manufacturing. Two days before the meeting, Adams published a lengthy essay under the pen name "Alfred." Building on the idea that Americans would have been reduced to absolute slavery if they had not fought the Stamp Act, Adams proclaimed that the people were more united than ever, that their opposition had been prudent and legal, and that they should continue their opposition until "every American grievance is redressed."

The town meeting did just what Adams outlined in his Alfred essay. The citizens endorsed a statement describing nonimportation as a legal, peaceful strategy that also had the best chance of successfully defending American rights. The merchants of Boston and the whole continent drew praise for "having nobly preferred the publick Good to their own private Emolument." Indeed, posterity would venerate them for their noble and public-spirited actions. The meeting then contemplated the few who were undermining nonimportation. It expressed astonishment and indignation "that any of its Citizens could be so lost to the feelings of Patriots, and the common Interest" as to keep buying British goods. Seven offending merchants were listed by name and thus held up to ridicule. The list included the three men Adams had openly denounced in his Populus essay: John Mein, Elisha Hutchinson, and Thomas Hutchinson Jr. Why had the offending merchants deserted their country in its struggle to protect its constitutional rights? Because they "preferred their little private advantage to the common Interest of all the Colonies." To enrich themselves, they had basely taken advantage "of the generous self denial of their Fellow Citizens for the Common Good." So the statement, which Adams probably helped craft, praised virtually the whole business community, the city's people, and even the rest of the continent for standing up for American rights. How could anyone openly vote against that? The pronouncement passed unanimously. By thus attacking the seven miscreants with loaded words, the town meeting's polemic reminded potential nonimportation slackers that public opprobrium might be visited upon them as well.

Adams had to be gratified when the October 4, 1769, town meeting prodded everyone to support nonimportation. Less than two weeks later, he had even better reason to smile. On October 17, the day before the town meeting was next scheduled to meet, Boston's merchant committee did what Adams had advocated. It proposed continuing nonimportation until Parliament repealed *all* the taxes. Then, when the town meeting convened the next day, the citizens approved a lengthy commentary written chiefly by Adams. The work's title revealed the basic goal: "An Appeal to the World; or a Vindication of the Town of Boston, from Many False and Malicious Aspersions" contained in the writing of Governor Bernard and others. The "Vindication" paraded the old themes of a profoundly peaceful Boston being overrun with soldiers because of the venality of Bernard, his cronies, and the customs commissioners. And, as he had been doing with increasing regularity, Adams also used "An Appeal" to urge Americans to defend their fundamental rights on a thoroughly consistent, not a piecemeal, basis. With simple clarity and thus with real force, Adams maintained that the colonists' grievances could never be truly redressed "till *every Act,* pass'd by the British Parliament for the express Purpose of raising a Revenue upon us without our Consent, is Repeal'd; till the American Board of Commissions of the Customs is dissolv'd; the Troops recall'd."

The public indignation expressed during the town meeting reflected the tension mounting in Boston from midsummer into the fall of 1769. It could be traced to much more than the physical attack on Otis. The anticipated evacuation of the last two regiments of redcoats had not materialized. In addition, Colonel Dalrymple, who resumed command of the British regulars in mid-August 1769, was not interested in placating Bostonians. As a result, repeated violence flared. On the evening of October 23, citizens exchanged insults with soldiers stationed at the guard post on Boston Neck at the outskirts of the city. The next day, a crowd assailed the soldiers as they returned to their barracks. Although several troopers suffered injuries, none of the assailants was arrested. Colonel Dalrymple speculated that this incident presaged something more consequential. Merchants who dared to keep importing British goods also experienced the people's wrath. Nathaniel Rogers, a nephew of Thomas Hutchinson, complained that his house had twice been "besmeared, the last time with the Vilest filth of the Vilest Vault." On October 28, John Mein had to scamper behind British sentries to escape an angry crowd. That night a crowd seized George Gailer, a man reviled as a customs official lackey. Gailer was tarred and feathered, hauled around Boston in a cart, and then forced to repent publicly for his offenses. Along the way, the crowd taunted a British sentry and threatened to pitch him into the cart.

Samuel Adams, always laboring to further the patriot cause, used the increased tension between soldiers and townspeople to press even harder for removing the troops. In late December 1769, about three weeks before the General Court was scheduled to reconvene, Thomas Hutchinson reported that "Adams has declared the troops must move to the Castle, and it must be the first business of [the General] Court to remove them out of the town." The British ministry in London, probably responding to the challenge made by Adams's " Appeal," had already sent orders that precluded that possibility. Acting on the home government's instructions, on January 4, Hutchinson decreed that the legislature would not meet until March. Adams fought back in a newspaper essay published four days later. He held that no person located three thousand miles away could understand when convening the legislature might be essential. Worse yet, if the assembly could not meet, the people would be deprived of their basic right of having their representatives petition for redress of grievances. Adams asserted that, under the charter, the acting governor could, and should, exercise his own independent judgment and call the legislature into session. Hutchinson naturally ignored Adams's pleadings. The General Court would not meet again until March.

Although the Whigs did not need the General Court to keep nonimportation going, Adams, who proclaimed himself an auxiliary to the merchants and who served on at least one merchant committee, knew that nonimportation faced mounting problems. His hopes for an energized and principled effort had been dashed because merchants in other cities refused to extend nonimportation until Parliament repealed *all* the revenue laws. They would not commit themselves to any more than continuing nonimportation until the Townshend duties were abolished. Left with little choice, Boston's business community accepted that plan at a meeting in October 1769. Some of the city's merchants, including Hutchinson's merchant sons, balked at doing that much. They considered themselves bound only by the original agreement. So, when it expired on January 1, 1770, those merchants began selling imported goods, especially tea, which fetched a high price. Adams rushed into print once again as "Determinatus." He tried to shame the slackers into continuing nonimportation until it succeeded. Reiterating that nothing worked as well as nonimportation, Adams accused those who sold imported goods of selfishly ignoring their obligation to society. Proclaiming that "the fate of *Unborn Millions*" of Americans hung in the balance, Adams urged the whole city to support the patriotic nonimportation effort. Everyone, not just the merchants, must insist on nonimportation "being *Strictly* adhered to."

Members of the merchant committee did their part by paying visits to individual slackers, but nine merchants still refused to comply. A large group of merchants and other inhabitants, including Samuel Adams, met at Faneuil Hall on January 23 and publicly denounced the nine as "obstinate and inveterate enemies to their country and subverters of the Rights and Liberties of this continent." The offenders would be boycotted and treated as outlaws. The meeting also made tea a special symbol by agreeing to abstain from drinking it. More than 300 married women soon pledged to do the same, except in the case of sickness, because they wanted to help "save this abused Country from Ruin and Slavery." Within two weeks, another 120 women signed an "Agreement of the young Ladies of this Town against drinking foreign TEA." They believed their abstinence might help "frustrate a plan which tends to deprive a whole community of all that is valuable in life." By mid-February, over 100 additional married women had subscribed to the anti-tea pledge, which meant that more than 500 Boston women had publicly endorsed the tea boycott.

As Adams prophesied, and probably hoped, the nine recalcitrant merchants suffered almost constant harassment. One favorite tactic involved simply identifying someone as an "importer." On the morning of February 22, young boys set up such a sign outside the shop of Theophilus Lillie, one of the nine slackers. Ebenezer Richardson, already despised as a customs informer, tried to destroy the sign. After exchanging insults with some adults, he retired to his nearby home. The boys, as they told the story, also had words with Richardson and his wife. Before long, the boys began tossing "light Rubbish of one Kind or other," which Mrs. Richardson pitched back at them. After cursing at the crowd and demanding that they leave, Richardson appeared at a window with a gun in his hand. The boys responded by pelting the house with whatever they could lay their hands on. Then, to everyone's amazement, Richardson fired. Young Sammy Gore fell wounded, but survived. Christopher Snider, who came from a poor German family whose name is sometimes given as Seider, was not so fortunate. Several large pellets tore into him; he died that night. Snider was only about eleven years old. Even Peter Oliver conceded that Richardson—who was subsequently tried, found guilty of murder, but ultimately pardoned—had "fired at Random & killed an innocent Boy."

Samuel Adams helped turn young Snider's death into a political event filled with powerful symbolism. On Monday, February 26, notices appeared in the press requesting that "the Friends of Liberty" attend Snider's funeral. The funeral procession began in the late afternoon at the Liberty Tree. On it, Sons of Liberty placed a sign that included the pious observation "The memory of the just is Blessed." Each side of the casket contained a message, in Latin, rendered in silvered letters. The inscription at the head of the casket translated into the lament *"innocence itself is no where safe!"* Newspaper accounts indicated that between four hundred and five hundred boys marched in front of the little casket. Six youths served as pallbearers. A cortege of more than thirteen hundred men and women walked behind the casket. About thirty horse-drawn coaches closed the procession. John Rowe also estimated that about two thousand people marched in the funeral, and John Adams confided to his diary that "my eyes never beheld such a funeral. The Procession extended further than can be well imagined." A sizable and bereft crowd watched this huge funeral procession. The *News-Letter* carried the observation that "young as he was, he died in his Country's Cause." An essayist called Snider "the little hero and first martyr to the noble cause." The publishers of the *Boston Gazette* assured their readers that a monument would be erected to perpetuate the memory of the young martyr. Patriotic gentlemen had, reportedly, already launched a subscription to achieve that goal. Lieutenant Governor Thomas Hutchinson understood the motives of Adams and other Whig leaders. He claimed that Snider's funeral, like other huge public funerals staged for political purposes, was designed to raise the people's passions in support of the cause the leaders espoused.

The press spread the news of the tragic death and magnificently patriotic funeral throughout the colonies. The Snider incident clearly had the potential of evolving into a significant landmark in the dispute between the colonies and Great Britain; however, it was soon overshadowed by an even more deadly confrontation. Many of the city's inhabitants, no matter what their political views, considered a bloody clash between Bostonians and the soldiers inevitable. All Bostonians, even Tories, disliked the way many redcoats behaved, but ordinary Bostonians had special and increasing reason to find their continuing presence offensive. Soldiers standing guard often treated the lower orders with disrespect, even threatening them. In addition, redcoats posed an immediate economic challenge. Because the British allowed off-duty troops to work, the people who typically formed the bulk of the city's crowds now often found themselves competing with soldiers for casual-labor jobs. That economic threat seemed even more menacing in early 1770. Nonimportation had caused the value of Boston's imports to drop by half, and this naturally reduced the number of jobs available in the city. To make matters worse, by late January 1770, ice clogged Boston's harbor, thus curtailing shipping and employment opportunities even more.

The combination of economic difficulties and mutual contempt bred by more than seventeen months of military occupation sparked a number of altercations. Fights on March 2 provided the immediate background of the catastrophe known as the Boston Massacre. As Patrick Walker, an off-duty soldier, strolled by John Gray's ropewalk in quest of work, a rope maker asked him if he wanted a job. When Walker replied affirmatively, the rope maker said, "then go and clean my shithouse." A fight followed. Getting the worst of it, Walker rounded up eight or nine other soldiers and came back for a rematch. But, when several rope makers joined forces, the redcoats again lost the tussle. Undaunted, Walker and the other soldiers regrouped and returned about forty strong. Anticipating the soldiers' action, the rope makers had obtained their own reinforcements. In the ensuing melee, the two sides went at each other with clubs and other weapons. Once again, the soldiers were routed. Over the next two days, rope makers and other civilians tussled with individual soldiers, and one, Private John Rodgers, had both his arm and skull fractured. Bostonians remembered soldiers exclaiming that they would have their revenge.

On Monday night, March 5, 1770, different groups of civilians and soldiers went looking for trouble. Private Hugh White, standing sentry duty near the customhouse in King Street, suddenly found himself being bombarded with snowballs and chunks of ice. He shouted for help, and soldiers from the Twenty-ninth Regiment, led by Captain Thomas Preston, rushed to White's defense. Estimates of the size of the crowd that gathered in front of the soldiers vary wildly from fewer than a hundred to well over a thousand, but there is no question that the crowd pressed close to the soldiers and taunted them mercilessly. Knowing the soldiers, clad in their scarlet coats, could not legally fire their weapons unless authorized by a civilian magistrate, members of the crowd shouted, "Come on you rascals, you bloody-backs, you Lobster Scoundrels; fire if you dare, God damn you, fire and be damned, we know you dare not." As the thunderous crowd pushed ever closer, one of the soldiers was knocked down. Then the soldiers did dare; they fired. They killed three civilians outright and wounded eight more, two of whom later died. Further carnage was avoided when acting governor Hutchinson courageously visited the scene and assured the people that the legal system would deal with the incident. Local authorities then arrested Captain Preston and his soldiers and held them for trial on murder charges. The Boston Town Meeting called the event a "Massacre"; the label stuck.

The Boston Massacre again illustrates why it is wrong to depict Samuel Adams as the "keeper" of a trained mob. Adams did not create the friction that produced repeated clashes between the soldiers and civilians, especially ordinary working people. Adams did not direct the members of the crowd who ventured into King Street that night. Equally important, the crowd was made up of individuals who had the most immediate and personal reasons to challenge the soldiers. John Adams probably exaggerated when he claimed that the crowd was composed of "a motley rabble of saucy boys, negroes and mulattoes, Irish teagues and outlandish Jack tars." His description is suspect in part because it implies that the members of the crowd came from the margins of society and were, in many cases, perhaps not even Bostonians. That depiction suited John's needs since he, like Samuel, wanted to downplay the image of a mobbish Boston. Nevertheless, even allowing for exaggeration, John's description seems generally accurate, and it is clear that the persons who pushed into King Street on that snowy night came primarily from the economically and socially less powerful segment of the populace. The five killed in the so-called Massacre were Samuel Gray, a rope maker; Samuel Maverick, a seventeen-year-old apprentice joiner; Patrick Carr, an Irish immigrant who worked for a leather-breeches maker; Crispus Attucks, a mulatto seaman; and James Caldwell, described variously as a "young seaman," a "sailor," and as a "mate"—a rank, which if accurate, would place his standing above an ordinary sailor. The lower orders opposed Britain's imperial policies and especially the military presence because those policies and those troops directly threatened their rights and their livelihoods. They took to the streets for their own good reasons.

Although Samuel Adams did not control the crowd that formed in King Street, he certainly used the Massacre to pry the remaining British troops out of Boston. On the morning of March 6, with blood still visible in the streets, the selectmen and other local officials visited the acting governor and demanded that he order the troops out of Boston. Although Hutchinson had the authority to issue such a directive, he claimed that he lacked the power to make the military redeploy. The town meeting convened in emergency session at eleven o'clock and established a committee of fifteen, which included Adams and other leading Whigs, to tell Hutchinson that only the immediate removal of the soldiers could prevent further violence. The governor responded in a written statement. Expressing sorrow over the events of March 5 and pledging that an inquiry and appropriate legal action would occur, Hutchinson reiterated his disingenuous claim that he could not command the troops to evacuate. Still, noting that the Council had asked that the troops be removed to Castle William and considering the role of the Twenty-ninth Regiment in the events of March 5, Hutchinson reported that Colonel Dalrymple, who was awaiting orders from General Gage in New York, had stated that the Twenty-ninth would be shifted to the castle. In addition, the main guard would be withdrawn from Boston and the activities of Fourteenth Regiment curtailed to prevent any further bloodshed.

When the town meeting reconvened that afternoon, Faneuil Hall overflowed with people, and the gathering moved to the Old South Church. Adams took the lead. He publicly read Hutchinson's letter and pronounced it inadequate. With one dissenting vote, the huge meeting concurred. The citizens then selected a seven-member committee to inform the acting governor of the vote and to renew the demand for the immediate removal of troops. When the delegation met with Hutchinson and his Council, Adams, serving as spokesman, conveyed the meeting's decisions. Hutchinson, with Colonel Dalrymple standing at his side, again claimed that he could not dictate troop movements. Adams responded in a cold, clear voice and in a manner Hutchinson himself remembered as showing "a strong expression of that determined spirit which animated all future measures." "If you have power to remove one regiment," Adams reasoned, "you have power to remove both. It is at your peril if you do not. The meeting is composed of three thousand people. They are become very impatient. A thousand men are already arrived from the neighborhood, and the country is in general motion. Night is approaching; an immediate answer is expected." Adams recalled how Hutchinson reacted. "I observ'd his Knees to tremble. I thought I saw his face grow pale (and I enjoyed the Sight) at the Appearance of the determined Citizens peremptorily demanding Redress of Grievances." Hutchinson asked the Council for advice. Once again unanimously recommending that all troops be sent to Castle William, the coun-

Paul Revere engraving "The Bloody Massacre" (1770). Courtesy, American Antiquarian Society.

cilors pointedly warned the acting governor that he would bear the responsibility if he failed to act and something horrible happened. Hutchinson and Dalrymple, who both tried to escape responsibility for the decision, surrendered. All the troops would be relocated to the castle. The accounts that British prime minister Lord North received of these events reportedly caused him thereafter to refer to the troops then stationed in Boston as "Samuel Adams's Regiments."

The Adams committee returned to the town meeting in triumph. Speaking for the committee, Adams reported that Colonel Dalrymple had promised, on his honor, that both regiments would be moved to the castle as quickly as possible. The redeployment would begin the next morning. After expressing great satisfaction with this news, the meeting decided a citizen night watch should be established until the troops actually departed. Adams and the other committee members who had wrung the concessions out of Hutchinson and Dalrymple volunteered to stand guard that night. The meeting agreed and authorized them to increase the size of the force and appoint a watch for the succeeding nights. Adams and John Hancock, William Mollinux, William Phillips, Joshua Henshaw, Samuel Pemberton, and Dr. Joseph Warren had, in effect, become the temporary police commissioners of Boston. Since the last soldier was not relocated to the castle until March 16, the citizens' night patrols continued for almost two weeks.

The town meeting was extraordinarily active during the three weeks after the Massacre. In addition to its emergency meetings of March 6, the town meeting convened on five separate days from March 12 through March 26. Adams, as usual, helped direct its activities. In the midst of repeatedly telling Colonel Dalrymple that he must quickly remove all the soldiers from Boston proper, the meeting arranged to publish its own history of the Massacre. And soon after ten thousand to twelve thousand people had attended the public funeral of four persons slain in the Massacre, the town meeting decided the legislature should consider erecting a monument "as a Memento to Posterity of that horred Massacre, and the destructive Consequences of Military Troops, being quartered in a well regulated City."

With Adams again spearheading efforts, the town meeting also tried to ensure that the trials of Captain Preston and the British troops would neither be delayed nor tarnish the image of a peaceful Boston victimized by a standing army. Right after the Massacre, the judges who would hear the cases considered postponing them. Speaking for a town meeting committee, Samuel Adams personally confronted the judges and demanded that the trials get under way forthwith. He wanted them held while the memory of the carnage of March 5 remained fresh. Intimidated by Adams's threats, the judges agreed to start the trials expeditiously. However, owing to what Hutchinson called a number of accidental occurrences, the trials did not take place until late fall.

Adams fared better when it came to ensuring that Boston would be presented in the best possible light during the trials. Desperate to get any lawyer to defend him, Captain Preston applied to Josiah Quincy, an ardent young Whig. Quincy accepted the case only after Samuel Adams and others convinced him he should take it and after John Adams agreed to work with him. The soldiers followed their officer's lead by having these lawyers defend them as well. Samuel Adams worked to get Quincy and his cousin John to serve as defense counsel because Samuel knew they would not denigrate the city in order to defend the British soldiers. He was also instrumental in getting Robert Treat Paine, another Whig, installed as the prosecutor. Moreover, at least once during the trials, Samuel provided Paine with commentary on the evidence and also made suggestions about courtroom techniques. There is no doubt Samuel labored hard to keep the trials from besmirching Boston's image.

In addition to dealing with issues rooted in the Massacre, the town meeting also used its numerous March 1770 sessions to champion nonimportation. On March 13, the citizens pondered what more they could do to strengthen the nonimportation agreement, discourage the consumption of tea, and provide employment for the poor by encouraging local manufacturing. To make nonconsumption of tea a prime symbol of support for nonimportation, the meeting created a committee to convince shopkeepers to stop selling tea until Parliament repealed the revenue acts. Three days later, the town meeting passed a resolution proclaiming that almost all American merchants embraced nonimportation and thus "nobly preferred the publick Good" to their own private benefit. Adopting Adams's line that nothing defended America's rights as effectively as nonimportation, the meeting excoriated the few merchants who did not back the effort. The gathering expressed astonishment and indignation that any Bostonian could "be so lost to the feelings of Patriotism, and the common Interest, and so thoroughly & infamously selfish." These few miscreants suffered what Adams considered the ultimate public humiliation: their names and villainy were recorded in the official town records for posterity. In all, thirteen merchants, two of them women, landed on the roster of shame. Given this kind of leverage, the committee charged with persuading shopkeepers to stop marketing tea did very well. It reported that, in less than two weeks of solicitations, 212 shopkeepers had signed the agreement.

As Adams and other Whigs had long emphasized, support for American manufacturing went hand in hand with nonimportation. So it made sense for the March 13 session of the town meeting to search for ways to increase the colony's manufacturing. There was another significant reason for promoting manufacturing, and that was, the meeting said, to provide work for "the Poor." The committee assigned to accomplish that goal reported back on March 26 and made it clear that it aimed to provide employment for "the Tradesmen" as well as for poor people. The committee understood that more than the poor faced hard times due to the business constrictions created by nonimportation. If the people in general could not find jobs, support for nonimportation might weaken, and the potential for violence would increase. Fortunately for the Whig forces, the committee succeeded. Asserting that shipbuilding constituted the best and most natural way to provide employment, the committee joyfully reported that it had arranged for the construction of three ships.

The popular forces accomplished a great deal in the immediate aftermath of the Boston Massacre. By March 16, all British troops had been relocated to an island in the harbor. By the end of the month, the town

meeting had taken strong measures to shore up nonimportation. Manufacturing had been bolstered and, at the same time, work provided for artisans
as well as for the poor. If the rest of America acted with equal vigor, the
British government might retreat from its latest effort to raise revenue
through parliamentary taxation.

The reconvening of the General Court offered Adams and the popular
party new ammunition against the imperial government and Lieutenant
Governor Hutchinson. The House was scheduled to resume its work in
Boston on March 14, but, on the basis of instructions sent from Britain,
Hutchinson ordered the representatives to assemble in Cambridge. The
assemblymen had complained when Bernard temporarily moved them
from Boston to Cambridge, and Hutchinson's explanation of yet another
forced removal played right into the radicals' hands. After hearing the acting governor's explanation, the House appointed a committee of seven to
fashion a response. The committee, which included Adams and the other
Boston representatives, reported back that afternoon and asserted that,
according to the charter, the House must meet in "its ancient Place, the
Court House in *Boston.*" While giving a number of practical reasons for
returning to Boston, the committee stressed that moving the legislature
because of instructions from Britain constituted "an Infraction of our
essential Rights, as Men and Citizens, as well as those derived to us by the
British Constitution and the Charter of this Colony." Hutchinson, who
considered these arguments a challenge to the king's prerogative, retorted
that he was obliged to follow the king's instructions. In quick order, the
House established three committees to enlist the Council's support, to
respond to another message from Hutchinson, and to prepare an analysis of
the situation in the province. The House staffing of those committees
demonstrates the importance the members placed on Adams's leadership.
He was the only leading Whig who served on each committee; the only
other representative appointed to all the committees was Daniel Leonard, a
new member from Taunton who was noted for his ardent Whig views.

In addition to persuading the Council to join in demanding that the
General Court be returned to Boston, the House members resorted to one
of Adams's favorite ploys. They asked Hutchinson to produce a copy of his
instructions. The acting governor refused on the grounds that the king had
forbidden sharing letters of instruction with colonial legislators. Although
this was true, the governor was made to appear stubborn, secretive, and
uncooperative. The House turned to its regular business only after stressing
that doing so could not be construed as acceding to its unconstitutional
removal from Boston.

As the lengthy fight over the relocation of the General Court unfolded,
Hutchinson inadvertently gave the representatives a new opportunity to
lambaste him. On April 7, he informed the House that a horrible riot in
the town of Gloucester demonstrated that the "executive Powers of Gov-

ernment" should be strengthened. The House appointed a committee to consider the issue, and, as usual, Adams was on it. The committee report submitted on April 23 illustrates why Hutchinson, when reviewing the events of this period, complained that Adams possessed an extraordinary "talent" for vilifying an opponent. Indeed, Hutchinson, who noted that Adams penned "most" of the House's pronouncements, maintained that Adams "made more converts to his cause by calumniating governors, and other servants of the crown, than by strength of reasoning."

Samuel Adams's reasoning had greater strength than the acting governor cared to admit, but Hutchinson was right about Adams being a master political mudslinger. The mud almost oozed from the April 23 report. Hutchinson's suggestion about strengthening the executive's power was scornfully dismissed as both unnecessary and possibly "dangerous to the Rights and Liberties of the People." Adams openly defended crowd actions and, in doing so, hinted that an increase in the executive's power might generate more violence. "It may justly be said of the People of this Province," he intoned, "that they seldom have assembled in a tumultuous Manner, unless they have been oppressed." The report chastised Hutchinson for bemoaning the Gloucester riot without even mentioning the horrible Boston Massacre. Piling accusation upon accusation, the report implied that, in his capacity as chief justice, Hutchinson had illegally aided the British soldiers when they attempted to muscle the residents out of the manufacturing building in Boston. The committee finished off its attack by again asserting that compelling the General Court to meet in Cambridge violated the legislature's constitutional rights.

An infuriated acting governor responded three days later. He complained that the House committee had used his message as an excuse to fashion a political harangue. Having clearly been put on the defensive, Hutchinson embarked on a lengthy account of the effort to evict civilians from the manufacturing house. He claimed he had nothing to do with the incident and was not even in the city when it happened. He tried to explain away his silence on the tragic events of March 5 by asserting that the facts were well known and legal proceedings were under way. With respect to forcing the General Court to meet in Cambridge, Hutchinson reiterated that he was following the king's orders. The acting governor then decreed that the legislature be dissolved immediately. Although Hutchinson had the last word, the exchange was a public relations disaster. He felt compelled to produce his lengthy defense because the House clerk had already had the House's report published in the press. Hutchinson, like Bernard before him, understood that many of the House messages Adams drafted were intended for the people, not some government official. Samuel Adams was again using the clerkship as a bully pulpit; and, as Hutchinson lamented, because he did it so ardently and skillfully, he was the most dangerous of the Whigs.

The exchange between the House and the acting governor became the opening shot of the annual colony-wide election contest. The 1770 election gave the popular party yet more power. In Boston, the voters reelected Samuel Adams, John Hancock, and Thomas Cushing, all well-known Whigs. Because of his increasing medical difficulties, James Otis was replaced by James Bowdoin, a solid Whig and longtime councilor whom Governor Bernard had negated off the Council in 1769. When Bowdoin regained a Council seat in early June, John Adams assumed Bowdoin's place in the House. Bowdoin's return to the Council caused Hutchinson even more headaches. The acting governor complained that "the good understanding and reciprocal communications" between Bowdoin and Samuel Adams meant that "the messages of council and house harmonized." From Hutchinson's point of view, the sad fact was: if the governor now encountered opposition from one branch of the General Court, he would also meet it from the other.

Hutchinson considered Samuel Adams his chief adversary because Adams was, as the acting governor said, "the most active member in the house." Adams's ardor "in the cause of liberty" made the difference. Indeed, his "constant application" to that cause "distinguished" him "from all the rest of the province." By the late summer, Hutchinson had become so fixated on Samuel Adams that he routinely described his opposition as being "Adams, &c." or "Adams and the Bostoneers." Hutchinson, like the members of the House who constantly called upon Adams's services in the cause of defending liberty, increasingly saw Samuel Adams as the indispensable Whig politician. In time, their judgment became history's judgment.

When the new legislature convened on May 30, the issue of forcing the General Court to meet in Cambridge quickly surfaced. It took the new House less than a week to escalate the fight into a full-blown constitutional crisis. On June 6, 1770, acting on a report from a committee that naturally included Samuel Adams, the representatives did more than restate their case against being forced to meet in Cambridge. Employing an argument Josiah Quincy had written into the Boston Town Meeting's instructions, the House maintained that the monarch's prerogative could be used only "for the Good of the Subject." If an exercise of the prerogative power injured the people, it must be opposed lest it "overthrow the Constitution itself." Boldly proclaiming that "it is our indispensable Duty, as the Guardians of the People's Rights, *now* to make a Constitutional Stand," assemblymen announced that they would not conduct any business until the House was returned to Boston. To signal the importance of the issue, the members took a roll-call vote and entered it in the permanent record. The militants carried the day, 96 to 6. With neither side willing to compromise, on June 25, Hutchinson suspended the legislature for a month. That only increased the House's resolve. When the representatives reconvened, they voted unanimously not to conduct any normal business until they were returned to Boston.

Thomas Hutchinson believed that the conflict took an especially dangerous turn when Samuel Adams drafted yet another of his lengthy statements for the House. This commentary, unanimously approved on July 31, was provocative. Adams asserted that the people faced real threats to their most valuable liberties, and he cited John Locke's argument about an aggrieved people having the right to rebel. Although he carefully said that the Americans had not yet been driven to that extreme, Samuel also advanced the stunning claim that the members of the Massachusetts House had the right to oppose any prerogative—even a legal and constitutional one—if it was "abusive." Indeed, if complying with the monarch's instructions would injure the people, those instructions "cease to be binding." And who would determine if that was the case? The people's representatives would decide. Hutchinson called this lengthy missive Adams's "treatise" and denounced it as a criminal and seditious production that hinted at revolution. The acting governor again suspended the House and dictated that it would not again meet until September.

Hutchinson could shut the House down, but he could not silence Samuel Adams. Understanding the value of using the media as well as any modern politician, Adams kept the controversy fresh in people's minds by carrying the fight into the press. Adopting the pen name "A Chatterer," he produced three essays that reviewed the whole controversy over forcing the General Court to meet outside Boston. In the process, Adams accused various unnamed colonial governors of having acted "like *Verres* . . . to oppress and plague the people they were bound to protect." Most readers of the *Boston Gazette* probably knew of Verres. As the Roman governor of Sicily, he had plundered the island and its people. Verres's crimes became so infamous that he was tried and eventually exiled. Hutchinson had good reason to rue Adams's skill at tarring an executive's image.

When the legislature reconvened on September 26, 1770, it faced a new constitutional crisis. Again following instructions from the British government, Hutchinson had relinquished Castle William to the British army on September 10. According to the charter, the governor controlled the castle, a military facility built and maintained by the province. Hutchinson had rather ably defended himself against the charge of violating the charter when he forced the legislature to meet outside Boston. That issue was not clear-cut. But, by complying with the British instructions to surrender Castle William, Hutchinson compromised the charter, and he knew it. He relinquished control surreptitiously and endeavored to make it appear that he had not subverted the charter. Not surprisingly, as Hutchinson admitted, many people responded to the transfer with "rage." "Adams, in particular," he said, "was inflaming the minds of the people, declaring that I had broken the charter by giving up the Castle."

Faced with this new and more threatening challenge to the charter, the House blinked. Rather than having Samuel Adams fire off yet another thunderbolt, the representatives used the transfer of Castle William as an excuse to resume normal business. A resolve offered to the House on October 9 put the best possible gloss on the retreat. It posed the question: faced with this new grievance which requires immediate redress, should the House return to conducting business while also, of course, continuing to protest the illegal removal of the general assembly from Boston? That resolve passed on a roll-call vote of 59 to 29 with the most ardent and prominent Whigs—including Adams, Hancock, and Joseph Hawley—voting no. They opposed the resolution because they feared that the assemblymen would begin carrying on all regular business. That is exactly what happened. Adams, who had insisted that the colonists must act on principle, was mortified. The British and Hutchinson had worn the representatives down. Too many were no longer willing to endure the hardships caused by pursuing what Adams would call a principled resistance.

Although a majority of the House retreated, it was not a rout. The representatives continued to claim that, on the basis of the charter, the General Court must be returned to Boston. And for the rest of the fall legislative session, especially in pronouncements Adams drafted, the assemblymen kept sniping at the acting governor on a range of issues. Above all, they relentlessly attacked Hutchinson for having complied with the instructions to surrender control of Castle William. The representatives and the acting governor dueled with pronouncements and counterpronouncements right through November 20, 1770, the last day of the session. On that final day, the representatives charged that, by relinquishing control of Castle William, Hutchinson had discarded "a Power of governing, which by the Charter is vested in you for the Safety of the People; and that it is a Precedent of the most dangerous Tendency." The representatives urged the acting governor, "in Tenderness to the Rights of this People," to redress this "very great Grievance." The unrelenting assault on Hutchinson led him, when he closed the session, to complain that the representatives had, "by every Way in your Power," sought "to impeach my Conduct."

The representatives did even more to undermine Hutchinson. Because their London agent, Dennys De Berdt, had died, the representatives needed to choose a new agent. Having selected Benjamin Franklin, the representatives took an important additional step. They created a committee of correspondence to communicate with Franklin and others in Great Britain. The committee, made up of Adams and four other noted Whigs, could function even when the General Court was not in session. Equally important, the committee was authorized to communicate with the Speakers of other colonial assemblies or with correspondence committees the assemblies had or might appoint. Although the Massachusetts House did not actually call upon the other colonial legislatures to create committees of correspondence, the representatives' action reflected an ideal that Adams and some other leading American Whigs had long advocated: establish intercolonial communication systems to link the defenders of American liberties.

Adams and other radical Whigs could take solace in the fact that the House still attempted to defend American liberties even though it had abandoned the position that it would not function until returned to Boston. Ardent Whigs could not, however, take any comfort in what was happening to the nonimportation effort. By the time the Massachusetts assembly retreated on the contentious issue of its meeting place, the nonimportation program was disintegrating.

In April 1770, Parliament repealed all the Townshend duties except the one on tea. Bostonians and the rest of the American colonists then faced a crucial decision. Should America keep up nonimportation until the British abolished the tea duty? Or should the colonists accept a partial victory by ending or severely curtailing nonimportation? For Samuel Adams the choice was obvious. Time and again he had stressed that nonimportation should be continued until Parliament rescinded all unconstitutional acts. The current agreement fell short of that, but it did say nonimportation would last until all the Townshend duties were abolished. If the colonists ended nonimportation merely because most Townshend duties had been repealed, it would not be a partial victory, it would be a defeat. For Adams, the question was precedent; the question was what it had always been: the true nature of the British constitution. Believing that one must uphold fundamental principles, Adams had urged sacrifice, and the Boston Town Meeting had vigorously supported nonimportation. But by repealing all the duties except one, the British government made it tempting for Americans to follow their immediate economic interests and, in so doing, hand Britain a constitutional victory. Over time, the temptation proved too alluring. As Adams attested with a measure of pride, Boston's merchants held remarkably firm for nonimportation. However, the rest of America's business communities did not. Despite the efforts of Massachusetts Whigs, New York City effectively abandoned nonimportation in July 1770. Philadelphia's merchants did the same in late September. Faced with economic ruin if they persisted alone, on October 12, Boston's merchants agreed that the general nonimportation would end. Henceforth, only tea and any other articles subject to revenue duties would be boycotted. Since most American merchants said they would not import duted tea, they could claim that they had not abandoned the cause of liberty. But the truth was the British had defeated nonimportation. The majority of American merchants had lost the will to carry on the fight against a cleverly scaled back but determined British insistence on the right to tax the colonists.

Writing in November, Adams claimed he always feared the nonimportation effort would "fall short of our Wishes." The merchants had actually supported it "much longer than I ever thought they would or could. It was a grand Tryal which pressd hard upon their private Interest." Faced with that reality, Adams increasingly came to emphasize that only the masses could be expected to oppose Britain's evil policies, and even more resolutely he trumpeted the possibilities of American manufacturing. In language clearly intended for English ears, Adams wrote to Franklin about what might befall Great Britain if the mother country kept treating the colonists "as bastards and not Sons." "The body of the people will vigorously endeavor to become independent of the mother-country for supplies, and sooner than she may be aware of it, will manufacture for themselves." If that happened, one of the major benefits the British derived from the American colonies would vanish. Adams worked to turn his predictions into reality by drafting, or helping draft, a House pronouncement calling upon the people of Massachusetts to promote and support "our own Manufactures." To achieve that goal, on November 6, the House created a committee to formulate a plan "for the Encouragement of Arts, Agriculture, Manufactures and Commerce." The committee, which included Adams, was to have its report ready for the next legislative session.

The day after the legislature completed its work, Adams summarized its accomplishments in a letter to a South Carolina Son of Liberty. For Adams, the vital achievement was the creation of a committee "to correspond with our friends in the other colonies." He added that "AMERICAN MANUFACTURES" should be "the constant Theme" of the committee's writings. Adams closed with a bold one-sentence paragraph: "Our young men seem of late very ambitious of making themselves masters of the art MILITARY."

Samuel Adams's defiant pronouncements and increasing emphasis on the power of "the body of the people" could not obscure the fact that the American resistance movement was in disarray in the late fall of 1770. Only a year before, the patriot efforts had been so strident that, as Hutchinson reported it, Adams revealed his true feelings at an October 1769 town meeting by boldly proclaiming, "Independent we are, and independent we will be." The progress toward a uniform and stalwart defense of American rights was going so well in early November 1769 that Samuel boasted to agent De Berdt that "Britain may fall sooner than she is aware; while her Colonies who are struggling for Liberty may survive her fate & tell the Story to their Childrens Children." However, skillful political maneuvering by the British government and Lieutenant Governor Hutchinson had, by late 1770, effectively blunted the American resistance movement. A majority of the Massachusetts House, anxious to get back to regular business, had retreated from their principled stand against being forced to convene outside Boston. More important, although Americans said they would continue to boycott dutied tea, nonimportation was dead. These unwelcome developments presented the revolutionary politician with perhaps his greatest political challenge. Samuel Adams had to find ways to keep the flame of liberty alive when most Americans had abandoned the ideal of consistently adhering to political, philosophical, and constitutional principle.

5

The Chief Incendiary

*A*merica's Whigs had been thrown on the defensive even before the increasingly timid Massachusetts General Court ended its 1770 fall session. The collapse of nonimportation suggested that many Americans placed economic self-interest above patriotism. Although Samuel Adams rued the dampening of patriotic ardor, he believed a politician could not "create events." The best the Whigs could do, he counseled, was "to be ready *for all Events,* that we may make the *best Improvement* of them." The revolutionary politician diligently kept looking for ways to "improve"—to exploit and capitalize on—British mistakes. But for more than two years, Adams found little he could effectively improve upon. British-American relations became so tranquil that scholars refer to "the quiet period" stretching from mid-1770 into 1773. Although others shied away from confrontation, Adams could not become passive. Driven by his belief that a political leader must sound the alarm when the people's fundamental liberties were threatened, he strove to keep the flame of resistance alive. Equally important, he played a central role in developing radical organizations that could take advantage of whatever missteps the British might eventually make. In doing so, Adams came to emphasize that only the people themselves could save America's liberties. His unrelenting efforts reinforce the judgment of Stephen Sayre, an American emigrant living in England, who in 1770 proclaimed that Samuel Adams was "the Father of America." Sayre and others in the English Society of the Supporters of the Bill of Rights, a group dedicated to democratizing British politics that also supported the American cause, demonstrated their appreciation of Adams by electing him a member of their society.

Throughout his arduous and often lonely struggles to rouse his fellow colonists from their lethargy during "the quiet period," Adams could draw comfort from two interrelated and fundamental facts. Even when they stopped actively resisting British policies, Americans still overwhelmingly rejected the claim that Parliament could bind them in all cases whatsoever. For its part, the British government remained determined to make the colonists acknowledge the supremacy of Parliament. The British thus seemed destined to provide an issue that, with proper Adams "improvement," might rekindle the flame of liberty. The administration of Prime Minister Lord North furnished that issue in mid–1773 when it devised a plan designed to help the ailing British East India Company and maneuver Americans into admitting Parliament's supremacy. That scheme produced extraordinary repercussions. It allowed Adams and his political protégés to devise innovative organizational advancements that shifted effective political power in Massachusetts into the hands of the people and, in the process, did rekindle resistance in America.

As soon as the Massachusetts legislature adjourned in November 1770, Adams set about improving on events by penning two essays for the *Boston Gazette*. These missives summarized the legislature's squabbles with acting governor Hutchinson. Although he reviewed long-simmering disputes, Adams focused on new dangers, and, as usual, portrayed his adversary as standing on the wrong side of basic rights issues. Pointedly observing that the British military used instructions from England to grasp control of Castle William, Adams described that as the introduction of government by instructions. He warned that this innovation—a development Hutchinson supposedly did not oppose—would destroy the Massachusetts Charter. Having put a Whig spin on the legislative session, Adams confronted the discouraging results of the Boston Massacre trials. A provincial jury acquitted Captain Preston on October 30, 1770; when the trial of the eight soldiers who fired into the crowd ended on December 5, the jury merely convicted two soldiers of manslaughter, not murder. Such verdicts seemed unimaginable only a few months earlier. Now, when coupled with the collapse of nonimportation, the juries' decisions made it even more difficult for Adams to sustain patriotic ardor. In eleven essays published between December 10, 1770, and January 28, 1771, the revolutionary politician labored to improve on the disheartening events. Writing as "Vindex," Adams dissected the Massacre and the subsequent trials to convince the public that the verdicts were unjust. He intimated that the judges favored the soldiers. Moreover, the jurymen were not Bostonians and therefore could not assess the veracity of eyewitnesses who presented conflicting testimony. Adams offered his assessments, though, and in one instance played upon anti-Catholic prejudice to discredit a key witness's testimony. Emphasizing that his analysis incorporated material not presented in court, Adams painstakingly reconstructed the Massacre. In Samuel's hands, the evidence revealed that "insolent" and "blood-thirsty" soldiers executed a prearranged plan "to assassinate" Bostonians. Describing how a soldier reportedly stabbed his bayonet five inches into the head of a victim who had already been shot, Adams depicted the assassins "murder[ing]" with "Savage barbarity." The grisly outrages of March 5 once again proved "how fatal are the effects . . . of posting a standing army among a free people!"

Thomas Hutchinson conceded that, owing to Adams's writings, "a great part of the people were induced to believe the aquittals unjust, and contrary to evidence; and the killing of the men was declared to be a horrid massacre, with the same freedom as if the jury had found those concerned in it guilty of murder." Despite Adams's propaganda victory, the Whigs kept losing ground. Hutchinson sensed the changing mood. He noted that, beginning in late 1770, "four or five months passed away in Massachusetts Bay, more quietly than any other space of time for seven years preceding." In a move calculated to perpetuate that quiet, the acting governor decided against reconvening the General Court for its normal winter session. As the political calm stretched into the spring, Hutchinson had special reason to rejoice. On March 14, 1771, he was officially installed as the royal governor of Massachusetts.

The decline of American patriotic ardor forced Adams to reassess the situation. As his Boston Massacre essays showed, he still had faith in the common people. Praising the ability of ordinary persons to "judge, as well as their betters, when there is danger of *slavery,*" he maintained that "the people in general seldom complain, without some good reason." Equally important, Adams advanced a democratic, and for the time radical, theory that government officials were the people's agents and that governments should serve the people, "the multitude." "The *multitude* I am speaking of," said Adams, "is the *body of the people* . . . for whose sake government is instituted; or rather, who have themselves erected it solely for *their own* good— to whom even kings and all in subordination to them, are strictly speaking servants and not masters." Samuel Adams was not spewing empty rhetoric; he truly considered himself "the Servant of all" the people.

Although he expressed a faith in the masses that few politicians of his day shared, Adams also believed political leadership played a crucial role in protecting the people's rights. He reasoned that most individuals would ordinarily have to focus on their material concerns, not politics. Therefore, political leaders had a special duty to sound the alarm when the threat of tyranny arose. Indeed, "the *true* patriot," upon detecting miscreants poised to subvert the constitution and enslave the people, "will stir up the people." The leaders' role was so crucial that "the Man who nobly vindicates the Rights of his Country & Mankind shall stand foremost in the List of fame."

Adams blamed the Whig leadership for the people's lethargy. In March 1771, writing to James Warren, the staunch Plymouth patriot, Adams chastised Whig leaders for letting the people be temporarily "hush[e]d into Silence." Opining that the leaders'"*mistaken* Prudence""springs from Indolence or Cowardice or Hypocricy or I know not what," Samuel contemptuously observed that "for the sake of their own Ease or their own Safety, they preach the People into paltry Ideas of Moderation." Seeking to buck up Warren, and perhaps himself, Adams asserted, "it is no Dishonor to be in the minority in the Cause of Liberty and Virtue." And while he admitted that Massachusetts's patriots faced many difficulties, Samuel said he was "fretful" rather than desperate. Building on this positive note—and looking as he habitually did to the judgment of "posterity"—Adams proclaimed that "our Sons, if they deserve it, will enjoy the happy Fruits of their Fathers."

To counter the "paltry ideas of moderation," Adams again resorted to the technique of turning anniversaries into public commemorations. On March 5, 1771, Bostonians heard bells ringing in the morning and the evening. At night a depiction of the Boston Massacre victims was exhibited in the city. A week later, the town meeting selected Adams and other notable Whigs to determine how best to perpetuate the memory of "the horred Massacre." They recommended having an oration delivered "to impress upon our minds the ruinous tendency of standing Armies in Free Cities" and to remind the citizens of the need to emulate the glorious resistance the Bostonians of 1770 had mounted to thwart "the designs of the Conspirators against the public Liberty." The first in what became a series of annual Boston Massacre orations was delivered on April 2; to enhance its influence, the town meeting had the speech printed. Governor Hutchinson admitted that the commemorations dampened "the spirits of all who were hoping for peace and quietness."

The governor's concern probably intensified because the General Court was scheduled to reconvene on April 3. Whigs would undoubtedly attempt to have the legislators stoke the fires of resistance. Adams tried but could not get the House to take a hard line on the old "grievance" of being forced to meet outside Boston. After maintaining that they should be returned to Boston, the representatives conducted normal legislative business. However, Adams soon uncovered a potentially explosive constitutional issue: who would pay the governor and other royal officials? On the basis of the charter of 1691, the General Court had supplied those salaries for eighty years. Following the established practice, the House passed legislation to pay Hutchinson. When he vetoed it without comment, it seemed obvious that the British government was compensating him and perhaps others as well. This was no minor issue. The charter clearly granted the legislature the right to pay such salaries, and, equally important, the representatives had long used their power of the purse as a political weapon. So, for both constitutional and pragmatic reasons, Whigs considered the new salary arrangements a threat to American liberties.

Although Hutchinson vetoed the salary legislation, he offered no indication that the British aimed to gut the legislature's power of the purse. Hutchinson's adroit political maneuvering made Adams yearn for the days when Bernard was governor. "Happy indeed it was for the Province that such a Man was at the Head of it, for it occasioned such a Jealousy & Watchfulness in the people as prevented their immediate & total Ruin." The clever Hutchinson would, Adams forecast, find a way of "artfully concealing his Independency" of the legislature. Prodded by Adams, the assembly tried to pin down the governor on this potentially explosive matter. However, Hutchinson skillfully evaded those efforts throughout the legislative session. So the issue of the governor's salary remained clouded as Whigs and the government party prepared for the annual election of 1771.

The race for Suffolk County registrar of deeds, voted on in April, offered an early test of strength. It pitted Samuel Adams against Ezekiel Goldthwait, the longtime registrar known for his conservative views. Adams faced a difficult challenge. Suffolk County included much more than Boston; the taint of his tax-collecting failures still marked him; and voters traditionally did not reject officeholders who had served for a lengthy period. Moreover, increasing numbers of citizens were losing interest in challenging Britain's imperial policies. Not surprisingly, Goldthwait won handily, 1,123 to 467. Although Goldthwait's victory could hardly be considered a clear bellwether, Tories grew bolder. John Adams, who had worked for Samuel's election, remarked that elated Tories stopped disguising their "bitter" hatred for Whigs. By late April, John, who had just attained a significant leadership position among Whigs, sounded thoroughly discouraged. Ruminating on his loss of income while toiling to defend the people's freedoms, he moaned, "now I reap nothing but insult, ridicule, and contempt for it, from many of the people themselves." John proclaimed himself ready to say "farewell politics," and he meant it. In short order, he decided not to stand for reelection in Boston, moved back to Braintree, and turned his back on politics.

The withdrawal of John Adams from politics in the spring of 1771 illustrated the loss of leadership vigor that Samuel decried. John's retirement did not diminish the Whigs' chances of carrying the May election in Boston, but it boded ill for the province as a whole. As Samuel struggled against the political indifference that might swing power to the government party, he naturally attempted to turn the governor's conduct and salary into campaign issues. Focusing on "the black art of Adams," Hutchinson alleged that "our sons of sedition are afraid of a change of members in many towns, and make a strong effort in the newspapers to prevent it."

The annual election did not significantly alter the balance of power in Massachusetts, but it quickly became apparent that the government party had reason to rejoice. James Otis, having been judged well enough to reclaim his House seat, began acting like a Tory. He opposed Adams's motion that the representatives refuse to conduct normal legislative business unless they were returned to Boston. Worse yet, by arguing that the governor could make the legislature meet anywhere in the colony, Otis undermined a constitutional issue Adams had carefully developed as a weapon against the governor. Hutchinson believed Otis's actions sprang from a desire to squelch "any design for a general revolt" and from a "dissatisfaction with the great influence Mr. Adams had obtained." The representatives still petitioned for a return to Boston, but, following Otis's lead, they

The wicked Statesman, or the Traitor to his Country, at the Hour of DEATH.

BOSTON : Printed by ISAIAH THOMAS : Sold at his Printing Office near the Market, and at his shop near the Mill-Bridge [Price 7 coppers single, and 20 s. old tenor the dozen.]

Paul Revere engraving of Thomas Hutchinson—"The wicked Statesman"—from the *Massachusetts Calendar . . . 1774.* Courtesy, American Antiquarian Society.

dropped the charge that forcing them to meet outside Boston violated the charter. Soon Bostonians began talking about Otis's "conversion to Toryism," and Hutchinson expressed hope that Otis might be "serviceable" in keeping radical Whigs in check. That hope soon evaporated when Otis's mental instability returned, but Hutchinson could take comfort in the fact that Otis was not the only Boston representative whose patriotic ardor had cooled. John Hancock and Thomas Cushing, philosophically moderate Whigs, also appeared willing to capitulate on the question of the governor's right to make the General Court meet outside Boston.

John Hancock's backsliding was particularly important. No one considered him a significant political thinker, but he possessed great popularity and immense wealth. Arch-Tory Peter Oliver derisively said that Adams siphoned that wealth to fund the radicals, and all observers agreed that Hancock's riches helped support the patriot cause. However, Hancock himself worried that Adams pushed the governor too hard. Moreover, from the early spring to the fall of 1771, Hancock seemed preoccupied with courting his future wife and shoring up his business interests. As a consequence, after supporting Otis on the issue of where the legislature should meet, Hancock essentially joined John Adams on the political sidelines. In addition, perhaps because his fiancée came from a venerable and conservative family, Hancock began hobnobbing with conservatives while, as Hutchinson described it, suddenly ending his friendship with Samuel Adams.

The House's bickering over how to challenge its banishment from Boston revealed that Samuel Adams was the only Boston representative still actively pursuing a radical Whig agenda. Moreover, the one established issue he had to work with in May 1771 had been tainted by Otis's arguments. Nevertheless, Samuel managed to raise the stakes—managed to improve on events—by making the issue more complex. Using language from his newspaper attacks on Hutchinson, Adams helped draft a House "Protest" that decried the horror of the legislature being moved to Cambridge "merely by Force of Instructions." The "Protest" also broached the potentially inflammatory salary issue. The House declared that the Massachusetts Charter made the legislature responsible for paying government officials. Adams rushed the "Protest" to the local press; he also composed newspaper essays skewering the governor for giving British instructions "the force of law" and thereby undermining the charter. These propaganda efforts fizzled. The people refused to be stirred up. Considering the retirements and backsliding that marked every member of the Boston delegation except Samuel Adams, it seemed that what Hutchinson called "this calm interval" might go on and on.

Given his personal situation and the public's apparent indifference to politics, Samuel Adams might have been tempted to emulate his cousin John and John Hancock by focusing on business and personal concerns. When the General Court adjourned in early July 1771, Samuel was almost fifty and already exhibiting the effects of palsy. And while he was notoriously unconcerned about acquiring wealth, he had a family to maintain. The family's only regular income apparently was the £90 a year he received as clerk of the House. The Adamses had a substantial home only because Samuel inherited it and other valuable property. Because their union did not produce children, Samuel and Elizabeth did not have the economic burden—or the joy—of raising young children on their middle-class but hardly lavish income. However, the children from Samuel's first marriage, Samuel Jr. and Hannah, had to be supported. In young Samuel's case, that included the cost of sending him to Boston Latin School and then to Harvard, where he graduated with the class of 1770. Fortunately, his prospects seemed bright. In 1771, he secured a medical apprenticeship with Dr. Joseph Warren, a noted physician who was also one of his father's political protégés. What the future might hold for Hannah, who turned fifteen in 1771, remained unclear.

Although personal and financial concerns prompted some leading Whigs to curtail their political activities, the idea of stepping back from active Whig politics apparently never crossed Samuel's mind. Governor Hutchinson's actions certainly support that view. He dismissed every suggestion that Adams might be bribed to cease his opposition to the British policies. Given Adams's precarious financial situation, he seemed a prime candidate for preferment—the well-established practice of offering politicians special favors to entice them into supporting the government's position. Hutchinson would have gladly exchanged preferment for Adams's silence, but, as the governor ruefully observed, Adams "could not be made dependent and taken off by some appointment to a civil office." Hutchinson believed that, on the question of seeking American independence, Adams had "a most inflexible natural temper." Adams's longtime adversary knew the Revolutionary politician cared about political ideals, not self-aggrandizement.

As the political calm stretched into the summer of 1771 and others pursued fortune rather than politics and, in some cases, cozied up to members of the government party, Samuel ventured into print. He labored diligently to awaken his fellow citizens to Britain's continuing attacks on their constitutional rights, and he emphasized that Governor Hutchinson aided and abetted the assaults. In midsummer Hutchinson, who stressed that no one matched Adams's unwavering advocacy of the radical Whig position, said of him, "I doubt whether there is a greater incendiary than he in the King's dominions." Adams proved Hutchinson right by launching a propaganda campaign on August 19 and then intensifying his efforts even after he became extremely ill. From September 9 through mid-October of 1771, each issue of the *Boston Gazette* carried another of Adams's "Candidus" essays. Turning history into a weapon, Samuel built each essay upon historical analysis. Although he also drew on ancient history, in the main Adams highlighted the meaning and significance of recent events, including the

Stamp Act controversy, the fight against the Townshend duties, the Massachusetts circular letter imbroglio, the horrors a standing army unleashed on Boston, and the legislature's continuing fights with Hutchinson. Adams developed two interlocking themes: The British government, aided by evil Americans lusting after power and wealth, conspired to smash America's constitutional liberties. As a consequence, the colonists must actively resist the conspiracy or be reduced to slavery.

When he fashioned his case against Britain and her colonial toadies, Adams constantly reminded the people that the British would use unconstitutional taxes to reduce the colonial legislatures to ciphers. He noted, for example, that the British had started paying Hutchinson an annual salary of £2,000 collected "from the Earnings and Industry of the honest *Yeomen, Merchants* and *Tradesmen,* of this continent, against their Consent." A governor who became financially independent of the legislature would, Adams warned, likely become a tyrant. Samuel then raised the more ominous specter of the American judicial system being corrupted: "We are told that the Justices of the Superior Court are also to receive fixed salaries out of this American revenue!"

Stressing that the colonial opposition reflected Lockean principles of defending basic rights against arbitrary power, Adams repeatedly urged the people to resist Britain's tax policies and the assaults on the colonial legislatures. Knowing Tories had floated the argument that the colonists had nothing to fear "as long as we continue quiet," Adams urged Americans to "beware of these *soothing* arts." They were, he insisted, part of a conspiracy against liberty. Indeed, since America's constitutional grievances had not been redressed, "what can be intended by all the *fair promises* made to us by tools and sycophants, but to lull us into that *quietude* and *sleep* by which *slavery* is always preceded."

As he developed this historical analysis, Adams warmly embraced continentalism. Each of the American colonies must, he maintained, "be upon their guard" and "take care lest by mutual inattention to the interest of each other, they . . . fall a prey to the MERCILESS HAND OF TYRANNY." Where the colonies' liberty was concerned, *"the cause of one is the cause of all."* It followed that "an attempt to subdue one province" should "be considered as an attempt to enslave the whole." Adams did more than delineate evils; he offered remedies to defeat the conspiracy. "It is by *united* councils, a steady zeal, and a manly fortitude, that this continent must expect to recover its violated rights and liberties." Adams thus continued to stress the importance of intercolonial councils, an idea he and other Whigs had championed since the time of troubles with England began. He reiterated that "I have often thought that in this time of common distress, it would be the wisdom of the colonists, more frequently to correspond with, and to be more attentive to the particular circumstances of each other."

Spurred perhaps by the growing political apathy, Adams's imagery became more graphic, his language shriller. In his October 7, 1771, essay, the next to last in the series, Adams sounded truly exasperated. Appealing to "the common sense of mankind," he pleaded, "To what state of misery and infamy must a people be reduced!" before they resisted? A week later, he thundered that "no people ever yet groaned under the heavy yoke of slavery, but when they deserv'd it." Truly, if a people did not have "*virtue* enough to maintain their liberty against a presumptuous invader, they deserve no pity, and are to be treated with contempt and ignominy." Pressing for action, Adams warned that "A Tyranny seems to be at the very door." "The Tragedy of American Freedom," he lamented, appeared "nearly completed." Looking as he so often did to "posterity"—to *"millions yet unborn"*—Adams insisted that the people had more than a right to resist when their fundamental liberties were assaulted. They had an *"indispensable duty to God and Their Country"* to resist *"by all rational means."* There could be no compromise, no halfhearted measures. "The liberties of our Country, the freedom of our civil constitution are worth defending at all hazards: And it is our duty to defend them against all attacks."

Samuel's acerbic pronouncements flowed from the soul of his political beliefs, and his thrusts *were* incendiary. By mid-October, when his Candidus mentioned Hutchinson, the word "tyrant" or "tyranny" appeared close by. On October 17, after enduring nearly two months of Adams's increasingly inflammatory manifestos, Hutchinson assessed the political scene. Hancock "is quiet at present, and so are most of the [Whig] party. All of them, except Adams, abate of their virulence." Adams was *the* troublemaker. He "would push the Continent into a rebellion to-morrow, if it was in his power."

From late October through late November of 1771, Adams sent only two essays to the *Boston Gazette*. The temporary decline in his propaganda output hardly gave Tories cause to celebrate. One Adams essay turned Hutchinson's own words against him. In early November, as tradition required, the governor issued a thanksgiving proclamation. But Hutchinson overreached himself by saying the people should give thanks for the continuance of their civil and religious liberties and for the marked improvement in the province's trade. Adams, who claimed that the proclamation outraged the people, penned an essay branding Hutchinson's message a threat to religious liberty. He then joined in coordinating a campaign that resulted in virtually all of Boston's ministers refusing to read the proclamation to their congregations. Depicting this affair as "an effort . . . to raise a commotion from a very trivial and innocent cause," Hutchinson nonetheless admitted it had "some effect." In fact, the opposition, lacking any real grievance, could not have employed "a more artful method of exciting the general attention of the people." Struggling as he was to gain the people's attention, Adams would have considered that a compliment.

Adams's second fall essay launched a series that, when completed in late January 1772, included eight publications. Pursuing the same goals enunciated in his historical-analysis essays, Adams vigorously reiterated that the colonists must steadfastly resist "the plan to enslave us." But in these essays, several of which countered publications by a government party writer, Adams highlighted political theory. Drawing upon numerous political theorists but emphasizing "the reasoning of the immortal Locke," Adams analyzed Massachusetts's constitutional relationship with Great Britain. He described the Massachusetts Charter as a "compact," a "contract," between the British Crown and the people. And that charter—the people's "constitution"—granted the citizens of Massachusetts, not the British Crown, the right to pay the governor. That essential right must be safeguarded, said Adams, since having the power of the purse had been consciously designed to keep "*imperious* governors" from subverting the people's liberties.

As he explored the constitutional relationship between America and the mother country, Adams even raised the possibility that Parliament might not have *any* right to pass legislation binding the colonists. A livid Governor Hutchinson called Adams "the Chief Incendiary" and warned that the radicals aimed to make "further advances until they have rejected every act of Parliament which controls the Colonies." Events proved Hutchinson right, but Adams did not go that far in these essays. He contented himself with the Whigs' cardinal arguments: Parliament had no right to tax the colonists, and Parliament's insistence on taxing Americans constituted a sinister attack on the people's basic liberties. Maintaining that those liberties "are originally from God and nature, recognized in the Charter, and entail'd to us and our posterity," Adams reiterated his fundamental view that "it is our duty therefore to contend for them whenever attempts are made to violate them." He again tried to spur denunciations of Britain's evil plans by warning his "countrymen" that their silence would be construed as acquiescence in the assault on their liberties.

From the close of the legislative session in July 1771 through early 1772, the Chief Incendiary probably spent a good deal on quills, ink, and paper. But, while Adams's impressive propagandistic endeavors helped keep the flame of resistance alive, he could not burn off the political calm. By late January 1772, he seemed to sense that; he did not craft another newspaper essay until the annual election season arrived. Although he turned away from newspaper warfare, Adams kept looking for ways to revitalize opposition fervor. He again participated in arranging what had become, owing in no small part to his efforts, the annual Boston Massacre oration. Starting in 1772, when an estimated four thousand attended, it occurred on the anniversary date. In the evening, large throngs viewed the Massacre exhibition presented at the home of Mrs. Clappams in King Street. Because the town meeting continued its tradition of publishing the oration, the Whigs again managed to remind citizens of the horrors of British policies. Just as important, this reminder came shortly before the annual legislative elections.

When Hutchinson finally reconvened the General Court in April of

1772, Adams quickly discovered he could not use the session to rekindle patriotic ardor. Knowing Hutchinson had intimated that the legislators could return to Boston if they spoke of inconvenience rather than constitutional rights, John Hancock urged the House to adopt that argument. Adams opposed Hancock's motion by again emphasizing the danger of according the status of law to British instructions. A scant majority backed Adams, but the open split with Hancock seemed ominous for the Whig cause. Once the legislators turned to their regular business, Hutchinson continued his practice of avoiding political fights. The session ended quickly and quietly. On April 28, shortly after dissolving the assembly and well into the second year of what he called the political calm, Hutchinson voiced confidence. Assessing his opponents, the governor remarked that "I think we have so divided the [Whig] faction that it must be something very unfortunate which can unite them again."

Although angered by Hancock's apparent duplicity, Adams put the best face on the situation and continued his efforts to awaken the people, as well as some Whig leaders. In late April, as he regularly did, Adams turned to the press in hopes of influencing the annual election. He presented a lengthy list of grievances. Some Tories, confident that the people had rejected Adams's brand of radicalism, struck back boldly. For years Boston's Tories had not even contested the election of Whigs, but in 1772 they tried to get the town meeting to dump the Chief Incendiary. The odious scent of his tax-collecting failures had not dissipated, and Adams's brand of fervent American patriotism had fallen out of favor. Still, although he received only 505 of a possible 723 votes, Adams, who like the other winning candidates was backed by the Boston Caucus, easily gained the final spot on the delegation. Although Tories had merely reduced Adams's victory margin, Andrew Oliver, the lieutenant governor, bragged about the sharp decline in popularity of the man "who has been so long the idol of the populace."

Even though they failed to unseat Adams, Tories had reasons to gloat. The Whig leadership had fractured, perhaps irrevocably. And the quiet period was about to enter its third year. This state of affairs, which made Tories optimistic and frustrated Adams, can be traced to a complex set of factors. Intriguingly, Adams and Hutchinson, who not only occupied opposite ends of the political spectrum but who also truly hated each other, offered similar explanations for this period of calm.

Adams firmly believed that a politician could not spur the people to action unless they believed their rights were being trampled. And even before the Boston Massacre, the British government and Hutchinson had made it harder for radicals such as Adams to capitalize, to improve, on events. From early 1770 on, the British cultivated a moderate policy and image. Parliament lowered the duties it imposed and eliminated every Townshend duty except the one on tea. The British ministry also waged its own propaganda campaign by suggesting that all taxes might be repealed—if the colonists continued to behave. The specter of a standing army had been diminished by withdrawing the troops from Boston proper. And when the British began paying the salaries of colonial officials, they did it surreptitiously. For his part, Hutchinson so dexterously evaded admitting the truth about his salary that Adams referred to the "silent" attack on constitutional rights. Moreover, in all his dealings with the General Court, Hutchinson endeavored to deny Whigs any flashpoint issues. Thus, the quiet period stemmed in part from Britain's policy of moderation and from the skillful way the British and their American friends implemented that policy.

Brightening economic conditions aided the British strategy. Even though he expressed faith in the people, Adams believed that individuals would usually be politically inattentive because they were "necessarily engaged" in earning a living. This assessment reflected the way events in Massachusetts had unfolded. People formed anti-British crowds when their livelihoods or freedom seemed in *imminent* danger from the Stamp Act or from impressment. And, while the economy was sour when the Stamp Act controversy erupted, by the early 1770s the economy hummed and the threat of impressment had dissipated. Consequently, the people became less active politically, and political crowds did not form. Hutchinson understood the importance of economic considerations. Speaking of developments from roughly 1770 into 1772, he gushed that "commerce never was in a more flourishing state" and, economically, Massachusetts was "the envy of all the other colonies." As both Adams and Hutchinson emphasized, events demonstrated that the people seemed more politically apathetic in good times.

The quiet period also stemmed from the fact that most Americans found extreme Whigs like Samuel Adams too radical. The British government and their American allies believed that the vast majority of colonists—including notable Whigs like Otis, Hancock, and Cushing—did not want independence. They were right. Virtually all colonists merely sought a return to the imperial relationship that existed before 1763. And while the majority of colonists rejected Adams's zealous patriotism, many of his fellow Whigs deemed his ideas on government too radical. When Adams argued that power flowed from the people and that government officials were the servants of the people, he voiced a democratic ideal anathema to many who later became revolutionaries. They advocated following a moderate course in part because they feared Adams's brand of radicalism might bring about a restructuring of American society.

The misguided effort to toss Adams out of the Massachusetts House in May 1772 helped subvert the political tranquillity Tories prized. Hutchinson admitted that the attempt, which had little chance of success, "proved a disservice to government" because it "caused an alarm" among Whigs. In response, they labored mightily to reunite Hancock and Adams. It took the better part of a year to achieve that reconciliation. In the meantime, Hutchinson effectively removed a Whig "grievance" by letting the General

Court return to Boston. Hutchinson claimed he acted "to prevent a dissatisfaction among the people of the province." However, it hardly seems mere coincidence that the governor informed the legislators about the return on June 13, the day he finally admitted that the British were paying his salary. The timing, it appears, was designed to dampen anger over the salary question. Hutchinson's ploy failed. The salary dispute gave Adams a powerful issue to improve.

Adams and his longtime ally Joseph Hawley, the two most ardent Whigs in the House, took the lead in drafting a committee report that put Hutchinson on the wrong side of a fundamental constitutional issue. The report branded the paying of executive salaries an "innovation" that violated the charter, that "most solemn contract" that bound the British Crown and the people of Massachusetts. Indeed, "the innovation is an important change of the constitution, and exposes the province to a despotic administration of government." Tory members of the House found the pronouncement "disquieting," and Hutchinson conceded that the report might make people think their charter rights had been "invaded."

After telling the representatives that they had misinterpreted the Massachusetts Charter, Hutchinson adjourned the legislature on July 14. But adjournment could not halt the growing controversy. It heated up considerably after the province learned in September that the British would also pay Massachusetts's superior court judges. Adams touched on this possibility in his 1764 instructions, openly broached this explosive issue again in 1768, and referred to it yet again in his propaganda blitz in the summer of 1771. As Adams kept emphasizing, the question of the British compensating judges seemed especially troubling because of the nature of judicial appointments. The Crown appointed judges. In England judges received appointments for life during good behavior. In the colonies, however, judges could be dismissed at any time for any reason. Making colonial judges financially dependent on the Crown thus raised the specter that they would do the monarch's bidding. The threat to judicial integrity touched a nerve with many people, not just ardent Whigs. Of course, the Tory Peter Oliver, chief justice of the five-member superior court, viewed it differently. With some justification, he charged that the legislature used its power of the purse to undercut judicial independence. But most citizens did not see it that way. They considered the "innovation" of the British paying judges a threat to their liberties. The fact that the judges would be paid out of revenues derived from the tea duty made the problem even more nettlesome.

When official confirmation of the new salary arrangements seemed imminent, Adams and other radicals leaped into action. In an October 5, 1772, newspaper diatribe, Samuel pictured "the iron Hand of Tyranny" raised to "ravish our Laws and seize the Badge of Freedom." He pleaded, "Is it not High Time for the People of this Country explicitly to declare, whether they will be Freemen or Slaves?" Seeking to spark yet another inflammatory issue, Adams linked the defense of political liberty to the preservation of religion and the people's morals. As he called upon "the *Body of the People*" to defend "their free Constitution," Adams professed that history was on America's side. Seldom, if ever, had even a small community of people "been kept long in Bondage, when they have unitedly and perseveringly resolv'd to be Free." To foster that necessary unity, Adams urged people to "converse together . . . and open our minds freely to each other" on the subject of the threat to American liberties. "Let it be the topic of conversation in every social Club. Let every Town assemble. Let Associations & Combinations be everywhere set up to consult and recover our just Rights."

Adams's impassioned pleas were calculated to generate support for a powerful new Whig organizational tool. Whigs, as well as other groups, had long used correspondence committees, and Adams and other leading Whigs had routinely promoted the idea of establishing an intercolonial correspondence system. While not abandoning the hope that an intercolonial network might one day be erected, Adams, Dr. Thomas Young, and possibly others in Massachusetts saw great potential in creating a town-based structure of committees of correspondence that would present a unified Massachusetts front against Britain's policies. Adams and his allies realized such a system could not be constructed until a sharp grievance presented itself. So they planned—Tories would say plotted—and waited for events that would let them implement their scheme. The volatile issue of who would compensate judges and Hutchinson's unwitting assistance afforded them the opportunity.

In addition to fashioning newspaper items to lay the groundwork for a committee of correspondence system in Massachusetts, Adams helped circulate petitions that urged the selectmen to call a town meeting to deal with the issue of the salaries of superior court judges. On October 27, the day before the meeting, Adams was already working to have other town meetings express their opposition to Britain's "Incroachments of Tyranny." One of the people he contacted was Elbridge Gerry of Marblehead, who, upon entering the House in May, became an instant ally of Adams. Gerry agreed that the legislature, not the British, should pay judges. Samuel spelled out the plan. Boston Whigs would have the town meeting ask the governor to call the assembly into immediate session while also demanding that judges declare whether or not they would reject Britain's "odious" new remuneration system. Promising to keep Gerry informed, Adams revealed his true goal: "I wish we could arouse the continent."

Boston Whigs did urge the town meeting to "expressly declare their natural & Charter Rights to their Representatives" and to press the governor to reconvene the assembly. When that moderate proposal did not garner support, ardent Whigs apparently decided against broaching their more radical proposal of asking judges to declare themselves. The best the Whigs could get was the formation of a three-member committee, headed by

Adams, charged with preparing an address to the governor to inquire if he had any knowledge about the Crown paying judges. Although Adams's committee denounced the idea of the British paying judges and reiterated the bedrock Whig argument that Parliament could not constitutionally tax the colonists, the address merely requested that the governor please inform the meeting if he had received information about this important issue. Given its deferential tone, it would have been hard to vote against the address. No one did.

As promised, Adams immediately informed Gerry of the meeting's actions. In doing so, he entreated, "I wish your Town would think it proper to have a Meeting." Indeed, "Pray use your Influence with Salem & other Towns." Adams reasoned that, if the towns declared themselves, "our Enemies would not have it in their power to divide us." He clearly hoped to use the issue of judges' pay to foment resistance throughout Massachusetts. And Adams pushed for action outside the metropolis even before Boston's town meeting established the committee of correspondence that was the key to developing the new organizational system he and Young envisioned.

Hutchinson refused to confirm or deny the report that the British planned to pay judges. But rather than being "equivocal" as Adams thought he might, Hutchinson told the town meeting that it should mind its own business, which he stressed did not include inquiring about imperial policies. Hutchinson, an experienced and often wily politician, should have realized his response would provoke the meeting. After considering the governor's comments, the meeting created a high-profile committee made up of Cushing, Adams, and Otis, who had at least temporarily regained his sanity. The meeting authorized the committee to draft a petition asking the governor to permit the General Court to meet, as scheduled, on December 2. Although Adams advocated even stronger action, the petition's moderation gave it broad appeal. After approving the petition unanimously, the meeting adjourned until November 2 to await Hutchinson's reply.

Hutchinson played right into the Chief Incendiary's hands. Although the town meeting had sent him deferential and moderate requests, Hutchinson again responded haughtily. Emphasizing that the "Royal Charter" vested the power to call or dismiss the legislature in the governor, Hutchinson again lectured the meeting on its proper duties, which he emphasized did not include meddling in the timing of assembly meetings. Adams had to smile with delight. Reiterating one of his cardinal political maxims, he informed Gerry that the meeting's requests of Hutchinson had been "so reasonable that in refusing to comply with them he must have put himself *in the wrong,* in the opinion of every honest & sensible man." As a consequence, "such measures as the people may determine upon to save themselves, if rational & manly, will be the more reconcileable even to cautious minds, & thus we may expect that Unanimity which we wish for." Adams was right. The town meeting responded to Hutchinson's blast by unanimously passing a resolution stating that the people always had the right to petition the king or his representatives for redress *and* the right to communicate their sentiments to other towns. At this point, Adams struck. He moved that Boston create a twenty-one-member committee of correspondence. It would issue a manifesto on the colonists' rights "as Men, as Christians, and as Subjects" and also formulate a statement of grievances. The committee would ask every Massachusetts town to send "a free communication of their Sentiments on this Subject." Since Adams's resolution spoke of the committee assessing infringements or violations of the colonists' rights as they "have been, or from time to time may be made," the committee could function as a protest clearinghouse. What Samuel Cooper called "a Number of the most respectable Friends of Liberty in the Town," including every Boston representative except Adams, opposed his proposal. They said the other towns would not respond. However, after discussion, the more timid Whig leaders backed down, and Adams's proposal passed unanimously.

Adams and Otis, now merely a shell of his former self, headed the committee. But prominent and wealthy moderates—including Hancock, Cushing, and William Phillips, who had replaced Otis in the House—declined to serve. For those who counseled moderation, that was a mistake. As Richard D. Brown, the modern historian of the Boston committee, notes, the committee was made up of staunch Whigs who recognized Adams as their leader. Indeed, eight of the twenty-one members, including Adams, belonged to the North End Caucus, one of the branches of the Boston Caucus. Adams and the other extreme Whigs had their instrument to rally and unify support for the Whig cause throughout Massachusetts.

The Boston committee held its first meeting on November 3, 1772, and began the process Adams hoped would result in Massachusetts towns presenting a united front against Great Britain. As committee members drafted position statements, Adams kept sending personal letters to Whigs in other towns to promote the creation of similar committees and to get them to endorse the actions of the Boston Town Meeting. He believed that once the towns established correspondence committees and shared their thoughts, it would demonstrate that the people were "united in Sentiments." That would naturally produce "a Confidence in each other, & a plan of Opposition will be easily formed & executed with Spirit." On November 14, Adams sounded even more like the Chief Incendiary. Again calling upon Gerry to increase support for a committee of correspondence movement, Adams expressed his desire to behold "the Love of Liberty & a Zeal to support it" enkindled in every Massachusetts town. Employing the same image, he later urged James Warren to spur Plymouth to action with the admonition that "where there is a Spark of patriotick fire, *we* will enkindle it."

On November 20, the Boston committee gave the town meeting its statement on the rights of the colonists, its list of grievances, and a copy of

the letter to the other Massachusetts towns. The section on rights, originally worked up principally by Adams, mainly restated well-developed
Whig arguments. Stressing and often quoting from Locke, Adams emphasized that the people had fundamental rights that could not be abridged.
The statement gave lengthy and special attention to suggesting that Americans' religious liberties might be as endangered as their political liberties.
The manifesto was also notable for incorporating a claim Adams had been
articulating more and more often: political officials were the "servants of
the society." The lengthy list of grievances offered a dozen numbered sections each festooned with detailed evidence, some carefully drawn from
other colonies. The covering letter asserted that Americans confronted "a
constant, unremitted, uniform aim to enslave us." This official letter, unlike
Adams's private correspondence, did not ask other towns to form correspondence committees, but it amounted to an invitation to do just that. It
suggested that Boston's observations should "be laid before your Town, that
the subject may be weighed as its importance requires, and the collected
wisdom of the whole People, as far as possible, be obtained." The committee made it clear that Bostonians believed the people outside the metropolis would agree that the colonists' rights were in mortal danger and must
be defended.

After making a slight revision in the list of colonial grievances, the meeting unanimously approved the pronouncements and ordered them printed
as a pamphlet. The committee members were authorized to send copies to
the selectmen of every Massachusetts township and to whomever else they
thought proper. It took ten days to get the pamphlets printed. Adams,
always known for his industry, put enormous effort into creating a colony-
wide communication system during this period. He kept up a steady correspondence with Whigs in several towns and pressed them to have their
towns take immediate action. As John Adams observed, "his time is all
employed in the public service." At the end of November, Samuel informed
Arthur Lee in England that, while the committee's pamphlets had not yet
been sent into the interior, "other towns are in motion of their [own]
accord." Adams could have added, but did not, that his letters urging action
helped stimulate the movement.

As he toiled to plant committees of correspondence throughout Massachusetts, Adams found a way to champion his goal of forging an intercolonial network. In one of the few actions that marred the quiet period,
Rhode Islanders had burned a British revenue ship, the *Gaspee,* in June of
1772. Invoking a recently passed law that allowed colonials accused of such
a crime to be tried in England, the British authorized a special commission
to investigate the *Gaspee* incident. In late December, with the commission
about to begin functioning in their province, Rhode Island officials asked
Adams for advice. Denouncing the commission's powers as a violation of
the first principles of government, the British constitution, and Magna

Carta, Adams counseled standing firm against the commission. Forcefully embracing the principle of unified colonial action, he suggested that Rhode Island's cause was the cause of all Americans; therefore, its assembly should send the other colonies a circular letter on this issue. This would "tend to the Advantage of the General Cause & R Island in particular." The Rhode Islanders, who consulted political leaders throughout the colonies, were thinking along similar lines. They sent out the type of circular letter Adams advocated.

It would take time before the results of Rhode Island's circular letter could be known, and, as 1772 ended, Adams focused on getting a committee of correspondence system up and running in Massachusetts. The Chief Incendiary and his colleagues on the Boston committee usually assembled once a week. They began by meeting from 5 P.M. to 7 P.M., and soon their gatherings extended to 9:30 or even later as the members, who jointly purchased and consumed Rhode Island beer, mixed committee work and conviviality. When responding to communications it received from the townships and districts of Massachusetts, the committee showed creativity by flattering the townships' wisdom and patriotism. To convey a sense of growing momentum, as additional townships contacted it, the committee emphasized the growing number of responses in its own writings. And as events worth "improving" occurred, the committee exploited them. Thus, when the news of the *Gaspee* investigation broke, committee members highlighted the new grievance in their missives.

Leading Tories snickered when the Boston committee came into existence. At the same time Adams thought of sparking "the Love of Liberty & a Zeal to support it" in every Massachusetts town, Hutchinson snidely observed that "to keep up a correspondence through the Province by Committees of the several Towns . . . is such a foolish scheme that they must necessarily make themselves ridiculous." By the end of November smirks turned into worried frowns. Finally realizing that the Boston committee was creating a powerful Whig organization throughout Massachusetts, Tories tried unsuccessfully to sabotage it. On December 8, Thomas Hutchinson scolded himself for having believed Boston's committee would have "little or no effect." He concluded that, as a result of the committee's efforts, a "doctrine of Independence upon the Parliament" was "every day spreading and strengthening itself." Although Hutchinson probably overstated the case, the Boston committee's messages, especially on judges' pay, were clearly helping to rekindle Whig ardor as 1772 gave way to 1773. Indeed, it was the issue of who would pay judges that brought John Adams and then John Hancock back into the political fray.

By early January 1773, many Massachusetts communities had gone on record opposing British policy. The task was made easier because, in some towns, Tories publicly conceded that it would endanger liberty to make judges depend on the Crown for their salaries. Hutchinson's anxiety about the impact of the expanding committee of correspondence system ballooned when he received reports that the radicals, after having shown what could be done in Massachusetts, planned to have the Massachusetts House issue a circular letter aimed at creating an intercolonial correspondence system. That chilling thought goaded the governor into taking a major gamble.

For almost three years, Hutchinson had endeavored to avoid giving Whig legislators issues they could exploit. He had been particularly careful about steering clear of the explosive question of what powers the British Parliament actually had over the colonies. But faced with the Boston committee's success and believing the radicals were plotting to establish an American committee of correspondence system, Hutchinson called the General Court back into session on January 6, 1773. Supremely confident in his own intellectual prowess and unrivaled knowledge of Massachusetts history, the governor appeared in person and delivered an address centered on the question of the supremacy of Parliament.

Admitting that "the government is at present in a disturbed and disordered state," Hutchinson blamed the difficulties on the Whigs' failure to realize that "it is impossible that rights of English subjects should be the same, in every respect, in all parts of the dominions." History proved that, from the start, the colonies formed part of "the dominions of the Crown of England" and thus "remain[ed] subject to the supreme authority of Parliament." Therefore, the resolutions recently passed by various towns that "deny the supreme authority of Parliament . . . are repugnant to the principles of the [British] constitution." Pressing the legislators to admit the supremacy of Parliament, Hutchinson put the issue starkly: "I know of no line that can be drawn between the supreme authority of Parliament and the total independence of the colonies." Hutchinson expanded the argument by picturing the dangers independence would bring. Shorn of British protection, the colonies would be gobbled up by a European power. Hutchinson openly challenged the General Court to prove him wrong. The governor's erudite address impressively marshaled the essential Tory arguments and voiced them in a calm manner. And his arguments were compelling—*if* one accepted the premise of Parliament's supremacy. Hutchinson certainly expected that, once they realized they were flirting with rebellion, the General Court and the people of Massachusetts would reject Whig ideas. He miscalculated.

Samuel Adams was the chief author of the House's lengthy response, but it was a collective effort in which Joseph Hawley played a central role. The House boldly maintained that, when created, the colonies were not annexed to the realm of England but were under "the absolute control of the Crown." Moreover, since the colonies were not annexed to the realm, "they are not a part of the kingdom and consequently not subject to the Legislative authority of the kingdom." The colonists could be subjected to

Parliament's authority *only* if the Massachusetts Charter authorized that, and it did not. Since the charter did not establish Parliament's supremacy, Parliament could not assert it now. Nor could the British cite the fact that Parliament had recently taxed the colonists as a precedent because "whatever is originally in its nature wrong, can never be *sanctified,* or made right by *repetition* and use." This radical claim, a claim Hutchinson had warned that the legislature would adopt, amounted to a denial of Parliament's right to legislate for the colonies.

Hutchinson paid dearly for arguing that no line could be drawn between independence and accepting Parliament's supremacy. Following Adams's dictum of putting an opponent in the wrong, the House placed the onus on Hutchinson for anything the representatives might say on that score. "We cannot but express our concern," they intoned, "that your Excellency, by your speech, has reduced us to the unhappy alternative, either of appearing by our silence to acquiesce in your Excellency's sentiments, or of thus freely discussing the point." The representatives said that, if no line could be drawn, the colonists were either mere "vassals of Parliament" or they were "totally independent." Turning to history, the legislators maintained that the colonial delegates who negotiated the 1691 charter agreement surely would not have reduced themselves to vassalage; therefore, they must have considered the colony independent.

After accusing Hutchinson of forcing the legislators to contemplate independence, Adams implied that the governor's address might necessitate calling an intercolonial gathering similar to the Stamp Act Congress. He claimed that "if your Excellency expects to have the line of distinction between the supreme authority of Parliament, and the total independence of the colonies drawn by us, we would say it would be an arduous undertaking, and of very great importance to all the other colonies." Accordingly, the legislators—even if they could discern a line of distinction—would not think of marking it out unless an intercolonial congress concurred in the analysis. Adams had once again found a way to point out the need for unified colonial action.

The governor counterattacked on February 16 by delivering an address laced with historical references buttressing his legal analysis. His scholarly effort merely caused the legislators to draft additional pronouncements that restated, even more emphatically, the essence of their original responses. Hutchinson now realized he had initiated a controversy that "may be lengthened out to perpetuity." The governor also misjudged when he condescendingly observed that many of the province's people could not understand the constitutional debate. As the many responses sent to the Boston committee indicated, the province's citizens had a lucid conception of their fundamental rights. The problem for Hutchinson and the British was that the Massachusetts vision was not their vision. The overwhelming majority of Massachusetts citizens insisted that there were limits to Parliament's power, that Parliament had no right to tax underrepresented people such as themselves, and that the Crown should not pay colonial judges.

Even as they engaged in a sophisticated constitutional debate with Hutchinson on parliamentary supremacy, Adams and his allies kept hammering on the easy-to-understand and sensitive issue of who would pay judges. Whigs recognized, as Adams put it, that the issue "was like Thunder in the ears of all but a detestable and detested few." In early February 1773, a House committee, with Adams as its driving force, finally made the governor admit that the British were funding the judges' salaries. The House quickly accused the judges of wrongdoing if they accepted pay from the Crown. "No Judge who has a due Regard to Justice, or even his own Character" would let himself be placed under the "undue Bias" of depending on the Crown for his compensation. Just before the legislative session ended, the House turned up the heat. It proclaimed that any judge who accepted payment from other than the General Court had no real understanding of "the Importance of an Impartial Administration of Justice, that he is an enemy to the Constitution, and had it in his Heart to promote the Establishment of an arbitrary Government in the Province."

Hutchinson refrained from again commenting on parliamentary supremacy until March 6, 1773, the day he adjourned the legislature. That tactic hardly guaranteed the governor the last word, and it even played into Adams's hands. Believing the controversy supported their Whig positions, the representatives had already voted to have all the official pronouncements of both sides in the "Controversy" printed as a pamphlet. In a move that reflected the methods of the Boston committee, the clerk of every town and every district in Massachusetts as well as all members of the General Court received a copy. The legislators did not fear having their debates with Hutchinson distributed throughout Massachusetts, and they were right. Hutchinson had committed a major tactical error. As Adams remarked to a fellow Whig, Hutchinson's defense of parliamentary supremacy "quickened a spirit of enquiry into the nature and end of government, and the connection of the colonies with Great Britain." When they learned what Hutchinson had done, British government officials winced. Hutchinson soon regretted having raised the issue in the first place, and that regret nagged him the rest of his life.

With Adams serving as a vital member of each body and clearly functioning as the liaison between the two, the Massachusetts House of Representatives and Boston's correspondence committee increasingly worked in close harmony. Right after the legislature adjourned, the Boston Town Meeting responded to Hutchinson's suggestion that Boston had no right to concoct resolves on imperial policy or to urge other towns to adopt its views. The Boston Town Meeting made Adams the head of a committee charged with preparing a report that would "vindicate" Boston against the governor's "gross misrepresentations and groundless charges." Adams drafted the lengthy report. Not surprisingly, it emphasized the crucial issue of judges' salaries and also put Hutchinson on the wrong side of another basic rights issue: the right of the people of Boston—or any Massachusetts community—to meet "together in a time of publick danger." Adams accused Hutchinson of attempting to keep the people "in ignorance of their danger, that they may be more easily and speedily inslaved." After unanimously approving the report, the meeting directed its correspondence committee to send copies to every town and district in the province.

By early March of 1773, Virginians had received copies of the Boston Town Meeting resolves on judges' pay, information on the establishment of Boston's committee of correspondence, and the pamphlet containing the addresses Hutchinson and the legislators had hurled at one another. Newspaper accounts about the *Gaspee* commission in Rhode Island had also reached Virginia. A member of Virginia's House of Burgesses indicated that the items sent from Massachusetts "were of use" when the burgesses decided what must be done. On March 12, they called for the development of intercolonial committees to gather and exchange information about Britain's flagrant attack on American liberties. The burgesses gave special attention to the new threat of Americans possibly being transported to England for trial. As soon as it learned of the burgesses' actions, Boston's correspondence committee held a special meeting. On their own initiative, the committeemen decided that the letter containing the burgesses' resolves should be published as a circular letter and forwarded to every township and district in Massachusetts. Adams and the rest of the committee transformed Virginia's actions into a ringing endorsement of Massachusetts's correspondence system. The Boston committee prefaced its circular with the flattering observation, "we congratulate you upon the Acquisition of such respectable Aid as the ancient and patriotic Province of *Virginia*." Reminding township officials of the value of correspondence committees, the circular contained the directive that it should "immediately" be given to the town's correspondence committee or, if none existed, to the selectmen so they could communicate it to the town.

By the spring of 1773, Adams could honestly boast that Boston's correspondence committee had produced "Effects which are extremely mortifying to our petty Tyrants." As he later phrased it, the committee's efforts "had raised the Spirits of the People, drawn off their attention from picking up pins, and directed their Views to great objects." Fellow Whig Samuel Cooper observed that the Boston committee "had an Effect beyond the most sanguine Expectations" of its friends. The great majority of Massachusetts towns had followed the committee's lead, said Cooper, and their actions proved "the Body of the People," not some small faction, believed "that their most essential Rights are violated." Adams observed that the towns and districts stressed "two capital Grievances": taxing the colonists without their consent and using that money to pay the governor and judges.

Cooper overestimated the groundswell of public action. By April 1773, slightly less than half the colony's townships and districts had responded to the Boston committee's missives. But the momentum remained, and in early April, Adams asserted that a great many Massachusetts towns, "& the Number is daily increasing," voiced full support for the positions taken by the Bostonians. In time, a majority of townships did react, but only 58 of the 260 townships and districts formed their own committees of correspondence. Although the committee network was never fully developed, the responses demonstrated that a clear majority of citizens opposed Britain's imperial policy. Equally important, the correspondence system provided a powerful organizational base when further action became necessary.

By mid-April 1773, when he began exchanging letters with the noted Virginia Whig Richard Henry Lee, Adams was so exuberant about Massachusetts's committee of correspondence system that he wanted to clone it. Recounting its impressive achievements in Massachusetts, he recommended establishing a similar system in every colony. If that development occurred, it might well "promote that General Union, upon which the Security of the whole depends." Adams added that "I have often thought it a Misfortune, or rather a Fault in the Friends of American Independence and Freedom, their not taking Care to open every Channel of Communication." Reiterating a theme Whigs had often voiced and employing terms he had publicly enunciated as far back as 1764, Samuel argued that by creating an intercolonial correspondence network, the united "Wisdom & Strength" of the whole continent could be "employed upon every proper occasion." Three days later, writing to the committee in Duxbury, Massachusetts, Adams asserted that creating a two-tiered committee of correspondence system would "strike Terror into the hearts of those who would enslave us."

What a difference a year made! In May 1772, deep into the quiet period, confident Tories tried to have Boston pitch Samuel Adams off its House delegation. Now, in 1773 as the colony-wide election approached, Tories languished. At least in Massachusetts, the quiet period was just a memory, and only a masochist would have challenged Adams's reelection. He garnered 413 of a possible 419 votes, and when Thomas Cushing, the Speaker of the House, could not serve as moderator, the town meeting elected Adams to that honorific post. The meeting also unanimously approved instructions produced by unflinching Whigs who heartily endorsed Virginia's plan of establishing intercolonial correspondence committees. The next day, Adams forwarded a copy of the proceedings to Arthur Lee with the comment that Boston's instructions served various good purposes, which included communicating Boston's "sentiments and spirit" to the other towns and beyond.

As Tories feared, the annual election further weakened them. When the new General Court met in late May, Adams's days of struggling to improve on the flimsy issue of the General Court's meeting place had given way to controversies over judicial independence and the right to a jury of one's peers. Moreover, Virginia's call for creating intercolonial committees of correspondence was ready for action. And if Governor Hutchinson proved foolish enough to renew the fight over parliamentary supremacy, that would supply yet more fuel to the growing resistance movement. Hutchinson understood the new realities. When he addressed the legislators on May 27, he uttered not a word about Parliament's powers. It did not matter. The damage had already been done.

The new House took immediate action on Virginia's resolutions. In what was probably a moment of extraordinary pleasure, and perhaps with a sense of accomplishment, Adams presented the motion that proclaimed the representatives "fully sensible of the Necessity and Importance of a Union of the several Colonies in America, at a time when it clearly appears that the Rights and Liberties of all are systematically invaded; in Order that the joint Wisdom of the Whole may be employed in consulting their common Safety." Instead of the small correspondence committee the House normally appointed, the members now established a standing committee of fifteen that, as in the case of the earlier correspondence committees, included Samuel Adams. Adopting the language of Virginia's resolves, the Massachusetts House ordered its committee to obtain all possible information about the important issues separating Britain and the colonies and to share that information by maintaining correspondence "with our Sister Colonies." Again following Virginia's lead, the commission of inquiry in Rhode Island, the *Gaspee* commission, received special attention. The House directed that a circular letter containing its resolves be sent to every colonial assembly and that those assemblies be urged to join Massachusetts in supporting "the wise and salutary Resolves of the House of Burgesses in Virginia." As other colonies also followed Virginia's lead, one of the cherished goals of many Whigs, not just of Samuel Adams, was being accomplished. The development of intercolonial committees of correspondence provides a prime example of how many colonists in many colonies worked together and shared ideas on the road to revolution.

Massachusetts's committees of correspondence proved especially vital since Governor Hutchinson, like the governor of every royal colony, could simply refuse to call the legislature into session or could dismiss it at any time. The committee of correspondence system allowed Whigs to establish a form of shadow government that constituted a way station on the road to installing extralegal governments in Massachusetts. As Adams later said in appraising the Massachusetts committee system, "by this Means we have been able to circulate the most early Intelligence of Importance to our Friends in the Colony, & to establish an Union which is formidable to our Adversaries." He hoped the other colonies would emulate Massachusetts.

In June of 1773, Samuel Adams orchestrated a political exposé that savaged

Governor Hutchinson's political reputation beyond repair and helped fuel the American resistance movement. For months, Thomas Cushing, the Speaker of the House, had possessed letters written in the late 1760s by Hutchinson, Lieutenant Governor Andrew Oliver, and other friends of the British government. Cushing got the letters from Benjamin Franklin, the House's agent, on the condition that they neither be copied nor made public. Believing the letters would sink Hutchinson, Adams longed to expose them. He finally managed to publicize them by once again working closely with John Hancock. Adams's methods even won Hutchinson's grudging appreciation for the Chief Incendiary's ability to manufacture propaganda.

Less than a week after the House supported Virginia's call for intercolonial committees of correspondence, Adams dramatically informed the representatives that he had matters of grave importance to communicate and requested that the gallery be cleared. Once that had been done, Adams told the members he had obtained letters prejudicial to Massachusetts and had received permission to share them with the House provided the members stipulated they would not be copied or printed. The members agreed, and Adams read the letters. That afternoon the House turned itself into a committee of the whole and considered the correspondence. Hancock reported that the representatives had concluded the letters were designed "to overthrow the Constitution of this Government, and to introduce arbitrary Power into the Province." The House approved that statement by a vote of 101 to 5. A week later, as Hutchinson twisted slowly in the wind of circulating rumors, Hancock said that he had acquired what apparently were copies of the infamous letters. The House initiated an elaborate process of authenticating the documents that, as Hutchinson justifiably complained, allowed Whigs to continue inflaming the public with vicious rumors about the still unreleased contents of the letters.

Adams used the Massachusetts committee of correspondence system to spread suspicion about the letters. On June 22 Boston's committee issued a broadside describing the uncovering of the letters as "a very fortunate important Discovery." The letters supposedly showed the need for "the strictest Concurrence in Sentiment and Action of every individual of this Province, and we may add, of THIS CONTINENT." Clearly, said the committee, "all private Views should be annihilated, and the Good of the Whole should be the single Object of our Pursuit." By standing united, Americans "shall be able to defeat the Invaders and Violators of our Rights." Massachusetts's religiosity and the traditional ideal of consensus were being blatantly exploited for Whig purposes. And, as Hutchinson lamented, all this happened without anyone directly quoting from any of the supposedly damning letters.

Hutchinson was clearly justified when he complained that his letters were being manipulated and that Adams engineered the manipulation. But the governor erred when he tried to dismiss his writings by saying they contained nothing more than what he had already said about Parliament's supremacy. When the letters finally became public, Hutchinson could not escape the devastating repercussions of his claim that, for the colonists, "There must be an abridgement of what are called English liberties." That line alone convinced many that Hutchinson cared little about American rights.

The assault on Governor Hutchinson, waged by all means fair and foul, culminated in the House approving a petition to the king by a vote of 80 to 11. Drafted by Adams, the document assured the king that "Nothing but a Sense of Duty we owe to our Sovereign, and the Obligation we are under to consult the Peace and Safety of the Province" could produce such a petition. Adams implied that the difficulties between Massachusetts and the British flowed from "misinformation" supplied by "evil Men in this province." They planned to annihilate America's liberties so they could gain wealth and political position. Governor Hutchinson and Lieutenant Governor Oliver were named as such miscreants and therefore should be replaced by "such good and faithful men" as the king might select. Once again this was not mere propagandistic bombast. The letters Adams wrote to Arthur Lee in England must be viewed as statements penned with the knowledge that they might be published. Still, writing to Lee, Samuel insisted that the notorious letters "show[ed] that the plan for the ruin of American Liberty was laid by a few men born & educated amongst us, & govern[e]d by Avarice & a Lust of power." Adams, like his principal adversaries, honestly believed evil men in Massachusetts played a central role in fomenting conflict between the colonies and the mother country.

As he led the assault on Governor Hutchinson and his supporters, Samuel Adams continued, as the governor ruefully noted, to be innovative in "even small circumstances." According to Hutchinson, Adams had, over the course of four or five years, transformed the political language in Massachusetts. Under his direction the House of Representatives had come to refer to itself as "his majesty's commons"; the House debates were styled "parliamentary debates"; what had been known as "the province laws" were now heralded as "the laws of the land." In language, at least, Adams made it seem that Massachusetts had already achieved a significant degree of autonomy if not outright independence.

By the time he adjourned the legislature in late June, Governor Hutchinson had been so beaten down by the unstinting attacks that he did not even mention the purloined letters, the question of judicial pay, or the petition asking for his removal. The quiet period in Massachusetts had obviously ended. And by the early summer of 1773 Massachusetts had a powerful new Whig organization, the committee of correspondence network, ready to combat Britain's assaults on the people's liberties. The American colonists had not yet fully awakened from their political slumber, but vital issues such as the right to a fair trial, who would pay colonial officials, and the possible limits of Parliament's power simmered in the public consciousness.

In mid-1773, the British stumbled into a confrontation with the colonists that finally shattered the quiet period throughout America. The new conflict stemmed from a plan Lord North's administration devised to rescue the tea-rich but cash-poor British East India Company from bankruptcy. The company's economic woes arose in part because Americans often consumed smuggled tea. To deal with these interrelated problems, Parliament passed the Tea Act in May 1773. Under this law, the East India Company could consign its tea to a few colonial merchants and ship the tea subject only to the Townshend duty. In practice, that meant the East India Company could undercut the price of smuggled tea. From the British perspective, the Tea Act seemed fair and brilliant. By disposing of tea that might otherwise rot in storage, the East India Company would be saved while the Americans would drink inexpensive tea. And, by enticing the Americans into buying the company's duchy tea, the colonists would be conceding that Parliament could tax them. The British administration thus bet that the colonists, then as fond of tea as they later became of coffee, could not resist cheap tea. The politicians realized that their scheme might alienate those colonial merchants squeezed out of the tea business. Still, the British government apparently believed that only tea smugglers, headquartered in Philadelphia and New York City, would howl about the Tea Act.

The North administration badly misjudged the situation. When news of the Tea Act reached America, opposition sprang up throughout the colonies, not just among smugglers. Philadelphia led the way. A massive town meeting of October 16 tore into the Tea Act in eight sharply worded resolutions that blended political principle with concerns about immediate economic interests. The meeting did not, of course, point out that the legislation threatened the livelihood of everyone from merchants to cartmen who smuggled tea. Rather, the meeting asserted that the Tea Act endangered all law-abiding classes and that low-cost tea would come at a horrific price. Merchants raised the specter of the British monopolizing all manner of businesses from selling tea to manufacturing chinaware. Thus ordinary citizens heard that the act might destroy their livelihoods just as it would ruin many honest merchants. Philadelphia's mass meeting also maintained that the Tea Act endangered America's liberties because it gave renewed vigor to the Townshend duty on tea. Adopting a tactic used against Stamp Act distributors, the Philadelphia meeting proclaimed that merchants who had signed on as consignees for East India tea must resign.

Although opposition began in a tea-smuggling port, it spread throughout the colonies. The most dramatic and influential challenges occurred in Massachusetts as a result of innovative actions spearheaded by Samuel Adams. In a circular letter of October 21 prepared for the House's correspondence committee, Adams called the Tea Act a "fresh" grievance. This "Scheme," he warned, would destroy the colonial economy and also support Britain's claim that Parliament could bind the colonies in all cases whatsoever. Here and throughout the developing controversy, Adams never lost sight of the goals of creating an intercolonial correspondence system and of achieving colonial unity. He asserted that, in the face of the new dangers, the colonies should be "united in their Sentiments." If any colony experienced an infringement of "the common Rights of all, that Colony should have the united Efforts of all for its Support." Thus he repeated his tireless refrain: all the colonies should establish committees of correspondence to achieve a unified defense of America's liberties.

Because many Americans, not just radicals like Adams, believed the Tea Act threatened them, most Tories and royal officials in America tried to ignore the legislation. Thomas Hutchinson was not interested in doing that. Having had his credibility shredded by the publication of purloined letters, Governor Hutchinson was about to leave office and sail to England. Defending the Tea Act afforded him one final chance to defeat the radicals. And, if needed, the governor had military muscle handy: British troops were still garrisoned at Castle William; British warships dotted Boston's harbor. Moreover, a majority of the East India Company's Boston consignees were related to Hutchinson by blood or marriage. The governor may not have been spoiling for a fight, but he hardly thirsted after compromise.

Since Hutchinson had canceled its fall session, the General Court could not launch an assault on the Tea Act. So Adams and the Boston Caucus sprang into action. In late October, the North End Caucus vowed to stop the sale of East India tea "with our lives and fortunes." On November 2, the members met at the Green Dragon Tavern. They voted that the tea "shall not be landed" and established a committee to arrange for the public resignation of the tea consignees at the Liberty Tree at noon the next day. A handbill invited the people to the proceedings. When the consignees indicated they would not come, the North End Caucus proclaimed itself "intolerably insulted." The members declared that if the consignees failed to appear, they would be considered "enemies to their Country." On November 3, Boston's church bells started ringing at eleven o'clock, and the town crier called the people to the Liberty Tree. By noon, at least five hundred people milled around the Liberty Tree, but the consignees refused to play their assigned part in the street drama. About an hour later, a large crowd appeared before a warehouse where several consignees had gathered. William Molineux, a noted radical merchant who belonged both to the North End Caucus and the city's committee of correspondence, walked at the head of the crowd. A delegation of nine, with Molineux as the spokesman, confronted the consignees. Using words the North End Caucus had adopted the night before, Molineux said the people's heavy resentment would fall on the consignees if they refused to resign. Shortly after the delegation left, some members of the crowd rushed the warehouse; the merchants hurriedly barricaded themselves in a second-story room. Although a consignee labeled this a "mob" action, he noted that no injuries occurred and that, within thirty minutes of the altercation, the merchants walked out of the warehouse, strolled up and down the street, and then went to their homes—all "without any molestation."

When the type of intimidation that had proved effective during the Stamp Act crisis failed, the caucus turned to the town meeting. On November 5 it considered a petition that proclaimed the Tea Act a nefarious plot aimed at destroying the colonial trade and exacting a "Tribute" that would crush the people's liberties. The petition's supporters cleverly asked if anyone wanted to defend the Tea Act. No one did. Pointedly embracing the ideal of colonial unity, the meeting then unanimously adopted the "Judicious Resolves lately entered into by our worthy Brethren the Citizens of Philadelphia." Further emulating Philadelphia, the gathering established committees to inform the consignees that the town expected them to resign. When the consignees tried to evade the question by sending a message declaring they lacked official knowledge of the East India Company's intentions, the meeting unanimously branded the response "*Daringly Affrontive* to the Town."

The town meeting assembled again on November 18 when the arrival of East India Company tea seemed imminent. The meeting appointed a new committee to demand the consignees' immediate resignation. When the committee, which included Adams, visited the consignees, they promised to respond by three o'clock. They met the deadline but continued to temporize. After unanimously voting the merchants' response unacceptable, the meeting immediately dissolved itself. Hutchinson said this unexpected action "struck more terror into the consignees than the most minatory resolves." "The inhabitants of Boston," the governor lamented, "were in possession of the powers of government."

With Adams at its head, Boston's correspondence committee stretched its powers and assumed leadership of the anti–Tea Act efforts. Promoting the unity Adams considered essential, a subcommittee, on which he served, arranged to meet with the correspondence committees from four adjacent townships. At that November 22 conclave, the five groups unanimously approved a circular letter drafted by a subcommittee that included Adams. The letter described the Tea Act as having been devised for "the purpose of enslaving us." The act must, therefore, be resisted to save the colony's "happy constitution." Then, on its own, the Boston committee added a lengthy addendum designed to prove that the Tea Act would hurt all Americans economically.

On November 28, as the Boston committee arranged for the printing and distribution of the joint call to action, the *Dartmouth* arrived in Boston harbor with a cargo that included East India tea. Although it was a Sunday, Adams convened the Boston committee in emergency session. The members pressured Francis Rotch, the owner of the *Dartmouth*, into withholding official notification of the ship's arrival until the last possible moment, November 30. That short delay allowed the committee time to arrange a gathering to prevent the tea from being landed. Adams quickly penned a circular letter asking the neighboring correspondence committees to ready their towns to help Boston save "this oppressed Country." The committees were invited to meet at Faneuil Hall on Monday at 9 A.M. and urged to bring supporters with them. Soon notices went up around town that cried out: "FRIENDS! BRETHREN! COUNTRYMEN! That worst of all plagues, the detestable tea . . . is now arrived in this harbour, the hour of destruction or manly opposition to the machinations of tyranny stares you in the face."

An observer later recalled that this mass meeting, which Adams was instrumental in organizing and which with adjournments stretched over two days, styled itself *"the People."* The meeting was also called "the body." These designations echoed Adams's depiction of the masses as "the body of the people." Thomas Hutchinson admitted that several thousand people came together in an extraordinary meeting so large it had to move to the Old South Meeting House. The gathering of *"the People"* resembled a town meeting. But as an assembly of *"the People"* of greater Boston, it was not bound by the legal restraints imposed on town meetings.

Adams opened the proceedings by introducing a resolution demanding that the tea be returned to England in the same ship that brought it. When Rotch protested that he would need the governor's authorization to do that, Adams offered the *Dartmouth's* owner some advice. After noting that cargoes and even vessels might be lost in storms, Samuel told Rotch he could argue he "was now compelled by a *Political* Storm to return the Tea." Indeed, he "might safely and honestly protest that he was compelled by a Mob of several Thousands to send the Tea back without the Duty's being paid and that it was necessary for the safety of his Person and Property so to do." Lest Rotch miss his less-than-subtle message, Samuel added that "the People" now had "the Power in their Hands" and would "carry their Resolutions into Execution at all Events." The meeting approved Adams's resolution, and Rotch promised to seek permission to reship the tea without any duty being paid. To ensure that the tea remained aboard the *Dartmouth,* "the body" created a twenty-five-member watch to guard the cargo. At this juncture, a spokesperson for the consignees stated that they had just received word from the East India Company and needed until the morning to respond. The body agreed to wait until the next day for their answer.

When *"the People"* reconvened on November 30, the sheriff arrived with a proclamation from Governor Hutchinson ordering them to disperse. The governor subsequently reported that the meeting refused to let the sheriff read the announcement "until Mr. Adams signified his acquiescence." As the sheriff read, boos and hisses filled the air. Adams then denounced Hutchinson and his proclamation. Samuel argued that "a free and sensible People when they feel themselves injured . . . had a Right to meet together to consult for their own safety." Moreover, the meeting was as orderly as the provincial assembly and even, as far as he could learn, of the House of Commons. After unanimously rejecting Hutchinson's demand, the body considered the consignees' letter. Pleading that they faced financial ruin if they returned the tea, the consignees volunteered to have it stored anywhere the people directed. Following motions by Adams, the meeting rejected the consignees' pleas and reaffirmed its demand that the tea be returned. Emphasizing that the tea must, in the meantime, remain under the people's control, Adams struck a militant note. After remarking that he kept his gun in good working order and by his bedside "as every good Citizen ought," Adams raised the possibility that the meeting's guards might be assaulted. If that happened, he "should not hesitate," and he expected no other person would hesitate, to respond appropriately. The people, pledging to achieve their goals "at the Risque of their Lives and Fortunes," decreed that copies of the meeting's resolves should be sent to England and the seaports of Massachusetts.

What Hutchinson described as these "bodies of the people collected together" frightened him. One saw in the meeting, he said, "a more determined spirit . . . than in any of the former assemblies of the people." Worse yet, everyone "had an equal voice," and many were "the lowest part of the people." Orderly government had, the governor moaned, given way to a democracy of the people, an unsavory development that raised the threat of violent anarchy. Nevertheless, Hutchinson conceded that the mass meeting had been surprisingly orderly; "no eccentrick or irregular motions . . . were suffered to take place." He accounted for that by saying the undertakings "seemed to have been the plan of a few, it may be, of a single person." Despite Hutchinson's implications, the man he called the Chief Incendiary did not manage everything by himself. A detailed account provided by an eyewitness indicates that others joined Adams as the "chief Speakers" at the mass meeting. Still, Hutchinson hit the mark when he underscored Adams's central role. Friend and foe alike testified that Samuel Adams was the leading light in Boston's fight against the Tea Act.

After the meeting of *"the People"* adjourned on November 29, Adams, speaking for the Boston correspondence committee, had ordered Rotch to have the *Dartmouth* moved to a town wharf. Rotch complied. Although Whigs controlled the tea ship, the custom officials could seize the cargo unless the Townshend duty was paid within twenty days. The grace period would expire at midnight on December 16. The anti-tea forces in New York and Philadelphia managed to avoid such problems because public pressure forced the consignees to resign, and government officials, wanting to avoid a confrontation, winked at the legal technicalities and allowed the tea to be returned to England. But, given Governor Hutchinson's unflinching position, Boston's Whigs knew they must act decisively or the tea would be landed and the duty paid.

The Boston Tea Party, a nineteenth-century depiction. Courtesy, American Antiquarian Society.

When two additional tea ships, the *Eleanor* and the *Beaver,* arrived, the local committees of correspondence, which had been holding daily joint meetings, ordered them tied up at Griffin's Wharf near the *Dartmouth.* As December 16, 1773—the day of decision—approached, Hutchinson believed "the town is as furious as in the time of the stamp act." The body of the people assembled again on December 14 and on December 16 to give the consignees and the owners of the tea vessels one last chance to return the tea without the Townshend duty being paid.

The December 16 gathering truly was a meeting of "the body of the people" of greater Boston. About 5,000 of the city's total population of approximately 16,000 joined the throng; another 2,000, some having traveled twenty miles to attend, came from areas outside Boston. Shortly after 6 P.M., with darkness having fallen, Francis Rotch reported that Governor Hutchinson would not let him reship the tea without paying the duty. Upon hearing that news, Adams declared that "he could think of nothing further to be done—that they had now done all that they could for the salvation of their Country." Although it has often been claimed that these words gave the signal to destroy the tea, the evidence is inconclusive. Still, Adams's declaration prompted the shouts: "Boston harbor a tea-pot tonight!"; "Hurrah for Griffin's Wharf!"; "The Mohawks are come!" And right after Adams spoke, men disguised as Indians advanced on Griffin's

Wharf. As they marched, Adams and the others who had been especially active in addressing the body remained very conspicuously behind in the Old South Church. Adams even suggested that Dr. Young should present a speech, which he did for fifteen to twenty minutes. Only after the huge gathering of 7,000 had dwindled to 100 or so did any of the leading Whigs stroll down to Griffin's Wharf. By then 90 to 130 men, who did their best to avoid damaging other property, were well into the task of breaking open 342 chests of East India Company tea and pitching it overboard. As a huge crowd watched silently, the "Mohawks" took about three hours to dump ninety thousand pounds of tea worth roughly £9,000 into the harbor. Adams, who was universally credited or blamed for leading the activities that produced this Boston Tea Party, proclaimed that it brought joy to all— "excepting the disappointed, disconcerted Hutchinson and his tools."

The day after the Tea Party, Adams hastily prepared an account of the proceedings. Paul Revere, who often served as an express rider in the Whig cause, rushed the message south. Revere reached Philadelphia by December 26. Samuel maintained that the news of the Boston Tea Party put starch into New York's anti-tea efforts. In late December, commenting on the fact that numerous areas of the colonies adamantly opposed implementation of the Tea Act, Adams happily asserted that the British government "could not have devised a more effectual Measure to unite the Colonies."

Samuel Adams, the revolutionary politician, had ample reason to celebrate in late 1773. Throughout the the quiet period when so many other notable Whigs temporized, Adams had unrelentingly persevered in defending America's liberties and in trying to awaken his fellow Americans to the threats against their freedom. In the process, Adams took the leading role in forging a Massachusetts committee of correspondence network and in setting America on the road to developing a similar intercolonial system. He had played a crucial role in shattering "the quiet period" in Massachusetts and then in the other colonies. Now the rekindled flame of resistance and the growing unity among Americans might light the way to independence. Nevertheless, Adams understood that the British could douse the flames if they chose. As he and others in the colonies and Great Britain had repeatedly said, the change in British imperial policy in 1763 set the time of troubles in motion. If the British returned to the imperial system that existed prior to 1763, the time of troubles would end no matter what the Chief Incendiary did. Of course, to do that, the British would have to respond with moderation to the Boston Tea Party, and they would effectively have to back away from their claim that Parliament could bind the colonies in all cases whatsoever. Adams was sure the British would not do that. He believed they would continue to provide issues that, once "improved," might allow the newly established committee of correspondence networks to light the way to the colonial unity he championed. The British administration did not disappoint him.

6

The Helmsman of American
Independence

*B*ritain's scheme to aid the beleaguered East India Company and maneuver Americans into admitting Parliament's supremacy did more than end "the quiet period." Lord North's bungling allowed Samuel Adams and his political protégés to shift effective political power in Massachusetts downward into the hands of the people. When the British subsequently responded to the Tea Party by lashing back in anger, Adams "improved" on events by using that response to help fuel the drive that produced inter-colonial congresses. He reached the zenith of his power and influence in the American congresses that met in 1774 and again in 1775–76. Adroitly employing his hallmark determination and consummate political skills, the revolutionary politician came to be seen as the man who successfully guided America to declaring its independence.

Although Bostonians worried about how Britain would react to the Tea Party, that response would not be known for months. In the meantime, fearing to do otherwise, Governor Hutchinson allowed the General Court to meet in early January. Adams quickly pushed the hot-button issue of judges' pay. By mid-February of 1774, the House had convinced every superior court judge except Chief Justice Peter Oliver to agree that only the legislature could pay them. When Oliver refused to yield, the House impeached him as "an Enemy to the Constitution of this Province," published its impeachment pronouncement in the press, and asked the governor in Council to remove him. Hutchinson naturally refused. Adams devised a way around the problem. He visited the Council room at the head of a House committee; when "officially" informed that the governor was absent, Samuel maintained that he was "presumed" to be present. Adams's innovative argument served as the pretense for claiming that the House had impeached the chief justice in the presence of the governor and his Council.

Adams soon engineered even more audacious assaults on established political practices. On March 7, the House adopted an Adams resolve that claimed the governor and Council constituted "a supreme court" possessing the power to remove judges for "crimes and misdemeanors." Moreover,

127

the powers of the Massachusetts governor and Council were so blended that the governor needed the Council's approval to negate laws. When this resolve was matched with Adams's assertion that the governor could be presumed to be in Council even when he was not, it meant the governor's powers would effectively be transferred to the Council. These arguments continued Adams's extraordinary efforts to shift authority from royal officials to the people or to legal entities responsive to the people. His arguments were not merely radical, they were subversive.

To fend off what he perceived as an Adams-led takeover of the government, Hutchinson, without warning, dispatched a message dissolving the legislature. Learning that the governor's directive was being read to the Council, the representatives employed a delaying tactic that proved useful more than once. After locking the door, they quickly endorsed several Whig measures. They declared that Hutchinson had opposed impeaching Oliver because the governor was also in the monarch's pay. In addition, the representatives instructed their correspondence committee to send letters to the other colonies and to the House's agent, Benjamin Franklin, outlining the citizens' grievances. Only then did the legislators open the door so the governor's message could be read.

Before the winter legislative session was so abruptly terminated, Adams had once again found a way to turn an attack upon the House's committee of correspondence to the Whigs' benefit. When the General Court reconvened in late January 1774, Hutchinson informed the legislators that the king disapproved of the House permitting a correspondence committee to function when the legislature was not in session. A House committee headed by Adams countered with a vigorous defense of the committee and the rights of all Americans. Adams, who authored the committee's response, pointedly declared that "the common Rights of the American Subjects" continued to face attack when colonial legislatures were not in session. Moreover, royal governors could call or dismiss legislatures whenever they desired; therefore, correspondence committees were necessary so the colonies could effectively "unite" to obtain redress of grievances. According to Adams, these committees helped achieve what he called "the great End" of government, which was "the safety and Welfare of the People."

Boston's committee of correspondence was already proving Adams's point by using the Tea Party as the occasion to initiate regular exchanges with other New England colonies. This interchange of messages inspired William Goddard, who had printing interests in Philadelphia and Baltimore, to suggest creating an American-run postal system. It would replace the tax-supported, and thus "unconstitutional," royal mail system. Realizing Goddard's plan would help unite the colonies and also keep Whig communications safe from prying British eyes, Adams eagerly embraced the idea. Supported by a circular letter Adams drafted for the Boston committee, Goddard quickly had the American postal system in operation from

Baltimore northward. In the summer he extended it south of Baltimore. Given these developments, Adams seemed justified in proclaiming in late March 1774 that "Colony communicated freely with Colony" and that colonial opposition to Britain's imperial policies had "become systematical." However, Samuel exaggerated when he added that the "whole continent is now become united in sentiment and opposition to tyranny."

Believing America must "cultivate and strengthen an Union" in the face of Britain's evil policies, Adams raised his voice in the growing chorus of advocates for holding an intercolonial congress. He had publicly espoused this idea for more than a year. John Hancock gave further support to the idea when he delivered the 1774 Boston Massacre oration, an oration Adams and others helped compose.

Realizing the Tea Party might be viewed as criminal vandalism, Adams devoted considerable time to explaining and defending it. When writing for the Boston committee or crafting personal letters, Adams stressed that the Bostonians, aided by many from the countryside, "acted upon pure & upright Principle." The people did not want to destroy the tea. But the intransigence of the consignees, the customs officials, and especially of Thomas Hutchinson left them no choice. Moreover, since nothing but the tea had been destroyed, the Tea Party was not the work of a "mob." Adams reiterated that message in a lengthy review of colonial grievances sent to Benjamin Franklin. Adams once again blamed the troubles on evil men in England *and* in the colonies. The colonists "wish for nothing more than permanent union with her [the Parent Country] upon the condition of equal liberty." That equal liberty involved protecting each colony's "Constitution," for the American people would never let the British "govern them arbitrarily, or without known and stipulated Rules."

Although Adams, like others, tried to persuade the British that they must abandon their theory of parliamentary supremacy if they wanted peace, he was sure they would not compromise. He even feared that the British might try to trick Americans by proposing that Parliament would exercise its full powers only in case of "absolute necessity." And "their Lordships will condescend to be familiar with us and treat us with Cakes & Sugar plumbs." That is why, as America awaited Britain's response to the Tea Party, Adams warned James Warren that the Whigs must be ready for anything.

While he spoke of being prepared for any response, Adams assumed the British would react to the Tea Party with brutal power. At a time when destruction of private property could be a hanging offense, the Tea Party would almost surely outrage the British. Benjamin Franklin, the House's agent, reflected the general view when he counseled the Bostonians to pay for the tea. Upon learning this, Adams reportedly remarked, "Franklin may be a good philosopher, but he is a bungling politician."

The British ministers did turn livid when they learned about the Tea Party. Their outrage stemmed from more than the destruction of private property, horrendous as that was considered. The Tea Party proved all the more galling because it occurred in Boston, long considered the hotbed of sedition. Heartily supported by George III himself, Lord North's administration aimed "to secure the Dependence of the Colonies on the Mother Country." Concluding that prior concessions had been a mistake, most British politicians accepted Prime Minister Lord North's argument that "we are now to establish our authority, or give it up entirely." The Earl of Dartmouth, who headed Britain's American Department, concurred. He concluded that, if the Americans refused to obey Parliament's laws, "they say in effect that they will no longer be a part of the British Empire." Even longtime defenders of the Americans, including Colonel Isaac Barré, agreed that the Bostonians must be punished. The result was the Boston Port Act, the first of Britain's Coercive Acts. Except for allowing limited local shipping, it closed the port of Boston as of June 1, 1774. It could not be reopened until Boston compensated the East India Company. Nor would it be reopened unless the king determined that trade could be carried on safely and that the customs officials could function without fearing for their lives. To tighten the screws of punishment, the Port Act also stipulated that Massachusetts's capital and the meeting place of the General Court would be shifted from Boston to Salem as of June 1. In addition, because Hutchinson had asked to be replaced, the British had another way to make Bostonians toe the line. George III appointed General Thomas Gage, commander of the British army in America, as the new royal governor.

General Gage and the text of the Port Act arrived together in early May, just after Boston's representatives to the House had been reelected. Flexing its now considerable political muscle and striving for a show of unity, Boston's correspondence committee quickly arranged for a May 12 joint meeting with the committees of eight neighboring towns. Just before that gathering opened, John Bowler, the Speaker of the Rhode Island House of Representatives, informed the Bostonians that every colonial assembly except Nova Scotia's had indicated it would join in united action for "preserving the Liberties and promoting the Union of the American Colonies." This electrifying news heightened the possibility that the colonists might mount a truly unified effort to assist Boston and in the process forge a unified American resistance.

The convention of towns chose Adams as chairman and approved sending all the colonies and America's port cities a circular letter he had written. The letter built on the premise that "Boston is now Suffering the stroke of Vengeance in the Common cause of America." If Boston failed to resist, every American colony would find its freedom endangered. Indeed, the Port Act was "intended to Intimidate and subdue the Spirits of all America." But "the joint efforts of all" could frustrate "this cruel Act." The greater Boston committee also endorsed a circular letter that would be forwarded to all Massachusetts towns. Although it did not specifically call for an economic boycott, the letter suggested as much by contending that, if America stopped trading with Great Britain, "the British manufacturer must *emigrate* or *starve.*"

The Boston Town Meeting convened in special session the next day and endorsed the proposals advanced by the greater Boston committee. With Adams serving as moderator, the meeting also adopted a resolution exhorting all the colonies to "come into a joint Resolution, to stop all Importations from Great Britain & Exportations to Great Britain & every part of the West Indies" until Parliament repealed the Boston Port Act. Doing that would "prove the salvation of North America & her Liberties." On the other hand, if the colonies carried on trade as usual, "the most Odious Oppression" would likely crush "Justice, Social Happiness & Freedom" in America. The Bostonians thus asked other colonists voluntarily to suffer Boston's fate because doing so would defend all the colonies. The meeting instructed Adams to have the news of its actions forwarded to the seaports and other American colonies. Paul Revere rushed south with the call for waging economic warfare.

In letters to Whig colleagues in various colonies, Adams spelled out the logic behind the movement for commercial warfare. Americans should take the offensive by making Britain "share in the miseries which she has unrighteously brought upon us." America should adopt a nonimportation and nonconsumption program so British manufacturers as well as British merchants would suffer. Adams believed a trade suspension "should be pushd as far as it will go & as speedily as possible." The colonists could not delay launching their economic reprisals until an intercolonial congress met. His theme became "A Congress is of absolute Necessity" but would take too long to arrange to help in "the present Emergency."

Adams emphasized that America's merchants could not be entrusted with carrying out the suspension of trade. Because their immediate self-interests were at stake, some merchants would hold back; others would actively oppose the endeavor. As a result, Adams increasingly counted on the "yeomanry"—as evidenced in the meetings of "the body of the people"—to make nonimportation and nonexportation work. He told Charles Thomson, a leading Philadelphia radical, that only the yeomanry's virtue could "finally save this Country." He voiced the same thoughts to Silas Deane, a leading Connecticut Whig. "The yeomanry," Adams stressed, "must finally save this Country." The fact was, he maintained, a suspension of trade could achieve "great Success" only if America's yeomanry enforced it. And if the plan was to have any chance of success, the colonies must aid Boston quickly lest "Misery and Want" cause the people "to yield to Tyranny."

In late May of 1774, with Adams in the moderator's chair, Boston's town meeting began waging economic warfare on the mother country. The meeting placed Adams at the head of a committee to prepare a "Non-Consumption agreement" and then furnish every Boston family with a copy.

The agreement should call upon Bostonians to abstain from buying any British manufactured goods that could be obtained from local producers. Moreover, reflecting Adams's belief that the yeomanry must spearhead the economic resistance, each family should "totally desert those who shall Counter-work the Salutary Measures of the Town." The town's correspondence committee was to inform the rest of Massachusetts of these actions so the nonconsumption movement could spread throughout the province.

By the time Boston fashioned its nonconsumption agreement, talk of holding an all-colonial congress percolated throughout the colonies. Adams planned to get the newly convened General Court, which opened on May 25, to endorse and arrange for the congress. But Governor Gage suddenly adjourned the legislature on May 28 and told it to reconvene in Salem on June 7. This unexpected development prevented Adams from raising the issue. But, during the brief recess, Samuel unlimbered his pen and championed a congress as an "absolute Necessity." He even asked Silas Deane of Connecticut if that colony's assembly could postpone its adjournment so the two colonies might "act in Concert" in promoting a congress.

When he wrote to William Checkley, a friend and relative of his first wife, to congratulate him on the birth of a daughter, Adams waxed eloquent on the possibilities of a united American resistance. Confronted with "the Malice of Tyranny," he found it "a consolatory thought, that an Empire is rising in America." He hinted at his own hankering after independence when he added that Britain "by her multiplied oppressions is now accelerating that Independence of the Colonies which she so much dreads, and which in the process of time must take place."

Dwelling on the influence of the birth of a child, Samuel speculated that the new father had added cause to participate "in the Struggles of your Country, as you hope your Infant will outlive you, and share in the Event." "We live in an important Period, & have a post to maintain, to desert which would be an unpardonable Crime, and would entail upon us the Curses of posterity." The allusion to posterity, a common allusion in Adams's writings, is telling. It demonstrates that, while Adams did not yearn for material prosperity, he did yearn for the approbation of posterity. And he believed, as he had said before, that "the Man who nobly vindicates the Rights of his Country & Mankind shall stand foremost in the List of fame." By pressing for immediate economic reprisals against Great Britain and by championing a colonial congress to unify America's resistance, Adams believed he was fulfilling his duty to posterity *and* helping to ensure his historical immortality.

The situation changed dramatically before the General Court could reconvene in Salem. On June 1, which ironically was the day Thomas Hutchinson sailed for England, never to return, the Boston Port Act took effect. To mark the sorrowful day, Bostonians walked the streets in mourning attire as the city's church bells tolled. In Philadelphia, the church bells rang out a muffled tolling, and ships' flags flew at half-mast. All of Virginia observed a day of fasting. June 1, 1774, was a bad day for Boston. June 2 proved even worse, and, for the revolutionary politician, more significant.

On June 2 Boston learned that Parliament had passed two more Coercive Acts. The Massachusetts Government Act, flagrantly overriding Massachusetts's charter, decreed that the provincial Council would now be appointed, not elected. In addition, while the charter accorded the councilors a significant role in selecting and dismissing provincial officials, the new act made the royal governor solely responsible for appointing and dismissing all judges, sheriffs, and other magistrates including justices of the peace. Moreover, juries could now be selected by the appointed sheriffs rather than, as they had been, elected. The law was also designed to emasculate the Massachusetts town meeting as a forum for protesting British policies. As of August 1, 1774, except for the annual meeting to elect local officials, no town meeting could occur unless the governor preapproved the agenda. The second piece of legislation, an act "for the impartial Administration of Justice," struck most colonists as anything but impartial. Under this law, if the governor so directed, the trial of anyone charged with committing a crime—including murder—while suppressing a riot in Massachusetts could be shifted to another colony or even to Great Britain.

In a letter to Richard Henry Lee, the ardent Virginia Whig, an indignant Samuel Adams labeled the Massachusetts Government Act an unabashed attempt "to destroy our free Constitution" and replace it with "an absolute despotic one." The so-called Administration of Justice Act was merely a way of "screening from Punishment any Soldier who shall Murder an American for asserting his Right[s]."

Confronted with these shocking new assaults on colonial rights, Boston's correspondence committee fashioned "a Solemn League and Covenant." That name alluded to an alliance formed against King Charles I during the English Civil War. The plan, apparently authored principally by Dr. Joseph Warren, Adams's closest friend and political ally, was sent off to all Massachusetts towns on June 8. The "Solemn League and Covenant" laid out a strident program of economic warfare. The people should come together and solemnly pledge to stop all commerce with Great Britain. No one should buy any British imports that arrived in America after August 31. To promote colonial manufacturing, as of October 1, no one should even use anything manufactured in Britain. The names of persons who refused to sign this or a similar pledge should be published so the patriots could boycott and ostracize them—forever. This agreement would remain in force until Parliament rescinded the Port Act and restored Massachusetts's charter rights.

The Solemn League and Covenant translated Adams's pronouncements about the yeomanry saving America into an action program. The people, not the merchants, would wield the effective power in an economic war to safeguard American rights. Adams and the other committee members tried to make it appear that their plan originated in the countryside. Tories and merchants, who generally denounced the plan, saw through that sham. In mid-June, they countered by asking the town meeting to "Censure" and disband its correspondence committee. Adams left his post as moderator long enough to defend the committee. The anticommittee resolution lost "by a great Majority."

As Adams helped formulate the Solemn League, he wondered whether Americans would see the Massachusetts Government Act and the Administration of Justice Act as attacks on one colony or "as part of a plan to reduce them all to slavery." Given Adams's theory that a political leader could not arouse the people unless they believed their rights were endangered, that was a crucial question. Since Adams and other radicals already believed a conspiracy was afoot to trample America's liberties, the question became: what would America's political moderates, including those with Tory leanings, think of the two new acts? The response of John Rowe, a political trimmer and wealthy Boston merchant who had socialized amiably with Governor Hutchinson, was typical and revealing. Rowe's diary consists mainly of social chitchat. When commenting on political issues, he rarely wrote more than a brief line or two. His June 1 entry on the Boston Port Act taking effect fits that description. But when he learned about the Massachusetts Government Act a day later, Rowe confided to his diary that the "Act strikes the very Charter Granted to this Province by King William & Queen Mary." He predicted that the act would produce "many Evils" in Massachusetts "& sour the minds of most of the Inhabitants thereof. I am afraid of the Consequences that this Act will Produce. I wish for Harmony & Peace between Great Britain Our Mother Country & the Colonies— but the Time is far off. The People have done amiss & no sober man can vindicate their Conduct [in the Tea Party affair] but the Revenge of the [British] Ministry is too severe."

When a man like John Rowe agreed with Samuel Adams that the British had mounted an unreasonable assault on basic rights, it suggested the great mass of colonists likely believed Great Britain *was* threatening American liberties. And the Coercive Acts *did* threaten American liberty. The Administration of Justice Act swept aside the ideal of trials by local juries, a principle that stretched back to Magna Carta of 1215. The Massachusetts Government Act was more frightening. If Parliament could unilaterally alter the Massachusetts Charter, it could do the same with any colonial charter. Even Edward Shippen, a moderate Pennsylvania Tory, graphically warned that the acts aimed at Massachusetts also contained the names of the other colonies "written with lime juice & only want the heat of fire to make them legible." If that happened, the colonial charters, which most Americans considered their constitutions, could offer no real protection against tyrannical actions. Because these latest in what came to be called the "Intolerable

Acts" were perceived as genuine threats to all the colonies, the warnings Adams had long been enunciating resonated throughout the colonies.

The two newly arrived Intolerable Acts heightened support for holding an intercolonial congress, and Adams's political adroitness helped ensure that the meeting took place. On June 9, having protested being forced to assemble in Salem, the Massachusetts House placed Adams at the head of a committee to report on the state of the colony and the Port Act. Every committee member except Daniel Leonard, who had increasingly turned conservative, was a committed Whig. Fearing Leonard would divulge their radical plans so Governor Gage could quickly dissolve the legislature, Adams and the rest of the members hid their intentions. At the committee's regular meetings, they discussed moderate measures, including possibly paying for the tea destroyed during the Tea Party. But in secret night gatherings that excluded Leonard, the Whigs, emulating the Boston Caucus, devised plans to call for an intercolonial congress and agreed upon a slate of delegates. Thus kept in the dark, Leonard saw nothing sinister when Robert Treat Paine, a fellow committee member, suggested they ride to Taunton.

With Leonard safely out of the way and after getting the gallery cleared and the House door shut and locked, Adams unveiled the results of the nighttime meetings. His committee proposed that all colonies send delegates to a congress that would convene in Philadelphia on September 1, 1774. The congressmen would "deliberate and determine upon wise and proper Measures to be recommended by them to all the Colonies, for the Recovery and Establishment of their just Rights and Liberties civil and religious, and the Restoration of Union and Harmony between Great-Britain and the Colonies, most ardently desired by all good Men." Having agreed that a circular letter containing this resolution would be forwarded to every colony, the House chose five men to represent Massachusetts at the congress: James Bowdoin, Thomas Cushing, Samuel Adams, John Adams, and Robert Treat Paine. Knowing Governor Gage would not authorize spending £500 to pay the delegates' expenses, the House took an extraordinary step. It recommended that Massachusetts's towns use their regular tax base to determine their share of the £500 and then forward that sum to Cushing in Boston. Doing that removed the governor from the taxing process and denied him his charter-given veto power.

Sometime during these deliberations, a House member feigned illness, was allowed to leave, and rushed to alert Gage about what was happening. The governor hastily scrawled an order dissolving the General Court and sent his secretary, Thomas Flucker, to read it to the House. But with Adams in possession of the key, Gage's secretary could do nothing more than read the governor's directive before the locked chamber door. As Flucker rambled on in vain, the legislators, having completed arrangements for a congress, passed a resolution supporting economic warfare. The House urged the people to stop consuming British goods "until the publick Grievances of America shall be radically and totally redressed." Only then was the door opened so Flucker could again read Gage's order dissolving the legislature.

Shortly after he dismissed the legislature, Governor Gage reportedly tried doing what Thomas Hutchinson had declared impossible—bribing Samuel Adams into abandoning his ideals. In June 1774, Gage had two reasons to hope Adams might be bought off. In midmonth, army units arrived and bivouacked on Boston Common. That deployment helped fuel a growing speculation that Adams, and others too, would be seized and whisked to England for trial and punishment. The possibility of being hauled away to an uncertain fate blended with a second consideration: the Adams family's shaky economic position. Since Adams was relatively poor for a person of his public stature, the loss of his salary as clerk of the House left questions about how the Adams family would subsist. That was the situation in late June when, according to Hannah Adams, Gage sent a Colonel Fenton to visit her father. Fenton verbally presented Gage's confidential offer. If Adams stopped opposing Britain's policies, he would receive "great personal advantages" and "make his peace with the King." As Hannah recounted it, having heard this proposal, her father responded: "Sir, I trust I have long since made my peace with the King of kings. No personal consideration shall induce me to abandon the righteous cause of my country. Tell Governor Gage it is the advice of Samuel Adams to him no longer to insult the feelings of an exasperated people."

Given the political tradition of preferment, the conditions in late June 1774, and his lack of knowledge about Adams, it made sense for Gage to tender Adams an offer. Thomas Hutchinson had known better. Neither threats nor inducements would dissuade Adams. They would not work for the same reason Samuel Adams could not, in "the quiet period," emulate John Adams and John Hancock and eschew politics to pursue personal economic gain. Samuel meant what he repeatedly said in public and private: he believed he had a duty to defend the people's constitution and liberties. The British assault on the Massachusetts Charter, a "constitution" that protected the people's rights, represented for Adams both an immediate political horror and the culmination of a conspiracy to destroy colonial liberty. Because many colonists were coming to share Adams's views, colony after colony agreed to attend the congress Massachusetts said should meet in Philadelphia on September 1. Thus, as the summer unfolded, Adams had reason to believe that the colonies would create "one firm Band of Opposition to the oppressive Measures of the British Administration."

During the summer of 1774, Adams diligently labored to make it possible for Bostonians to hold out against Britain's attempt to force them into submission through misery and want. He actively sought charitable donations from throughout the colonies and helped distribute the contributions in greater Boston. Fearing a lack of jobs might produce counterproductive violence, he also helped increase employment opportunities, especially for the poor. To do that, the Boston Town Meeting launched several public works projects.

In August, as he prepared to attend the intercolonial congress, Adams himself became the beneficiary of an anonymous gift, a complete gentleman's wardrobe. John Andrews, a Boston merchant who described the arrival of the clothes and accessories, noted that Adams also received a gift of money. In addition, individuals replaced the family's dilapidated barn and repaired the Adams home. Writing to a friend, Andrews said he recounted the examples of generosity bestowed on Adams "to show you how much he is esteemed here. They value him for his *good* sense, *great* abilities, *amazing* fortitude, *noble* resolution, and *undaunted* courage."

As others worried about his appearance and his family's comfort, Adams thought about keeping an organized resistance going in Massachusetts. He helped arrange a convention of towns like the one he had promoted in 1768 to oppose the arrival of British troops. To circumvent the prohibition against unapproved town meetings, Adams and Dr. Joseph Warren devised a plan for holding county meetings. By the end of August, delegates from four counties had produced an outline for a provincial congress that would effectively become the extralegal government of the colony. Significantly, the delegates suggested the provincial congress should urge the people to sharpen their military training and preparedness.

When Samuel Adams and other Massachusetts delegates climbed aboard a coach on August 10 for the journey to Philadelphia, he was leaving Massachusetts for the first time in his life. He hoped the congress would fashion a unified and vigorous resistance that would lead to independence. But, contemplating what awaited him in Philadelphia, Samuel knew that two decidedly different groups had promoted the congress. Radical Whigs wanted the congress to pursue the kind of vigorous resistance embodied in the Solemn League and Covenant. On the other hand, the moderates, including most merchants in the major cities, did not want to suffer severe business loses nor flirt with rebellion. In fact, some moderates, especially those in New York, had pushed for a congress to undermine the radicals' demands for initiating economic conflict with the British. As the Massachusetts delegates traveled south and conversed with other colonial leaders during their nineteen-day trip, it became clear that ardent Whigs and moderates had different agendas. The congress would surely turn into a crucial test of strength between the groups.

The situation proved all the more nettlesome because Samuel Adams and his fellow Massachusetts delegates had to walk a political tightrope that figuratively stretched from backcountry Massachusetts to Philadelphia. The delegates wanted their province to resist the British actively, and they wanted the congress to adopt vigorous countermeasures against Britain. At the same time, the Massachusetts contingent believed that attaining colonial unity, especially among the congressional delegates, was essential to the American cause. Therefore, to keep timid Whigs and Tories from undermining unity, the people of Massachusetts must show prudence and forbearance. But Massachusetts's landholders were threatening to cast prudence and forbearance aside. Adams had long maintained that Britain's claims of parliamentary supremacy could endanger the colonists' landholdings. He raised that specter in his famous 1764 instructions and during the quiet period had chided landholders for being "too unconcern'd Spectators" in the fight against the British policies that threatened *all* colonial property, including land. However, the message of lands being endangered resonated rather too well in the fall of 1774 and threatened to produce extreme actions that might scare moderate delegates and thus undermine unity at the intercolonial congress.

On September 12, Dr. Joseph Warren informed the Massachusetts delegates that the people, especially farmers, feared "molestation" of their lands. The fear was so strong, he said, that many in Massachusetts, "and almost all in the western counties," wanted to overthrow the established government and return to the first Massachusetts Charter. Under the 1629 charter, the people elected the governor. Warren stressed that many people believed that, even if the 1691 charter were fully restored, "the possession of their lands may be rendered precarious by any alterations in the charter which parliament shall think to make." He pleaded, "I beg you would give me immediate advice." Adams had to consider that question within the framework of fostering a strong resistance effort in Massachusetts without having that resistance alienate congressional moderates. Upon reflection, Adams suggested that Warren strive to unite the people behind fashioning a government based as much as possible on the current Massachusetts Charter. Reminding Warren that "there is a charm in the word 'constitutional,'" Adams counseled prudence and moderation so the British, not the colonists, would appear the aggressors. As he reiterated time and again, he wanted to put the onus on the British because "it is a good Maxim in Politicks as well as War to put & keep the Enemy in the wrong."

A paucity of sources makes it difficult to fathom the inner workings of the First Continental Congress. The delegates adopted a solemn pledge of secrecy, and their official journals contain only a bare-bones record of actions taken. Although the sources are frustratingly scanty, the Congress that met from September 5 through October 26, 1774, clearly split into two factions, the moderates and the ardent Whigs. Moderates dominated the important New York and Pennsylvania delegations; Joseph Galloway of Pennsylvania emerged as a chief spokesman of that faction. Although the moderates believed America had grievances against the British, they were committed to maintaining union with Britain. Thus they supported petitioning for redress, but, as Galloway put it, strove "to avoid every measure which tended to sedition, or acts of violent opposition." Moderates disliked economic warfare and especially so since, in their view, it would be implemented "by illegal conventions, committees, town meetings, and their subservient mobs, which would soon put an end to all order, and destroy the authority of Government."

Despite Galloway's assertions, ardent Whigs were hardly anarchists, even if some, including Samuel Adams, would have happily shifted political power downward. The more radical Whigs, who dominated the Massachusetts and Virginia delegations, were themselves not in total agreement. In 1774, as William Gordon noted, few shared Samuel's conviction that America must become independent. However, ardent Whigs agreed on two crucial general points. They believed, as Whigs had argued since the time of troubles began in the mid-1760s, that Parliament could not bind the colonists in all cases whatsoever. They also maintained that the colonists must do more than petition for redress; they must use economic and other forms of coercion to force the British into acknowledging America's fundamental rights.

When Congress convened on September 5, the Massachusetts delegates knew they themselves posed a danger to congressional unity. Samuel observed that some congressmen considered Massachusetts "intemperate and rash" and its delegates too domineering. His political acumen helped blunt those negative views. As the delegates began deliberations, Thomas Cushing recommended opening Congress with prayer. Several speakers said the delegates' differing religious persuasions made any joint worship impossible. At that point, Samuel rose and remarked that "he was no Bigot, and could hear a Prayer from a Gentleman of Piety and Virtue, who was at the same Time a Friend to his Country." Adding that he had heard that the Reverend Duché, an Episcopalian, was such a man, Adams moved that he be invited to speak. The motion carried, and Adams's ecumenical attitude softened the hostility some delegates had toward Massachusetts.

Speaking in private, George Read, a delegate from Delaware, called Adams's motion a "masterly stroke of policy." The stroke was enhanced by the fact that, on the evening before Duché spoke, news, incorrect as it turned out, reached Philadelphia that British warships had bombarded Boston. In that charged atmosphere, Duché offered a rousing patriotic prayer. The psalm of the day (Psalm 35) made his presentation especially inspiring. Psalm 35, as Duché would have read it, implores the Lord to "fight thou against them that fight against me" and defiantly proclaims, "Let them be as dust before the wind, and the angel of the Lord scattering them."

The masterful stroke of having Duché lead a prayer set the tone for Congress, but Adams improved on events even more by employing what Galloway called "continual expresses" between Philadelphia and Boston. Congress's committees and subcommittees had not yet even reported when Paul Revere arrived in Philadelphia on September 16 with the results of the Suffolk County convention Adams and Dr. Warren had planned. The convention had sent a letter to General Gage that pictured Bostonians being subjected to military oppression. More important, the convention had adopted a lengthy list of grievances. These Suffolk Resolves depicted the Coercive Acts "as the attempts of a wicked administration to enslave America" and advanced the subversive argument that the citizens need not obey unjust laws. The resolves, which advocated nonimportation and non-consumption, called for holding a provincial congress in Massachusetts and outlined ways for governing without accepting the Coercive Acts. While pointing out that the people of Massachusetts had not engaged in riots or tumults, the resolves emphasized, "we are determined to act merely upon the defensive, so long as such conduct may be vindicated by reason and the principles of self-preservation, but no longer."

The Suffolk Resolves jolted moderates. In Galloway's mind, the claim that Parliament's laws could simply be ignored constituted "a complete declaration of war against Great-Britain." He was horrified when, on September 18, Congress adopted a general endorsement of the Suffolk Resolves. And following the pattern Adams established during his clerkship of the Massachusetts House, Congress directed that its endorsement and the Suffolk Resolves be printed in newspapers. Over the next ten days, Congress called upon Americans to cancel orders sent to Britain and to begin non-importation on December 1.

In desperation, moderates proposed a Plan of Union drafted by Galloway. It envisioned the formation of an American legislature that would have to vote its approval before acts of Parliament could take effect in America. Galloway presented this plan on September 28, and it generated two days of heated debate. As Adams saw it, the Plan of Union, like calls for petitioning rather than waging vigorous economic warfare, amounted to a delaying tactic that could lead to the loss of America's liberties. Radicals effectively quashed Galloway's plan by tabling it. Congress then decreed that nonexportation would begin in September 1775 if America's grievances had not been redressed.

Radical Whigs dealt the moderates another sharp blow when Congress issued its Declaration of Rights on October 14. Although much of the declaration reiterated established Whig arguments, it broke new ground by explicitly denying that Parliament had any right to legislate for the colonies. Delegates like Galloway considered that treasonous. Congress softened its radical pronouncement by saying the colonists would cheerfully allow Parliament to regulate the empire's trade—so long as no taxes were involved. Even as modified by this concession, Congress's renunciation of Parliament's power marked a major advance along the road toward casting off British control.

Less than a week later, Congress formulated an "Association" to enforce the economic warfare. The association stipulated that nonimportation would begin in December and escalate to include nonconsumption and nonexportation in September 1775 unless Britain abandoned "the ruinous system of colonial administration adopted by the British Ministry about the year 1763, evidently calculated for enslaving these Colonies." Citizen committees would be chosen in every town, city, and county of America and charged with ferreting out anyone who violated the agreement. The names of such "enemies of American liberty" would be published so the people could "break off all dealings with" them. The endorsement of extralegal entities went even further. Congress recommended that the enforcement committees, as well as provincial conventions, "establish such farther regulations as they may think proper" to achieve the aims of the association.

The association decimated moderates. The only consolation they achieved, and it was a minor one, came from the stipulation that association committees should be elected by those eligible to vote for members of the colonial assembly. Since every colony had a property requirement to vote, Congress's directive, if followed, would stop poor people from determining who served on those committees. Although the association constituted a disaster for them, many moderates believed they had to accept it. As Galloway later explained to Parliament, he signed the association agreement to prevent Congress from adopting even more "violent measures."

The First Continental Congress took some actions that might be described as aiming at reconciliation. The delegates, accepting a proposal advanced by moderates, petitioned the king for redress of grievances. In addition, Congress presented addresses to the English and the American people. These pronouncements spoke of wanting reconciliation. But given Congress's frontal assault on Britain's economic interests and the way the association promoted extralegal entities, no one could deny that the ardent Whigs had carried the day. To ensure that the resistance program did not wither, the delegates authorized holding another Congress if the British rejected this Congress's positions. If needed, a second Continental Congress would open in Philadelphia on May 10, 1775.

Many delegates contributed to the triumph of the ardent Whigs in the Continental Congress of 1774. The Virginia delegation, acting on instructions Adams would have been proud to have authored, played a central role. The Virginia instructions praised the noble Bostonians for defending America's rights and denounced Gage's implementation of the Massachusetts Government Act as "the most alarming Process that ever appeared in a British Government." Even within the Massachusetts delegation itself, Samuel shared the limelight with his cousin John. Nevertheless, the reaction of moderates in Congress illustrates why Samuel Adams was considered the helmsman who steered America toward independence. When Joseph Galloway assessed what had happened in the Congress of 1774, he traced the achievements of what he called the "violent party" to one person—Samuel Adams. Galloway saw Adams as "a man, who though by no means remarkable for brilliant abilities, yet is equal to most men in popular intrigue, and the management of a faction." In short, Samuel Adams had the skills of a master politician. In addition, Galloway joined many others who expressed amazement at Samuel's energy and dedication. Galloway observed that Adams "eats little, drinks little, sleeps little, thinks much, and is most decisive and indefatigable in the pursuit of his objects." Having lost more than one political tussle with Adams, Galloway came away almost transfixed by what he considered Adams's evil political genius. "It was this man," Galloway opined, "who by his superior application managed at once the faction in Congress at Philadelphia, and the factions in New England."

Galloway, like Hutchinson before him, erred in attributing major Whig triumphs solely to Samuel Adams. Adams did not, could not, direct the politics of Massachusetts and Congress all by himself. But Galloway's reference to the management of factions accurately reflects the fact that, in Congress, the revolutionary politician effectively employed the political skills he had sharpened in the Boston Caucus, the Boston Town Meeting, and the Massachusetts House. Above all, Adams pursued his political goals with an unflinching single-mindedness that impressed his allies and exasperated his foes. Adams carefully planned ahead, as when he and Dr. Warren devised plans for holding provincial conventions. And, always seeking to improve on events, a process that included putting his enemy in the wrong, Adams helped arrange the express communications between Massachusetts and Philadelphia that allowed Whigs to build upon the Suffolk Resolves and the supposedly outrageous actions of Governor Gage's soldiers.

In the Congress of 1774, as in Massachusetts, Samuel achieved fame not only for his extraordinary energy and remarkable clarity of vision, but for what Galloway called "Adams's art." Contemporaries agreed that Adams exhibited an amazing, perhaps unparalleled, ability to lobby other delegates and make arrangements for pursuing joint objectives. Given the praise—and hatred—American politicians lavished on Adams's political prowess, it is hardly surprising that many British politicians shared Galloway's assessment of Samuel's extraordinary political skills. Josiah Quincy, one of the ardent young patriots Adams mentored, learned about Adams's exalted reputation in person. In December 1774, writing from England, Quincy told his wife that the estimation of Samuel Adams "runs very high here. I find many who consider him the first politician in the world."

Throughout his arduous labors in the 1774 Congress, Samuel Adams had a special source of strength, his wife. We can only catch glimpses of the relationship between Samuel and "Betsy," as he called Elizabeth. But a letter she sent Samuel in September, a letter written in a clear, forceful style, is instructive. The love and warmth the two shared is evident, even given the stilted language conventions of the day. Saying she had written three letters and impatiently awaited news from him, Elizabeth observed "indeed (my dear) I am never more happy than when I am Reading your letters or scribbling to you my self." Calling herself "your affectionate Wife," Elizabeth let Samuel know that "I long for the happy day when you will return

... [although] I know it will be to a new Scene of Cares." Her reference to the struggles that lay ahead underscores another vital aspect of Samuel and Elizabeth's relationship: both were fervent, articulate Whigs. She denigrated the lying, "the infamous" Thomas Hutchinson. Ruminating about Tories who had flocked to Boston, Elizabeth informed Samuel that "the once happy Boston is now become a den of thieves, a Cage of Every unclean Bird—[tea] consignees, Commissioners, and tools of every denomination have made this town their ark of safety."

By the time Samuel returned to Elizabeth on November 9, 1774, the government of Massachusetts had been transformed—but not in the way Parliament envisioned when it passed the Massachusetts Government Act. Governor Gage had dissolved the General Court even before it could meet. The representatives, joined by others selected at town meetings, had countered by forming a provincial congress that usurped the province's taxing power and set Massachusetts on a war footing. Under Dr. Warren's energetic leadership, the provincial congress's Committee of Safety continued military preparedness after the extralegal gathering adjourned in late October. The committee wanted to turn thousands of militiamen into "minutemen," citizen soldiers who would literally stand ready to fight at a moment's notice. Having long trumpeted the need for military preparedness, Adams heartily supported the effort. Writing to Dr. Thomas Young from Philadelphia in mid-October, Samuel remarked that "I have written to some of our friends to provide themselves without delay with arms and ammunition, to get well instructed in the military art, . . . and prepare a complete set of rules, that they may be ready in case they are called to defend themselves against the violent attacks of despotism."

When it reconvened in late November, the provincial congress added Adams and the province's other Continental Congress delegates to the Committee on the State of the Province, which formulated recommendations for the rest of the members to consider. Before dissolving their gathering on December 10, the delegates endorsed the Continental Association and exhorted the minutemen to become skilled soldiers. To keep their powerful extralegal form of government functioning, the delegates authorized the citizens to elect a second provincial congress and scheduled it to meet on February 1, 1775.

Despite the limitations the Massachusetts Government Act imposed, the Boston Town Meeting, with Samuel Adams serving as moderator, devised a way to continue operating. Using the ruse that its meetings were merely adjournments of a meeting held before the new regulations took effect, the town meeting functioned in late 1774 and into 1775 without submitting its agenda for the governor's approval. In early December Boston's citizens appointed Adams and the city's other noted Whigs to a sixty-two-member Committee of Inspection to enforce the association and the Continental Congress's other directives. As he assumed yet more duties in the Whig cause, Adams remained active on Boston's Donations Committee. Here, as always, he sought to improve on events and promote intercolonial unity. When he sent out letters of thanks to those who had contributed to the relief of Bostonians, Adams routinely emphasized that, sustained by the noble assistance of "sister colonies," the people of Massachusetts would persevere in their defense of the rights of all Americans.

To heighten patriotic ardor, Adams and his fellow Boston Whigs continued the tradition of having an oration delivered on the anniversary of the Boston Massacre. In 1775 that seemed a dangerous undertaking. Rumors circulated about Boston's leading Whigs being arrested, and people knew Governor Gage had more than twenty-five hundred redcoats available for the undertaking. Indeed, as Adams phrased it on the day before the oration was to occur, "Every Art has been practiced to intimidate our leading Men on the popular side." So it took courage for Dr. Warren to deliver the speech and for Adams to preside at the ceremony.

The events of the 1775 oration illustrate more than courage. They show how Adams could, as he so often did, turn a difficult situation to the Whigs' advantage. As the people gathered at the Old South Meeting House, Adams anticipated trouble. It came in the form of about forty British officers. As Samuel remembered, "I took Care to have them treated with Civility, inviting them into convenient Seats &c that they might have no pretence to behave ill, for it is a good Maxim in Politicks as well as War to put & keep the Enemy in the wrong." Adams's report, confirmed by other accounts, had the officers behaving "tollerably well" until Dr. Warren finished and the usual motion was offered to arrange for the next anniversary commemoration. That prompted hissing from the officers, which, Adams believed, was designed to provoke an incident and break up the meeting. Despite some exchanges of unpleasantries, "order was soon restored & we proceeded regularly & finished."

During the winter and spring of 1775, Samuel Adams devoted his energies principally to the Second Provincial Congress and to preparing for war. Again working closely with Dr. Warren, he gave special attention to Canada. In mid-February, probably at Adams's urging, the provincial congress authorized Boston's correspondence committee to solicit the support of influential men in Montreal and Quebec. Warning that their rights were also endangered, Adams urged Canadians to send delegates to the Second Continental Congress scheduled to convene in May. John Brown, a recent Yale graduate then living in western Massachusetts, carried these letters. He went north on February 21 with the committee exhorting, "We hope you will make utmost Dispatch to Canada, as much depends upon it." Adams and Dr. Warren counted on Brown to be more than a mailman; they instructed him to assess the military situation. Brown did so in late March and advised that Fort Ticonderoga in New York must be captured as soon as hostilities began. Fortunately, said Brown, New Hampshire men stood ready to undertake the task. Capturing Fort Ticonderoga would serve the patriots in two vital ways. The fort occupied a strategic location on the route between Canada and the American colonies, and it had many cannon, a crucial weapon in short supply among the colonists. Adams concurred with Brown's analysis and promoted an attack on Fort Ticonderoga when the appropriate time came.

Adams also prepared for the seemingly inevitable hostilities by seeking alliances with Native Americans. In late March, he chaired a small provincial congress committee charged with establishing favorable relations with the Indians of the Six Nations. The committee wrote to the Reverend Samuel Kirkland, a noted missionary who worked with the Mohawks. The committee urged Kirkland to convince the Mohawks, and through them the rest of the Six Nations, to join the colonists. If that proved impossible, he should attempt to keep the Indians neutral. Adams drafted a lengthy letter for Rev. Kirkland to give the Mohawks. Adams tried, as he did in his letters to Canadians, to convince the Native Americans that "you as well as we, are in danger." Warning that the British wanted the colonists' *and* the Indians' lands, Adams urged the Mohawks "to whet your hatchet, and be prepared with us to defend our liberties and lives." Given the American colonists' dismal record of breaking promises made to Native Americans, Adams's pronouncements had a hollow ring.

As a member of the powerful Committee on the State of the Province, Adams's efforts to form alliances extended to the New England colonies. On April 8, the committee urged the provincial congress to send delegates to Connecticut, Rhode Island, and New Hampshire with a proposal that they join Massachusetts in creating a New England army. The provincial congress overwhelmingly assented and began the process of forming this consolidated force before adjourning on April 15, 1775.

Samuel Adams knew he would not be at the next session of the provincial congress. He and the other Massachusetts delegates from the First Continental Congress had been selected to attend the Second Continental Congress in Philadelphia in May. After the provincial congress adjourned, Adams and John Hancock, who had been added to the province's congressional delegation, traveled to Lexington to spend a few days with the Reverend Jonas Clark. According to reports, British troops wanted to arrest Adams and Hancock. Despite such speculation, Adams believed that if the troops marched, it would be to capture military stores, not individuals. As Adams and Hancock rested in Lexington, it was not yet clear how the British intended to respond to the colonists' demands. They soon learned.

The actions of the First Continental Congress convinced the British that only brute force would bring the Americans, and more particularly the people of Massachusetts, to their senses. In November 1774, responding to the Suffolk Resolves and the Continental Congress's support for these radical pronouncements, Lord Dartmouth proclaimed that Massachusetts was "plainly in a state of revolt or rebellion." King George III agreed. "Blows," he said, must decide if the colonists would "be subject to this country or independent." By mid-February 1775, the king had officially declared Massachusetts in a state of rebellion, and measures expanding Britain's army and navy had been approved. In fact, the fatal step occurred even earlier. Lord Dartmouth believed that "a vigorous Exertion of . . . force" would stop the "acts of treason & rebellion." So, on January 27, he issued orders for General Gage to arrest the principal leaders of Massachusetts's provincial congress. He also advised Gage to capture military supplies colonists had taken from British depots. Although he left the implementation of these directives to Gage, Lord Dartmouth made it clear that Gage would face severe censure if he failed to act decisively. Dartmouth's letter reached Gage on April 16, 1775; he took immediate action. Gage ordered about seven hundred troops to move, as secretly as possible, to Concord, where colonists had stashed military stores. Despite Dartmouth's instructions and recent reports of possible upcoming arrests that swirled around the colony and caused leading Whigs to flee Boston, Gage's plan did not include having soldiers capture Samuel Adams or any other Whig leader.

The British operation began on the evening of April 18. Adams and Hancock received word of the British troop movement about midnight. When the soldiers appeared in the vicinity early on the morning of April 19, Adams and Hancock were prevailed upon to move to the nearby village of Woburn to avoid capture. It is not clear if the two men heard the exchange of gunfire between the redcoats and the Lexington minutemen that turned protest into war. But, according to the historian William Gordon, who talked with him later in 1775, as Adams and Hancock moved through the fields, Samuel proclaimed *"O! what a glorious morning is this!"*

Adams naturally put the British in the wrong when he penned comments on "that memorable Battle" of April 19. "I rejoyce," he professed about a month later, "that my Countrymen had adhered punctually to the Direction of the General Congress, and were at length driven to Resistance through Necessity. I think they may now justly claim the Support of the confederated Colonies." Adams displayed his imaginative use of language and his sense of America as a country by referring to the British troops as "The Rebel Army." The Americans were fighting "the mercenary Soldiers of a Tyrant." And, as Adams often reminded those to whom he wrote, that tyrant was George III.

After hostilities commenced, Adams made a revealing change in his writing. During the political sniping that preceded the war, Adams rarely invoked religious imagery. Once war erupted, he employed religious allusions more often. Thus, he observed that "Righteous Heaven will surely smile on a Cause so righteous as ours is, and our Country, if it does its Duty will see an End to its Oppressions." He was also much more inclined to see, and seek, God's intervention in America's affairs. Samuel even expressed the hope that "Divine Vengeance" would come crashing down on the tyranni-cal George III.

Samuel wrote about "Divine Vengeance" while attending the Second Continental Congress. Except for a brief recess the members took to avoid the August heat, Samuel toiled in Congress from the spring of 1775 through the formal declaration of independence and beyond. The August 1775 recess, which allowed him to make a quick trip home, provides an example of his famous physical stamina. Believing it would benefit Samuel's health, cousin John urged Samuel to return to Philadelphia on horseback. Although he had rarely been on a horse, Samuel agreed. He completed the three-hundred-mile journey with ease. In fact, by the end of the trip, Samuel apparently was, John admitted, the better horseman of the two.

As Samuel labored in Philadelphia, his family was much on his mind, and his concern naturally increased because the war was being contested in Massachusetts. Samuel's apprehension intensified after June 12, 1775, when Governor Gage offered a pardon to the American rebels who laid down their arms. Samuel Adams and John Hancock were the only rebels explic-itly excluded from the offer; their offenses were deemed so villainous that they must be punished. Samuel's anxiety probably intensified when he learned that his closest friend and political soulmate, Dr. Joseph Warren, had been killed on June 17 at the battle of Bunker Hill. Writing to Elizabeth, Samuel said he found solace in remembering that Dr. Warren "fell in the glorious Struggle for the publick Liberty." Samuel added that "my great Concern is for your health and Safety." To help ensure that safety, the Adams family had moved to Dedham. But the younger Samuel Adams, having recently completed medical training, remained in Boston and could not now get out. Samuel pleaded with Elizabeth for any news of his son and expressed elation when he learned in late June "that my dear Son has at length escapd from the Prison of Boston."

Samuel's concern for his only son, a son "for whom my Anxiety is great," led him to ask James Warren to assist young Samuel in securing an army post if he did not yet have one. Samuel tempered his request by saying War-ren should help young Dr. Adams only "as far as he shall appear to have merit." When Samuel received reports about his son behaving well on the battlefield, he wrote to Elizabeth: "Nothing gives me greater Satisfaction than to hear that he supports a good Reputation." Samuel's insistence that his son earn a position on merit as well as his emphasis on the importance of deservedly acquiring a good reputation reflected his own deep concern with being worthy of the public trust and doing one's patriotic duty.

Throughout the weary months in Philadelphia, Samuel inquired about everyone in the family household. He asked to be remembered not only to his family and friends but also to Surry, the family servant, and to Job, an apprentice boy. On occasion, Samuel exchanged letters with his son and with his daughter, Hannah. And, as in the days of Congress of 1774, he drew strength from the support of his wife. She was, he told her, his "dearest Betsy, his true partner in life." Although many of the couple's letters have not survived, they wrote regularly. Each pleaded for more letters, and each waited, as Samuel put it, "impatiently" for the other's letters to arrive. The simple truth was, said Samuel, "it is painful to me to be absent from you," and the arrival of "your Letters would in some Measure afford me Reliefe." One feels the warmth of their affection in a letter that also conveys a sense of the long hours he spent at his desk after Congress adjourned for the day. Samuel closed a letter of June 28, 1775, saying: "Pray my dear let me have your Letters more frequently—by every opportunity. The Clock is now striking twelve. I therefore wish you a good Night."

Elizabeth was far more than an affectionate wife to Samuel. In an age when few marriages reflected anything approaching equality, Samuel and Elizabeth's union was built on a great measure of equality. Samuel praised Elizabeth's "Prudence" and counted on her "usual Discretion" in difficult times. Elizabeth also apparently managed the family's finances. Samuel wrote from Philadelphia that "when I am in Want of Money I will write to you." And while most men—and women—stressed that women should not be involved in politics, Samuel and Elizabeth shared a passion for politics. When Samuel wrote to his dearest Betsy saying, "We must be content to suffer the Loss of all things in this Life, rather than tamely surrender the publick Liberty," he was writing to another ardent Whig. Elizabeth commented on the politics of the day when she wrote to Samuel. And he responded to a letter from Elizabeth—one that unfortunately has not survived—with the comment, "I am much pleasd my dear with the Good Sense and public Spirit you discoverd in your Answer to Maj^r Kains Message." Far from wanting Elizabeth to eschew politics, he lamented Congress's secrecy rule and told her, "I wish I could consistently inform you what is doing here." Samuel did send Elizabeth accounts of the latest intelligence from England as well as clippings on politics from the Philadelphia press. And when Thomas Paine's polemical pamphlet *Common Sense* appeared, he promptly sent Elizabeth a copy.

Pride as well as love glistened when Samuel recounted to Elizabeth how a Roxbury man "wrote me that he had often met with you and was surprised at your Steadiness & Calmness under Tryal." Samuel was not surprised. As he said, "I am always pleasd to hear you well spoken of, because I know it is doing you Justice." Elizabeth's strength and political drive, as well as her love, helped sustain and nourish Samuel, for theirs was a symbiotic relationship, and both labored to defend American liberties.

Samuel's efforts to further the American cause in the Second Continental Congress during the crucial period from the outbreak of war through the formal declaration of independence cannot be recounted with precision. The Second Continental Congress continued both the secrecy rule and the policy of providing minimal reports about deliberations. Because of

John Singleton Copley, Samuel Adams (ca. 1772), oil on can-
vas. Deposited by the City of Boston. Courtesy, Museum of
Fine Arts, Boston. Reproduced by permission. ©2001 Museum of Fine Arts, Boston. All rights reserved.

his understandable concern about keeping sensitive political letters from
falling into an opponent's hands, Adams revealed little in his letters. Moreover, he typically did not keep copies of his own correspondence, and he
destroyed "whole bundles of letters" so that "Whatever becomes of me, my
friends shall never suffer by my negligence."

Despite the paucity of sources, it is clear that Samuel Adams remained a
dominant, and perhaps the dominant, figure in Congress. Although he
never carried a gun or commanded troops, he played a significant role in
military efforts, especially in the first two years of the war. Adams revealed
his keen concern about military matters even before he began serving in
the Second Continental Congress. As he traveled to Philadelphia in late

April 1775, he and John Hancock stopped in Hartford. They met secretly with the Connecticut governor and Council to help arrange an attack on Fort Ticonderoga. The attack resulted in the capture of that strategic location and its invaluable cannon on May 1.

As a congressman, Adams devoured military intelligence and devoted himself to strategic planning. He quickly came to the conclusion that New York and Canada were vital and that the British planned to cut the colonies in half by driving through New York. Reflecting Adams's concern about the province, Congress placed him on a committee to determine what military measures should be taken in New York. Having already implored Canadians to join their southern neighbors, Adams was a natural to work on the committee drafting an appeal to the Canadian people. Adams also took a special interest in naval power. He served on the committee delegated to consider the possibility of developing an American navy, and he lobbied for creating such a force. When Congress approved building thirteen warships in December 1775, Adams said, "I wishd for double or treble the Number." He did not press for a bolder shipbuilding program out of fear that doing so might produce divisive acrimony in Congress.

Adams's deep interest in military matters was reflected in other important assignments Congress conferred on him. He served on a committee charged with obtaining military stores, especially ammunition. Samuel took this task seriously and even forwarded designs for a powder mill to Massachusetts. He was quite active on committees that assessed the defensive needs of various colonies. He held a seat on the powerful committee that evaluated the applications of all who sought to become officers in the Continental Army. As a member of this screening group, Adams showed a sensitivity to obtaining military talent from an unexpected quarter. He did that by supporting the appointment of British-born Charles Lee as a general. Making that appointment might, Adams believed, induce English officers to volunteer "in the Cause of Liberty in America." Adams's contributions to battlefield success did not go unnoticed. Thomas Jefferson, who served with Adams on important military committees, stressed the central role Adams took in prosecuting the war.

Adams devoted himself to military affairs because doing so could help procure what he had long believed was necessary to protect American liberties: American independence. Once hostilities commenced, Samuel hammered on the theme that the British remained determined "to establish arbitrary Government in the Colonies by Acts of Parliament and to enforce those Acts by the Sword." Chastising "moderates" for exacerbating America's problems, he repeatedly admonished his correspondents against succumbing to the illusionary and dangerous view that Britain might seek a peaceful resolution to the hostilities. Adams struggled to convince everyone he dealt with that hope of reconciliation with Great Britain could cause "the Shipwreck of America." Any British talk of possible reconciliation on reasonable terms was, he cautioned, merely a ploy to divide Americans and give the British a better chance of enslaving America. If Americans believed Britain wanted reasonable reconciliation, "it would be a Delusion leading directly to Destruction."

For Adams, independence offered the only alternative to political slavery. He also claimed that America actually became independent on April 19, 1775. Indeed, "the Moment we determin'd to defend ourselves by Arms against the most injurious Violence of Britain we declar'd for Independence." Given his views, Adams lamented that Congress did not issue a formal declaration of independence as soon as hostilities broke out, and he was bothered by Congress's continued reluctance to do so. He did not press more aggressively for an early declaration of independence for the same reason he kept counseling Massachusetts to be prudent and remained silent when Congress authorized fewer warships than he would have liked. Americans must, he stressed, preserve the unity "upon which everything we wish for depends." Also, he was well aware that it would take time "to convince the doubting and inspire the timid" members of Congress. As he said in one of his favorite aphorisms, one must give the fruit time to ripen.

Although he had long emphasized that a politician could not control events, Adams developed and pursued a vision of how Americans should defend their liberties and ultimately achieve independence. The first step involved organizing new governments in each of the colonies. Adams championed the creation of new governments because he believed it would have a domino effect leading to the establishment of an American confederation, the second vital step in his plan. He theorized that once the people of a colony installed their own government, they "will feel their Independence." When that occurred, "the Way will be prepared for A Confederation, and one Government may be formed with the Consent of the whole." America would thus become "a distinct State composed of all the Colonies with a common Legislature for great & General Purposes." Creating a confederation government was, for Adams, linked to obtaining the foreign assistance Americans needed to fight the world's greatest military power. As soon as hostilities commenced, Americans sought, and received, some military supplies from abroad. But Adams judged, and rightly so, that Americans must obtain full alliances with foreign powers if they were to win independence. Such alliances would, he reasoned, naturally follow once Americans established a true continental government. Looking to the future, Adams longed for the time when America's trade would be open to every nation except Great Britain. These developments—creating new provincial governments, forming a continental government, and forging alliances with other nations—would culminate in, and be crowned by, a formal declaration of American independence.

From Adams's perspective, Congress began moving toward his ultimate goal of independence on June 9, 1775, when it responded to a letter from the Massachusetts Provincial Congress. Proclaiming that Britain was waging war against the "peaceful and loyal subjects" of Massachusetts, Congress authorized the people to disobey an act of Parliament that altered the colony's charter. The people did not owe any allegiance to officials, such as the appointed governor and lieutenant governor, who were endeavoring to "subvert" the charter. Given these points, Congress, in language that reflected Adams's position, instructed the people of Massachusetts to form a government that conformed as nearly as possible to "the spirit and substance" of the colony's charter. Accordingly, the provincial congress should call upon the townships to elect representatives who would then elect a council. The council would exercise the governor's powers until the king appointed an executive who would govern according to the charter.

Since George III had no intention of replacing Governor Gage, Congress's recommendations smacked of independence. Still, in June 1775 Massachusetts was a war zone, so what happened there did not necessarily establish a precedent for other colonies. That is why Adams rejoiced when the movement for creating new governments spread. In mid-October, New Hampshire citizens asked Congress what should be done about their nonfunctioning government. Congress responded on November 3 by authorizing the colony's provincial congress to "call a full and free representation of the people." If those representatives deemed it necessary, they should establish "such a form of government" as the people thought would best produce happiness while securing peace and good order in the province during the present "dispute" with Great Britain. The same day Congress made that recommendation, it appointed a committee to assess the situation in South Carolina. Since Adams served on that committee, it is hardly surprising that it reported back the very next day and recommended that South Carolina be authorized to form a new government. Congress agreed.

The events of November 4 made Samuel wildly optimistic. That evening he wrote to James Warren and reported: "I believe the Time is near when the most timid will see the absolute Necessity of every one of the Colonies setting up a Government within itself." Almost giddy with delight, Adams prophesied that George III and the British administration "will necessarily produce the grandest Revolutions the World has ever yet seen. The Wheels of Providence seem to be in their swiftest Motion. Events succeed each other so rapidly that the most industrious and able Politicians can scarcely improve them to the full purposes for which they seem to be designd." Samuel even proclaimed he should be replaced since "Men of moderate Abilities, especially when weakened by Age are not fit to be employed founding Empires." Adams's continuing handiwork in helping to establish new colonial governments belied his self-deprecating comments. Responding to the royal governor's declaration of martial law in Virginia, in early December a committee Adams chaired recommended that Congress invite

Virginians to form their own government. Congress adopted the committee's recommendation.

Although new provincial governments were being authorized, Adams soon admitted he had been too optimistic when he proclaimed that "the Wheels of Providence seem to be in their swiftest Motion." As 1775 drew to a close, Congress had not yet moved toward creating a confederation government, much less toward declaring independence. Samuel complained to James Warren, "We go on here by Degrees, though not with the Dispatch I could wish." However, events in the new year quickly dispelled Samuel's gloom. On New Year's Day 1776 a British fleet bombarded Norfolk, Virginia. When the news reached Philadelphia on January 7, Americans expressed outrage. Adams, who believed events often exerted a controlling influence on politics, suggested that the cannonading of Norfolk would do far more than reasoning could to bring about a confederation.

Americans became even angrier when they learned of George III's response to Congress's pleas for redress of grievances. A copy of the king's pronouncements appeared in the *Pennsylvania Evening Post* of January 9. The king, doing what Adams said he would, insisted that the Americans must accept Britain's authority. The colonists had to realize, the king stressed, that only "submission" and "allegiance" would end hostilities. Believing many deluded Americans wanted independence, George III announced that the British military presence in America would be increased so it could force the colonists to yield. By chance, the *Evening Post* carried the king's speech on the same day Thomas Paine's stunning pamphlet *Common Sense* appeared. In powerful yet simple language ordinary people could understand, Paine savaged monarchy in general and George III in particular. And, much to Adams's delight, Paine constructed powerful arguments for America declaring its independence.

To fuel the growing sentiment for independence among ordinary Americans, Adams once again utilized the press. Writing for a Philadelphia paper in mid-February under his well-known Candidus signature, Adams built a case for independence. He began by praising Paine's pamphlet and then mounted a frontal attack on the claim that the colonists might yet reach a peaceful reconciliation with Britain. Although it was still Congress's official position, Adams savaged the idea that the empire might find peace if Britain returned to the pre-1763 imperial system. In the first place, said Adams, Britain would not consider returning to the old ways. And even if the British did agree, America's constitutional status would still be too vague, too precarious. That was especially true because, according to Adams, George III wanted to establish an absolute tyranny over *all* the people of the British Empire, not just over Americans. Turning to those who warned that Americans faced a protracted, bloody war if they declared independence, Adams boldly asserted that "the puling, pusillanimous cowards" had it backwards! Declaring independence, he reasoned, constituted "the only step that can bring the contest to a speedy and a happy issue." Why? First, once they declared independence, Americans would be on an equal footing when negotiating with Great Britain. Second, the nations of Europe, especially the maritime nations, "will find it in their interest (which always secures the question of inclination) to protect a people who can be so advantageous to them." Cleverly posing the question in a way that put his opponents in the wrong, Adams challenged the proponents "of returning to a state of dependence on Great Britain" to argue their case openly. Then to counter such efforts even before they might appear, Adams again put his opponents in the wrong by calling up, as he so often did, one's duty to posterity. "Shame on the man who can court exemption from present trouble and expense at the price of their own posterity's liberty!"

By early April 1776, Samuel openly spoke of linking the creation of a solid confederation to declaring independence and forming alliances with powerful nations. It was, he argued, time to embrace independence "and under God trust our Cause to our Swords." In late April, after reviewing the situation in each colony, he informed Samuel Cooper that "the Ideas of Independence spread far and wide among the Colonies." Adams also passed along the news that the British were expected to attack in the South. Samuel anticipated that prospect with pleasure because the South was well prepared to defend itself and because he believed such an attack would hasten independence. "One Battle would," he asserted, "do more toward a Declaration of Independence than a long chain of conclusive Arguments in a provincial Convention or the Continental Congress."

The "great object" Adams strained for so passionately seemed tantalizingly close in early June. By June 6, Adams knew his close political ally Richard Henry Lee would introduce a resolution calling on Congress to declare the colonies independent. Since he desperately wanted that resolution accepted unanimously, Adams certainly did not want events in Massachusetts spooking the more timid congressmen. The night before Lee's resolution of independence was introduced, Adams wrote to James Warren and implored him "to exert your Influence to prevent unnecessary Questions in the [Massachusetts] Assembly which may cause Contention. Now if ever Union is necessary—Innovations may well enough be put off, till publick Safety is secured."

On June 7, Lee offered the resolution that embodied the goals Samuel Adams had been advocating. The resolution declared the colonies free and independent, stipulated that foreign alliances should be formed expeditiously, and directed that a plan of confederation be produced. Although it postponed the vote on Lee's proposal until July so delegates might obtain instructions on independence, Congress appointed a committee to draft a declaration of independence. Less than a week later, Congress established a committee, made up of a congressman from each colony, to formulate a plan for a confederation government. Samuel Adams represented Massachusetts. Congress then created yet another committee and instructed it to prepare treaties that could be proposed to foreign powers. Then on July 2 Congress voted, unanimously, that "these United Colonies are, and of right, ought to be, Free and Independent States." Two days later the delegates approved the language of the Declaration of Independence. At least on paper, Adams's dream of American independence had been achieved.

Samuel Adams played a prodigious role in the movement that led to declaring independence. From 1764 on, his single-minded determination to defend the constitutions that protected the people's liberties and his consummate political skills set him apart from other American Whigs. Writing in April 1774, and not for public consumption, John Adams called his cousin Samuel perhaps "the most elegant writer, the most sagacious politician, & celebrated patriot" of anyone who had figured in the struggle for American liberties in the ten years since the time of troubles began. John was marveling at the political skills Samuel had employed and sharpened in the Boston Caucus, the Boston Town Meeting, the Massachusetts legislature, various extralegal committees, and as political author. Mercy Otis Warren, the sister of James Otis and the wife of James Warren, in an 1805 history of the American Revolution proclaimed that Samuel was "indefatigable; calm in seasons of difficulty, tranquil and unruffled in the vortex of political altercation; too firm to be intimidated, . . . his mind was replete with resources that dissipated fear, and extricated in the greatest emergencies." Adams had, she noted, "stood forth early, and continued firm, through the great struggle, and may justly claim a large share of honor, due to that spirit of energy which opposed the measures of [the British] administration, and produced the independence of America."

Whigs who served with Samuel Adams in Congress during 1775 and 1776 offered similar and even stronger assessments. Elbridge Gerry marveled that Adams worked day and night. And, as he had in Massachusetts and in the 1774 Congress, Samuel won fame for his clarity of vision and ability to forge alliances. Speaking of his cousin's work in the Congresses, John Adams, sounding like Joseph Galloway, depicted Samuel as a less-than-brilliant man who was, nevertheless, a brilliant politician. According to John, Samuel possessed "the art of commanding the learning, the oratory, the talents" of others. Moreover, Samuel did this "without anybody's knowing or suspecting he had it, but himself and a very few friends." Reflecting on the Second Continental Congress, which he joined in June 1775, Thomas Jefferson offered a strikingly similar assessment. Jefferson, who stressed that Samuel was "immovable in his purposes," said Adams gained everyone's attention when he rose to speak because he was "so rigorously logical, so clear in his views, abundant in good sense, and always master of his subject." Nevertheless, in Jefferson's view, Samuel Adams achieved greatness not as a debater but as a political organizer. Samuel "was constantly holding caucuses of distinguished men . . . at which the generality of the measures pursued were previously determined on—and at which the parts were assigned to the different actors, who afterwards appeared in them." And while John Adams was a "Colossus" in debate, he had little part in Samuel's caucuses. Intriguingly, Jefferson offered his most telling assessment of Samuel Adams in conversations that focused on Richard Henry Lee. Since Adams was not the subject of the discussion, there was no reason for Jefferson to give undue emphasis to his importance. Nevertheless, Jefferson emphatically attested that, if there was a helmsman of the American Revolution, "Samuel Adams was the man."

7

"Zealous in the Great Cause": Winning Independence

$\mathscr{D}$eclaring independence was, Samuel Adams emphasized, not the same as "securing" it. From the day Congress proclaimed independence until Britain officially recognized America as a nation, Adams followed the advice he gave all Americans. He was "Zealous in the great Cause." As he labored to help fashion a military capable of winning independence on the battlefield and the seas, Adams also endeavored to help create a continental government and gain the foreign assistance he considered essential to winning the War for American Independence. For congressman Adams, the great cause involved more than the ultimate military victory that would establish America's independence. The great cause also meant establishing independence on a firm geographical foundation that would allow the Americans' posterity to flourish.

As a member of Congress, Adams continued to play a vital leadership role in the military conduct of the war once independence had been declared. He served on many important committees including the Marine Committee and the Board of War, the major committee on army affairs. He worked so exhaustively creating an effective military and developing viable strategies that some analysts in Britain linked him to the most infamous military opponent of England's monarchy. One commentator called Adams "the would-be Cromwell of America"; another dubbed him "the Cromwell of New England." In America, Thomas Jefferson, thinking back on the work of Congress, asserted that Adams "had, I think, a greater share than any other member, in advising and directing our measures, in the Northern war especially." "Indeed," said Jefferson, "in the Eastern States, for a year or two after it began, he was truly the *Man of the Revolution*."

Knowing that winning independence required an adequate military, Adams worked diligently to provide the tools of victory in what he routinely called "the great" or "the glorious" cause. He zealously pushed for keeping army enlistments up and for meeting the supply needs of the armed forces, including the small navy. The difficulties of maintaining an effective army in the field forced the revolutionary politician to advocate measures that bumped against his fear of military power. Believing the military cast of mind endangered liberty, Adams had long advocated using militia, citizen soldiers who served for limited periods under their state's control. While he still championed the militia, Adams said the vicissitudes of war presented the revolutionaries with "a choice of difficulties." His own eyes quickly convinced him that America needed professional soldiers. He reached that conclusion in August 1776 after visiting the troops in New York and speaking with George Washington, the commander in chief of the Continental army. Writing to a fellow congressman, Samuel proclaimed "it would be a pity" to lose experienced troops. He recommended offering a more generous bounty—$20 and a hundred acres of land—provided an "old Soldier" reenlisted for at least three years. On September 16, with Samuel back in Philadelphia, Congress authorized a $20 bounty for noncommissioned officers and soldiers willing to serve "during the present war." A sliding scale of land grants offered ordinary soldiers the hundred acres of land Adams had recommended.

Making long-term enlistments more attractive did not help the immediate situation, and it soon turned grim. As the leaves changed color and fell in 1776, British forces, including Hessian mercenaries, smashed through sections of New Jersey and Pennsylvania, raping and pillaging as they went. By early December Adams spoke of the British tyrant having unleashed "the powers of earth and hell to subjugate America." Soon thereafter, most congressmen fled Philadelphia as a British force drew near. Adams and three colleagues who had not yet left the city learned the enemy had just put ten thousand men into Rhode Island. Calling it their "Duty," the congressmen informed George Washington and, observing that the area lacked a commanding general, recommended that he appoint either General Gates or General Greene because each was known in the region and that might make recruiting easier. America's military prospects had dimmed so precipitously that even the indomitable Washington said on December 18 that "I think the game is pretty near up."

By the time Congress reassembled in Baltimore shortly before Christmas, the military situation seemed almost hopeless. As Thomas Paine said in "The Crisis," "These are the times that try men's souls." A desperate Congress ordered Adams and two other members to propose appropriate action. They recommended, and on December 27, 1776, Congress agreed, that Washington be accorded extraordinary powers to make the army function. Those emergency powers, which would expire in six months, allowed Washington to make every effort, including giving bounties, to spur enlistments and secure supplies for the army. The congressmen explained that they took this drastic step because they had confidence in Washington and because of the abysmal military situation.

Victories at Trenton and Princeton together with the British decision to shut down the campaign for the winter eased the immediate danger. When campaigning reopened, Adams demonstrated that his own temperament favored aggressiveness. "I am apt to be displeasd," he admitted, "when I think our Progress in War and Politics is Slow." Despite his own penchant for bold military action, the lessons of war soon made Adams value military caution. By the spring of 1777, Washington was following what Adams labeled "a Fabian War" because it emulated the great Roman general's military strategy. As Adams reported, Washington attacked only when his army had the advantage. In the meantime, smaller units harassed and diminished the British forces by continual skirmishes. Quickly grasping the value of the Fabian strategy, Samuel contemplated the possible British capture of Philadelphia by asking, "What will it avail them unless they beat our Army?" In late June of 1777, Adams confessed to having been "very wrong headed" for ever having denigrated the Fabian approach. He now predicted that America's warriors faced "a long and moderate War." He continued to hope, as he put it in 1778, that "an early Stroke" would inflict "a mortal Wound" on the British. But he understood the military realities and in the fall of 1778 praised the generals who were wisely following a judicious Fabian approach even though it was not a popular strategy.

No matter what strategy they followed, the revolutionaries needed to field an experienced army, and Adams pursued that goal vigorously. In 1779, he supported the Massachusetts program of offering a $300 bounty to men who reenlisted for the duration of the war. When he happily reported to John Adams in early 1780 that many soldiers had rejoined, Samuel sounded positively militaristic. Maintaining that a soldier's "Courage" in combat often sprang from military discipline, Adams proclaimed that Washington would soon have the best American army ever because the longer soldiers served, the more disciplined they became. By the end of 1780, Samuel asserted that he had no choice but to support Congress's plan of forming "a permanent Army" to win the war. More than four years of fighting had convinced him that no person "in his Senses who wishes the War may be carried on with Vigor" would prefer a temporary militia "to a permanent and well appointed Army!" Adams thus demonstrated that, despite his distrust of the military, he could be flexible if the cause of liberty required it.

When personally confronted with the need to make a command decision, Adams showed his willingness to carry on the war with vigor. In June 1780, Adams and Elbridge Gerry, who then was also a Massachusetts delegate to Congress, met by chance in Hartford and learned that a large British force was unexpectedly threatening the strategic fortifications at West Point. The two congressmen ordered General John Fellows, commander of Massachusetts's Berkshire County militia, to secure provisions, get wagons wherever they could be found, and march his forces "forthwith" to relieve West Point. While admitting they acted *"without Authority,"* Adams and Gerry assumed, rightly, that the state's legislators would approve of their conduct "in Consideration of the very critical Situation of the Army."

A lengthy conversation Samuel had in December 1780 with the Marquis de Chastellux, a French major general serving in America, illustrates the zealousness Adams brought to the great cause. The discussion also reveals something of his political style and personality. Chastellux, who remarked that "everybody in Europe knows that he was one of the prime movers of the present revolution," found Adams impressive. "I experienced in his company," Chastellux marveled, "the satisfaction one rarely has in society, or even the theater, of finding the person of the actor corresponding to the role he plays." Echoing views held by both Whigs and Tories, Chastellux described Adams as "a man wrapped up in his object, who never spoke but to give me a good opinion of his cause and a high idea of his country. His simple and frugal exterior seemed intended as a contrast to the energy and scope of his thoughts, which were wholly focused upon the republic, and lost nothing of their warmth by being expressed with method and precision, just as an army, marching towards the enemy, appears no less daring for observing the laws of tactics."

Wanting all Americans to be as wholly focused as he was, throughout the war years, Adams used his considerable skills as political polemicist—as propagandist—to foster zealousness in the great cause. He wrote "private" letters for others to use in support of positions he advocated, just as he used letters sent to him. Adams occasionally read letters he received to government bodies, or he inserted appropriate extracts in the press. The optimistic military forecasts he put in private letters formed part of his propaganda efforts. He lobbied for greater effort by exuberantly depicting each new campaign as a critical one where extra exertions could produce victory. More than once in 1777 he suggested that one major American victory might well "put a glorious End to the present Campaign & very probably the War." In early 1778 he wrote of longing for America's forces to begin the military campaign "very early the next Spring." In mid-1780, one of his propagandistic newspaper essays used eye-catching type to proclaim that, if amply supported, America's soldiers had a "GOLDEN OPPORTUNITY" to make the current campaign "DECISIVE and GLORIOUS." Adams constantly exhorted the people of Massachusetts, of New England, of America to be "Zealous in the great Cause," and he lavished praise on them for pouring labor and money into the war.

When he wielded his pen to bolster the war effort, Adams highlighted two core arguments: America was defending her liberties against a barbarous enemy, and more than American liberty was at stake. He made the link emphatically at the end of 1776 when America's military situation seemed almost hopeless. The tyrant George III was determined "to subjugate America" because, Adams boldly asserted, "the lamp of liberty" burned there and nowhere else. By the summer of 1777, adapting the phraseology of Thomas Paine's *Common Sense,* Adams was proclaiming that America's great cause was "the Cause of Mankind." Indeed, liberty was under assault around the globe, so the friends of liberty looked to America as an asylum. America was thus on a dual mission for freedom: "We are contending for the Rights of our Country and Mankind."

Strident propaganda efforts seemed necessary because only a minority of Americans actively supported the war. To his dismay, many Americans attempted to maintain what Adams called "a dastardly and criminal Neutrality." A significant minority of Americans, at least one in five and possibly as many as one in three, wanted to remain in the British Empire. The British thought these loyalists, those Americans the revolutionaries maligned as Tories, could prove decisive. Adams shared the British view. His fears centered on Tories who might surreptitiously undermine the war effort. They were, he soon came to believe, more dangerous than loyalists who took up arms. By early 1777, and then throughout the rest of the war, Adams carried the argument further. "The secret Machinations" of Tories, he asserted, posed a greater threat to the glorious cause than the British military did. All manner of Tories must, he insisted, be squelched.

Soon after fighting commenced in 1775, Adams began translating his strident anti-Tory views into congressional action. He chaired the first congressional committee appointed to develop policies for dealing with Tories. Congress approved the report in January 1776. It called upon citizens to educate any well-meaning but uninformed Americans who were being deceived by Britain's supporters. The local governmental units, including conventions and committees, should speedily adopt measures "to frustrate" the "mischievous machinations" of persons working against America. All Tories should be disarmed; "the more dangerous" should be locked up or forced to post bonds for their good behavior. Since Adams's hatred of Tories never subsided, it is no surprise that he regularly served on congressional committees charged with recommending ways of "suppressing toryism."

The major antiloyalist efforts occurred at the state and local levels. So, even while he attended Congress, Adams kept pressing for vigorous action back home. Massachusetts did quickly pass a test act that incorporated the Adams committee recommendations. All free adult males were required to take an oath of allegiance to the Revolution. Those who refused would be disarmed; moreover, they could not hold public office nor hold posts as teachers or ministers. The extralegal committees and local magistrates would enforce these regulations. Adams soon called for sterner measures. Writing home in early 1777, and often thereafter, he insisted that measures, "and the most vigorous ones," must be taken quickly "to root out these pernicious Weeds." If the Tory weeds were not ripped out, America's struggle would fail. When these hints failed to produce results, Adams escalated his rhetoric. In June he proclaimed that Tories should be cast out of society. Although it took longer than he wanted, a September 1778 Massachusetts law banished upwards of three hundred Tories by name and threatened them with death if they returned. In April 1779, the Massachusetts legislature authorized the confiscation of Tory property.

While he considered patriotic fervor and the suppression of internal enemies essential to winning independence, Adams maintained that forming a confederation government was also a prerequisite to securing true independence. He was therefore gratified when Congress finally appointed a committee in early June 1776 to produce a frame of government for the confederation. He was, no doubt, happier yet when Congress placed him on it. The committee did not keep a record of its deliberations, so Adams's contributions are not known. However, it is clear the members clashed sharply over many provisions. The committee issued its recommendations a month later. The title of the government, the Articles of Confederation, highlighted the fact that "The United States of America" was a "Confederacy." To protect their liberties and promote "their mutual and general welfare," the states were creating "A League of Friendship," not a unified national government. The states that formed this perpetual union would retain "sole and exclusive" control of their internal affairs, provided their actions did not conflict with the Articles. The voting system and the rules for amending the Articles underscored that the government was a confederation: no matter what its size or wealth, each state would have a single vote in Congress and, once the Articles were adopted by a unanimous vote of the state legislatures, every state must give its approval before they could be altered.

The proposed frame of government obviously reflected America's colonial experience. As members of the British Empire, the colonists expected a central government to control foreign policy and mutual defense. The committee was, however, understandably determined to deny the central government the kinds of coercive powers that had produced the time of troubles and then revolution. Accordingly, the confederation government could station troops in forts, but it could not maintain standing armies. Except for financing a postal system, Congress could "never impose or levy any Taxes or Duties." The state legislatures would meet the confederation's financial needs by supplying funds based on a formula linked to a state's population. The confederation government was not, however, given any power to force states to comply with its requests for money.

While the Articles of Confederation that Congress sent to the states in November 1777 retained the essential features of the original plan Adams helped draft, the taxing formula was changed so assessments would be based on the value of each state's lands rather than its population. In addition, Congress's revisions clarified two important points. Congress would still have authority to settle land disputes arising from colonial charters or colonial land grants; however, the brief statement in the original plan had given way to a complicated system for adjudicating land disputes. In addition, a revised Article 2 spelled out unequivocally the principle of state's rights: "Each State retains its sovereignty, freedom and independence, and every power, jurisdiction, and right, which is not by this confederation expressly delegated to the United States, in Congress assembled."

Adams proclaimed himself reasonably satisfied with the final form of the Articles of Confederation. With its careful limitation on the power of the central government, the Articles seemed well suited to ensuring that the government could not endanger the people's liberties. The Articles' emphasis on state sovereignty—an emphasis Adams approved—reflected the fact that the revolutionaries had dual loyalties. Although they thought of themselves as Americans, at least to the extent of supporting the Union, many gave a preference to their state. It could be seen in the sharp debates in Congress about how land claims would be settled. It could be seen in the fact that many Americans, including Adams, kept referring to their state as their "country."

Once the Articles reached the states, Adams turned to established lobbying techniques. He wrote letters to his Massachusetts correspondents and impressed upon them the importance of approving the Articles. Putting a positive spin on the question while reflecting his own view that compromise was necessary when forming governments, he said he expected the General Court would approve the plan, "even those parts which it may be wishd had been different." This would be done "for the Sake of that Union which is so necessary for the Support of the great Cause." He also drafted a resolution, which the Boston Town Meeting unanimously approved, that proclaimed the Articles "well adapted to Cement the Union of the ... States." The town meeting translated those words into action by instructing its representatives to vote for the Articles.

The importance Adams attached to the Articles of Confederation shines in a letter he penned to Elizabeth on July 9, 1778. "I now write at the Table in Congress, having just put my Hand to the Confederation with my Colleagues [from Massachusetts] & the Delegates of seven other States." He indicated that two more states had also agreed to sign. However, owing in large measure to concerns about western land claims, the Articles were not adopted until March 1781, when Maryland became the last state to approve the Confederation.

The formal establishment of the confederation government could not obscure the fact that the revolutionaries were awash in economic difficulties. Despite foreign aid and loans, the revolutionaries had to issue paper money. Roaring inflation, especially in 1778 and 1779, created economic havoc, and numerous attempts to regulate prices failed. To remedy the problems on a long-term basis, Adams advocated levying high taxes and reducing the amount of money in circulation. At the same time, he insisted that the people should be sensitive to the needs of the poor. But Americans generally opposed high taxes. Given what was at stake in "the Great

Cause," Adams found it irksome that people were unwilling to sacrifice for the public good and for the good of posterity.

As the war dragged on, Adams grew increasingly convinced that some revolutionaries were selfishly pursuing their own economic interests. When circumstances reduced the supply of food, greedy people drove up the prices by withholding goods from the market. Public anger soon boiled over, and at least three dozen "food riots" erupted by the end of 1779. More than 40 percent of these riots took place in Massachusetts, and half of those happened in Boston. Samuel Adams was not involved in these disturbances; indeed, he was not even in Boston when food riots occurred there. Once again the evidence demonstrates that people did not need the influence of someone like Adams to form crowds to deal with crucial problems that touched their vital interests and that seemed to require their immediate action.

While Adams detested the monopolizers, he was no enemy of free enterprise. As he and others had pointed out time and again over the decades, his beloved Boston was "a commercial town." Adams also acknowledged that conducting trade in wartime conditions was both risky and expensive. It was, he said, only "natural" that business people would want a substantial profit. Nevertheless, all people had a duty to protect liberty, and, when liberty was in mortal danger, the people should not let "private Interest" compete with the larger interest "of the great Community." Writing in early 1778 from Boston, he lamented that "the Spirit of Avarice . . . prevails too much in this Town." Still, he exonerated the ordinary people—the yeomanry—by proclaiming that the evil "rages only among the few, because perhaps, the few only are concernd at present in trade." It was merchants, the same kind of people who had so often undermined colonial-era efforts to protect liberty, who shirked their duty as citizens.

Although Adams did not initiate the food riots in Massachusetts, he seemed to endorse them. In January 1778 he said he considered the suppression of monopolizers nearly as crucial as supplying the American army. Discussing how that might be done, Adams observed that price-control legislation seemed ineffective. He then suggested that, if "the Popular Indignation" could be raised "to a suitable Pitch," the price gouging would stop. He proclaimed himself ready to join in any measure that would achieve that goal. Adams did not have to direct crowd actions to use the threat of them as a club against monopolizers.

By early 1779, Adams believed that malevolent people were doing more than artificially driving up the price of goods. He feared that "a Combination of political & Commercial men" were "aiming to get the Trade, the Wealth, the Power and the Government of America into their own Hands." Two weeks later he voiced his suspicions more emphatically: "I am sorry to be obligd to think, that a Monopoly of Trade, and not the Liberty of their Country, is the sole object of some Mens Views. This is the Cake which they hope shortly to slice and share among themselves." By late February he was more apprehensive. He warned that men were plotting to grab America's best land as well as monopolize its commerce.

Adams detested politicians and business people who tried to enrich themselves through monopolies. Their behavior was the exact opposite of what he considered appropriate. Public figures should, he said, act "from pure and *unmixed* motives." He put the idea succinctly when he proclaimed that his first concern was "for the Honor & Safety of my Country." Those who truly loved their country would, he maintained, willingly make any sacrifice necessary to protect it. Adams summed up his ideals of public service, ideals he believed he measured up to, when he observed, "It would be the Glory of this Age, to find Men having no ruling Passion but the Love of their Country, and ready to render her the most arduous and important Services with the Hope for no other Reward in this Life than the Esteem of their virtuous Fellow Citizens."

Even as he vigorously labored to help create the confederation government and thwart those who sought to enrich themselves at the expense of their endangered country, Adams expended tremendous energy in the effort to acquire the foreign assistance he considered vital to winning independence. Since it had long contended with Britain for dominance in Europe and North America, Adams believed that "France is the natural ally of the United States." At first, France willingly aided the revolutionaries, but not openly and only on a limited basis lest she be drawn into war with Britain. Still, the arms and powder France supplied in the early phases of the war proved crucial to the American forces.

Once independence was declared, his fellow congressmen, recognizing Adams's ardor on the issue, placed him on a special committee charged with obtaining foreign aid. Adams wrote many letters intended for French eyes or ears. He pointed out numerous reasons why France's "true Interest" dictated helping America instantly and to the utmost. Military success, not words, finally swayed the French. It was the stunning American victory at Saratoga in October 1777 where a British army of more than five thousand surrendered that convinced the French to enter an alliance with America. When word of France's action reached America in the late spring of 1778, Adams was ecstatic. Congress acknowledged his diligence in pursuit of a French alliance by placing him on the three-member committee that arranged the formal welcome for France's ambassador.

As a political realist, Adams understood that America required the aid of France, especially of its navy. When hurricane winds and inferior numbers caused the French admiral D'Estaing to withdraw his fleet from a planned attack against the British in Rhode Island in the fall of 1778 and consequently endangered American ground forces, Adams did his best to quell the anti-French grousing of many New Englanders. As Samuel told his cousin John, he consciously employed his pen to blunt negative comments that could weaken the newly formed alliance and thereby give the British aid and comfort. He defended D'Estaing's withdrawal as militarily reasonable, and he also bluntly called it "impolitic" to traduce the French admiral. Adams's efforts on behalf of first acquiring aid from France and then avoiding rifts in the alliance were amply rewarded when French aid, in the form of a naval fleet as well as ground troops, proved essential in achieving the decisive victory at Yorktown in October 1781 that effectively ended the war.

Although he courted French aid and labored to make the alliance function smoothly, Adams had no illusions that the Catholic monarchy was assisting the revolutionaries for altruistic reasons. Nations, he insisted, pursued foreign policies "consistent with their Ideas of their own Interest." Adams certainly believed America should follow that dictum. In April 1783, he articulated his own sense of what America's long-term foreign policy should be. Contemplating what the American people should do in a peacetime world, Adams said, "I hope we shall never intermeddle with the Quarrels of other Nations." An independent America should, he believed, pursue a course of judicious international neutrality.

Given his own realpolitik view, Adams acted on the principle that American foreign policy should be based on America's interests, which, in Adams's mind, often neatly coincided with the interests of New England and especially of Massachusetts. The revolutionaries, he insisted, could accept peace only on terms that "shall be honorable & Safe to our Country." Independence was a "mere Charm" unless America secured "those Advantages," especially access to the fishing waters off Newfoundland, necessary to maintain that independence. The revolutionary politician pursued "those Advantages" relentlessly. From the opening of hostilities, he cast covetous eyes northward. He advocated annexing Canada and Nova Scotia too. Looking south, he also mentioned acquiring Florida. His suggestions about gobbling up land and his occasional declarations about America as an "empire" stamp him as an ardent expansionist. Yet, he explicitly denied that America fought for empire. In his case, that was true. He did not advocate acquiring Canada and Nova Scotia so America could develop an empire. He wanted those territories to ensure that Americans, especially New Englanders, could continue to fish Canadian waters. As he indicated, the possession of Canada and Nova Scotia would be "a great & permanent Protection to the Fishery." Adams's concern about "the Fishery" glistened in the congressional committee report on getting foreign assistance he helped draft in late 1776. The report stipulated that, if they wrested Newfoundland, Cape Breton, and Nova Scotia from Britain, the French and Americans would share the fishery equally while excluding all others.

Throughout the war years, Adams thought of acquiring lands to protect the invaluable fishery. Congress gave him an excellent opportunity to translate his desires into policy when it placed him on the committee charged with formulating America's war goals. The committee report of February 1779 listed several points as "absolutely necessary for the safety and independence of the United States." The right of fishing in Newfoundland waters and curing fish on the shore must, the report indicated, "be reserved, acknowledged, and ratified to the subjects of the United States." And while the committee recommended acquiring Nova Scotia and Florida, its report demonstrated that those lands were expendable. If Britain ceded Florida, Congress could sell it to Spain. Any claims to Nova Scotia should be sacrificed if doing so gave America an equal share in the fishery. Nova Scotia was valuable as a bargaining chip, not for itself. Congress debated the recommendations until August 1779 and then issued instructions that waffled on the question of the fishery.

Although the final military victory had not yet been gained and the fisheries had not yet been secured, by 1781 Adams believed the time had come to retire from Congress. Adams felt justified in leaving Congress in part because by March 1781, when he formally asked to be replaced, the great cause was doing very well at the continental level. All the original states had—finally—approved the Articles. Spain and Holland had become belligerents in the war against Britain, thus brightening the long-term military situation. In fact, the decisive victory he so yearned for occurred soon thereafter in October. The fishery still needed protecting, but Samuel could direct that effort from Boston. In addition, as he had repeatedly said and honestly believed, Massachusetts had many men who could perform admirably in Congress.

Samuel Adams, who spoke longingly of rejoining his family and tasting "the Sweets of Retirement," found the thought of returning home attractive for many personal reasons. He was approaching his sixtieth birthday and had taken to referring to old age creeping up on him. Those who knew him said he possessed a strong constitution, but that hard work was taking its toll. As he aged, the Adams family malady, palsy, grew progressively worse. The involuntary movements of his hand and head increased; his speech became more tremulous. Writing letters was an essential part of his political work, and by late 1780 he complained that his shaking hand was unfit to guide a pen. Specimens of his writing vividly show he was right. Samuel had also recently experienced major bouts of ill health, as had Elizabeth a year before.

After Adams retired from Congress in the spring of 1781, he no longer needed to exchange letters with his beloved Betsy, the woman he told his daughter Hannah was "a rich Blessing" to them both. In one sense that is unfortunate. What can be discerned about Samuel and Elizabeth's relationship comes primarily from their letters. The letters they exchanged from 1776 through mid-1781, like their earlier letters, reveal a loving relationship. As before, each pleaded with the other to write more often, and Samuel once said he would not consider it a burden if he received six of

Facsimiles of Samuel Adams signatures reproduced from William V. Wells's *Life and Public Services of Samuel Adams* (1865).

her letters at once. And when Elizabeth had sufficiently recovered from an illness so she herself could write, Samuel said getting her letter was "like cool Water to a thirsty Soul." Samuel expressed concern about the family members' safety and comfort as they moved about to avoid the British, but Elizabeth apparently continued to control her own finances. Each of them routinely inquired about the other's health, and Samuel gently chided Elizabeth because one of her letters did not "expressly" tell him she was well. He insisted she must always do that. Yet, Samuel withheld medical news he knew would worry her. Even as he scolded Elizabeth for not reassuring him about her health, he altered his letter by expunging a statement that Philadelphia "has for some time past been a complete Hospital, and many are still sick."

The relationship between Samuel and Elizabeth, as well as his general view of the place women should have in society, became clearer in these years. Although he did not say he was giving his personal view of a woman's proper role, Samuel once noted that society said women should occupy a subordinate position. A few months after giving Thomas Wells permission to marry "the dear Girl whom I pride myself in calling my Daughter," Samuel wrote to Thomas with advice about marriage. "The Marriage State," he observed, "was designd to complete the Sum of human Happiness in this Life." Saying that it required "Judgment on both Sides" to discern the proper conduct toward each other, Samuel remarked that "though it is acknowledged, that the Superiority is & ought to be in the Man, yet as the Management of a Family in many Instances necessarily devolves on the Woman, it is difficult always to determine the Line between the Authority of the one & the Subordination of the other." His own suggestion was "not to govern too much." He seemingly endorsed a sense of equality by adding that "when the married Couple strictly observe the great Rules of Honor & Justice towards each other, Differences, if any happen, between them, must proceed from small & trifling Circumstances."

On two occasions Adams voiced traditional stereotypes about women. Knowing Congress had fled Philadelphia in December 1776 to avoid the onrushing British, Elizabeth wrote Samuel that she "was greatly alarmd" to hear about the British occupation. That prompted Samuel to observe: "I have long known you to be possessd of much Fortitude of Mind. But you are a Woman, and one must expect you will now and then discover [the] Timidity so natural to your Sex." Then, in a letter of August 1777, Samuel ended a discussion on military matters with the comment, "But I forget that I am writing [to] a female upon the Subject of War."

Despite his occasional articulation of contemporary and stereotypical views about women, Samuel increasingly relied on Elizabeth's active participation in political matters. Their letters demonstrate the gradual but steady change. Writing in late 1776, Samuel observed, "it has not been usual for me to write to you of War or Politicks." He revealed that Elizabeth wanted to discuss such issues by then adding, "but I know how deeply you have always interrested yourself in the Welfare of our Country and I am disposd to gratify your Curiosity." By February 1777, he was leaving his expense vouchers under her control. In March he suggested he might be trying her patience with long letters about politics, but he wrote them nonetheless. It was in the late summer of 1777 that he mentioned not writing about military affairs to a woman. Intriguingly, he was well into that discussion of military matters before figuratively catching himself writing

to a woman on military topics. And he seemed to dismiss his own stereotypical observation by immediately adding the comment that "I know your
whole Soul is engagd in the great Cause." As 1778 progressed, Samuel no
longer mentioned any possible lack of interest on Elizabeth's part because
she was a woman, and he filled his letters to her with commentary on the
war and the political scene.

Samuel drafted Elizabeth into active political service by the end of 1778.
Deep into a lengthy letter on public matters, Samuel indicated that he had
read and then sent to James Warren a recent publication concerning a
political struggle raging between two American diplomats. He requested,
"I wish you would invite him to a Dish of Tea, and desire him to let you
see it [the publication] and my Letter which inclosd it." For her part, "You
may read this Letter to him and other Confidential Friends, but dont let it
go out of your own Hands." The general societal view still assumed women
should not even think about politics, much less participate in them. Thus
Samuel's request that Elizabeth engage in political discussions is intriguing.
His request was, in fact, remarkable because he spoke of "other Confidential Friends" without naming them. Samuel trusted Elizabeth to know who
should see his letter. In February 1779, he reiterated his faith in Elizabeth's
political judgment by telling her that she could show his letter "to such of
my Confidential Friends as you think proper." What makes that letter even
more illuminating is the fact that it came in response to one from Elizabeth in which she urged Samuel to resign his post as Massachusetts secretary of state.

Elizabeth's active participation in Samuel's political world reached a pin-
nacle in 1781 shortly before he retired from Congress. In a letter covering
various political matters, Samuel told her that his old friend, the Reverend
Samuel Cooper, had stopped writing although Samuel had requested specific information. Having expressed the hope that Cooper did not find the
correspondence "troublesome," Samuel sounded a hostile note. He
observed that, as Elizabeth knew, he was inclined to "retaliate" when someone chose to stop writing. He then added that when he thought an old
friend had done wrong, "I let none know it, but him & you." Samuel told
Elizabeth she could show the letter to Cooper but no one else. So, Samuel
shared his thoughts with Elizabeth on a special basis, and he left it up to her
to decide whether she wanted to initiate contact with her husband's
offending friend. She did and with good success. Cooper resumed writing
to Samuel and praised Elizabeth Adams for how she "communicated" the
original letter to him. "I am glad she did it in a Manner so acceptable,"
Samuel noted. "Indeed," he added, "I never found Reason to doubt her
Discretion." By the time Samuel returned home in June 1781, he was
rejoining the person who had become an active partner in his political
labors.

The Samuel Adams who returned to Elizabeth in the spring of 1781 was serious about retiring from Congress. In 1782 when once again appointed to the post, he recounted his lengthy congressional service and asked to be excused, which he was. And once having quit Congress and again taken up residence in Boston, Adams never again left Massachusetts. However, even as he contemplated leaving Congress, Adams, who was elected to the state senate before he returned to Boston, had no intention of retiring from politics. He merely planned to confine himself to what he called a more limited sphere. In addition, he had no intention of abandoning his efforts to achieve victory in the great cause and to rest independence on a secure foundation. He most certainly made sure Congress did not forget about the fishery. Again acting on his often repeated wartime statement that God helps those who help themselves, Samuel kept peppering congressional leaders with letters that emphasized the importance of protecting the fisheries. He argued that New England's and America's vital interests demanded that the fishing rights be guaranteed in any peace treaty. He harped on the idea that, in addition to being essential to New England's economy, the fishery provided "a Nursery for Seamen," the seamen America would need for its navy. Adams did not manufacture arguments to suit the political situation. He had long stressed that America would require a strong navy because the country would have an extensive merchant marine. To increase the political pressure, in late 1781, Adams chaired a Boston Town Meeting that enunciated the same pro-fishery points and called upon New England's towns to spread the word.

Exasperated French diplomats, who felt compelled to counter Adams's political campaign lest it prolong the war, testified to his effectiveness and to the fact that he did not have to be in Congress to wield considerable influence in that body. In early 1782, the Chevalier de la Luzerne, the French ambassador to the United States, complained that Adams "has employed all the influence he can bring to bear on the other [congressional] delegations to induce them to support the claims of Massachusetts." Reflecting the commonly held European view of Adams's role in fomenting the Revolution, the ambassador added "that Mr. Samuel Adams who at the beginning of this revolution directed in an astonishing manner the movements of the people by forming them into Committees" was doing it again. He was "adapt[ing] this same machinery to the affair of the fisheries," and, unfortunately, it was working. New Englanders, having been riled up, had held many meetings. According to Luzerne, several reasonable and moderate congressmen had informed him that they knew the New Englanders "and the difficulty of stopping them once they were in motion."

François Barbé de Marbois, the secretary of France's legation, offered a similar analysis in March 1782. Adams was "making every effort" and pouring "his constant labors" into ensuring that any peace treaty protected New England's use of the fisheries. If thwarted, Adams would then employ "all his resources, all his intrigues" advocating the conquest of Canada and Nova Scotia so he could secure the same result. Sounding rather like Adams's prewar opponents, the secretary argued that Adams "takes pleasure in troubles and difficulties" and "glories in forming a party of opposition." Yet, even as he denounced Adams as a supposedly incorrigible rebel, Marbois admitted that Adams could not have selected a better issue to sow the seeds of violent opposition in New England. Marbois, like Luzerne, realized that New Englanders generally, not just Samuel Adams, considered the fisheries essential. Thus, although the French, like the British before them, wanted to blame the undesirable political uproar on Adams's evil manipulations, they had to admit that, while he orchestrated the political fight, it was successful because the people believed their personal interests were at stake. The campaign Adams spearheaded aimed to pressure the French into defending America's fishery rights whether they wanted to or not. In the end, the French did not have to take a resolute stand because America's peace treaty negotiators got the British to stipulate that an independent America would have "liberty" to use the fisheries.

Great Britain agreed to a preliminary peace treaty on November 30, 1782, and formally acknowledged America's sovereignty and independence in the Treaty of Paris signed on September 3, 1783. This was the day Samuel had anticipated longingly when, writing to Elizabeth in 1777, he spoke of "the happy Day when Tyranny [shall] be subdued and the Liberty of Our Country shall be settled upon a permanent Foundation." When he knew independence was at hand, the revolutionary politician expressed his sense of accomplishment by saying, as well he might, "We have done our Duty. Future Generations can never curse the present for carelessly surrendering their Rights."

When he spoke of doing one's duty, Samuel Adams was talking about more than finally achieving American independence. For Adams, the great cause had always involved more than winning independence and more than gaining what he called the gifts of nature necessary to sustain independence. Adams stressed that independence would be worth little if his country of Massachusetts did not create a government and a society that would protect the people's liberties. So, even as he worked at the continental level to secure a declaration of independence and then to win America's independence, Samuel simultaneously worked to create a new Massachusetts government that would, by protecting the people's rights, be worthy of being jealously defended.

8

"The Principles of Liberty": The Massachusetts Scene

*E*ven before independence had been declared, Samuel Adams reached the conclusion that "his Country" of Massachusetts must create a new frame of government. Reflecting his core political values, he called for "the Establishment of a Government upon the Principles of Liberty, and sufficiently guarding it from future Infringements of a Tyrant." The reference to the future articulated one of Adams's core ideals: working for posterity, for the "millions yet unborn." As he pondered how to fashion a government that would protect liberty, Adams reached the conclusion that Massachusetts's society, as well as its government, needed to be transformed. He came to stress that Massachusetts revolutionaries had a duty to foster "Virtue" because virtue was "the Soul of a republican Government." So, even as he labored in Congress and worked to establish a new government for his "country" of Massachusetts, Adams spent considerable time contemplating how "the Virtue of my Countrymen may be secured for Ages yet to Come" and trying to turn his contemplations into social reality.

The question of reformulating the Massachusetts government officially surfaced in June 1775 when Congress authorized establishing a new frame of government modeled as nearly as possible on the charter of 1691. As a consequence of Congress's directive, from the summer of 1775 into the early winter of 1776, Adams spent considerable time ruminating about the nature of government and then endeavoring to translate his thoughts into action. "I have," he admitted, "a strong desire that our Colony should excell in Wisdom and Virtue." In the heady days of late 1775, Samuel dared hope that Massachusetts's legislators could emulate "that venerable Assembly, the Senate of Areopagus in [ancient] Athens." Its actions were so "eminently upright" that foreign governments asked it to mediate disputes. Events soon tempered Adams's optimism. Rather than emulating a great Athenian senate, the Massachusetts House of Representatives and Council bickered over control of the militia. Each body seemed more concerned about grasping power than promoting the public good. Only the forceful intervention of Samuel and his cousin John, who both wrote home and stressed that Congress would not become embroiled in the dispute, kept the unseemly quarrel from reaching Congress. The fall elections of 1775 also proved disappointing. Elbridge Gerry reported that some voters made their choices based on a candidate's wealth. Samuel, who considered the right to vote a sacred trust, found that mortifying. "Giving such a preference to riches is," he lamented, "both dishonourable and dangerous to a government."

The views Adams enunciated in the fall and early winter of 1775–76 were not idle philosophical musings. He crafted his letters, especially those to James Warren and Gerry, so his friends could use them to persuade Massachusetts's inhabitants and legislators to support the ardent Whig positions Adams, Warren, and Gerry advocated. Stipulating that government must, of course, rest on the consent of the governed and protect the people's liberties, Adams highlighted a number of specific issues.

He dwelled on the military. While admitting that government might occasionally have to rely on seasoned military men, he still insisted that "a standing Army, however necessary it may be at some times, is always dangerous to the Liberties of the People." There were ways, he maintained, to check the inherent danger the military posed. The legislature must control the military, and that requirement held true for the American army. Adams stressed that the militia must remain a vital part of the military because the militia constituted the "natural strength" of a free country. He reasoned that, since they were "free Citizens," militiamen would not trample their own rights but would, instead, steadfastly defend them from outside attackers. Maintaining state militias and keeping them under the control of the individual states would, Adams stressed, help safeguard the people from the military power.

As he pondered how to deal with potential evils, more than the military bothered Adams. The process of government itself contained inherent dangers. Reiterating a commonplace view, Adams intoned that "all Men are fond of Power." Indeed, the love of power did not evaporate merely because men entered legally constituted legislatures. Even legislators, he warned, often coveted more power than the public wanted them to possess. Fortunately, Massachusetts had, he observed, found ways to bridle the corrosive lust for power. Each branch of the legislature could thwart the excesses of the other. The legislators were, in turn, kept in check through annual elections. Adams considered annual elections a special bulwark for protecting liberty because the legislative power "frequently reverts into the hands of the People from whom it is derivd." Provided the voters scrutinized those who sought and held public office, yearly elections made public officials truly accountable. For Adams, theory and history demonstrated that Massachusetts must have a republican government that incorporated appropriate checks and balances. At the same time, it must rest on the consent of the governed and also give the people control over their elected political servants.

Adams gave special attention to plural officeholding, a vexing problem in colonial Massachusetts illustrated most egregiously by Thomas Hutchinson serving in all three branches of the government at the same time. While conceding that an attack on plural officeholding would cause inconveniences, Adams urged both Gerry and Warren to ensure that no one could hold political posts "incompatible with each other." He was particularly adamant about ensuring that no official could exercise both legislative and judicial powers. The evil of plural officeholding must, Adams insisted, be confronted, and "it is my opinion that the remedy ought to be deep and thorough."

No matter what issue he assessed, when thinking about the nature of government in late 1775 and early 1776, Adams eventually linked the topic to the question of moral character. His intense focus on character was probably influenced by his cathartic responses to the dramatically different actions of two talented young men he had befriended and promoted as defenders of America. In mid-October, Adams had to face the shocking news that Dr. Benjamin Church had sold out to the British. That disheartening revelation and the contrast it formed to Dr. Joseph Warren's patriotic death at Bunker Hill accentuated the importance of the question of character. As he discussed what should be done in Massachusetts, Adams repeatedly stressed one point above all: "virtue is the surest means of securing the public liberty." "Virtue" is not self-defining. In addition, Adams often spoke of the virtue*s* necessary to preserve liberty. Still, he defined virtue as "the Feeling of moral Obligations" in one's "private connections." When referring to what he labeled political virtues, Adams specifically mentioned fidelity to one's country and opposition to bribery, luxury, and extravagance. Speaking more generally of republican virtues, he mentioned piety, justice, moderation, temperance, simplicity, industry, and frugality.

Adams, who maintained that one's actions in private life typically paralleled what one did in public life, used the sad case of Dr. Church to illustrate the tie between private and public virtue. Church's infidelity to his wife had been "notorious" before the betrayal of his country was discovered. For Adams, the lesson was clear: those who were upright in their personal lives were not likely to be unfaithful to their country. He carried that idea further by repeatedly asserting that "the disposition and manners" of a people—their virtue or lack of it—determined whether they were fit for freedom or for slavery. In fact, he maintained that no country could long retain its freedom unless virtue was "supremely honord." He later provided a strong illustration of the personal importance he placed on virtue when he remarked to Elizabeth that "My Children cannot imagine how much Comfort I have in believing they are virtuous." Massachusetts *must* find ways to promote virtue. Adams suggested looking to the past.

In the fall of 1775 in letters to James Warren, Adams spoke of "the golden opportunity of restoring the ancient purity of principles and manners in our country" and emphasized education as the key to securing good government. Calling up the ideal of Massachusetts's noble ancestors, Samuel claimed the founders of the colony had laid an excellent foundation for defending liberty by quickly establishing an extensive public education system. Given the importance he assigned to education, Adams was horrified to learn that some Massachusetts towns had closed their local schools, reportedly because of the high cost of the war. In lines obviously intended for many eyes, Samuel urged society's leaders to impress upon the people the necessity of continuing to support an education system "well calculated to diffuse among the Individuals of the Community the Principles of Morality, so essentially necessary to the Preservation of publick Liberty." Adams sought to clinch the argument—and give the supporters of public education valuable ammunition—by proclaiming that "no People will tamely surrender their Liberties, nor can any be easily subdued, when Knowledge is diffusd and Virtue is preservd. On the Contrary, when People are universally ignorant, and debauchd in their Manners, they will sink under their own Weight without the Aid of foreign Invaders."

Adams even incorporated the idea of education for good government into his January 1776 proposal that Boston help overcome America's lack of trained military officers by establishing a military academy. The "young Gentlemen of a military Genius," Adams emphasized, should learn more than the art of war. They should be "taught the Principles of a free Government, and deeply impressd with a Sense of the indispensible Obligation which every member is under to the whole Society." Although he raised the possibility more than once, Boston did not establish a military school. But if one were established, Adams wanted to ensure it inculcated republican ideals as well military knowledge.

Adams considered religion essential for developing people's morals. Yet, in 1775–76 when he focused on formulating governments, he only occasionally linked religion to his quest for attaining a moral society. In fact, he did not specifically join the two until the spring of 1776 when he wrote to John Scollay, a longtime selectman of Boston. After expressing joy about the British finally quitting Boston, Adams reprised his theme of the previous fall by speaking of "the happy opportunity of reestablishing ancient Principles and Purity of Manners." He maintained that one of Britain's goals had been to destroy the people's "Sense of true Religion & Virtue" so the British could more easily enslave Boston. Stressing that God rewarded—or punished—communities "according to their general Character," he maintained that "the publick Liberty will not long survive the total Extinction of Morals." Without specifying exactly what the officeholders ought to do, Adams reminded Scollay that Boston's morals depended upon the selectmen's vigilance.

Adams was a religious man, an old-fashioned Puritan in the eyes of many, who believed in family readings from the Bible. He told his future son-in-law that "Religion in a Family is at once its brightest Ornament & its best Security." Like most other Americans, Adams considered public support for religion appropriate, and in late 1776 he commented to Elizabeth that "I wish we were a more religious People." During the war, he often mentioned God's intervening hand. And many historians have highlighted the fact that Adams spoke of Boston becoming "the *Christian* Sparta."

Although he believed in public support for religion, Samuel Adams considered religion primarily a personal and family matter. While he spoke during the war years of God's intervening hand, he rarely used such imagery before the fighting commenced. This suggests that he considered religious appeals especially appropriate—and potentially powerful—during wartime. Moreover, throughout the war, he repeatedly emphasized that God helped those who helped themselves. Furthermore, it is misleading to place great stress on Adams's reference to Boston becoming "the *Christian* Sparta." Too often that comment has been forced to bear an interpretive weight it cannot sustain. That phrase appears only *once* in all of Adams's published writings, and Samuel did not speak of consciously building the Christian Sparta. Rather, he used the term in a December 1780 letter in which he complained bitterly about Bostonians, including "Men of Religion," living a life marked by extravagant entertainments complete with "Superfluity of Dress & Ornamentation." Adams's reference to Boston's possible religious transformation was, thus, meant to reprove the Boston of late 1780. After recounting many examples of Boston's vices, Adams lamented: "But I fear I shall say too much. I love the People of Boston. I once thought that City would be the *Christian* Sparta. But Alas! Will men never be free! They will be free no longer than while they remain virtuous. [The political philosopher] Sidney tells us, there are times when People are not worth saving. I pray God, this may never be truly said of my beloved Town."

Since he normally tried to influence people by holding up the image of a nobler standard, Adams's reference to the Christian Sparta may have been no more than a ploy to reform his beloved, but far too unvirtuous, Boston. The evidence shows that, when he spoke of promoting religious ideals, he had in mind the maxim of doing unto others as you would have them do unto you, not of championing a specific religious sect. The evidence shows that, despite his own personal religiosity, when it came to government developing a virtuous citizenry, Adams looked to the schoolhouse every bit as much as he looked to the church.

The observations Adams advanced in the fall and early winter of 1775–76 constituted a primer on forming a republican government and developing the virtuous society he believed a republican society needed to survive. He did not alter his basic views as the war progressed and as Massachusetts continued to have difficulty creating a new frame of government. But his thoughts were naturally colored by the process of seeking independence, by seeing it declared, and by the travails of war. Some of his concerns, especially about the issue of character, intensified in the lengthy period it took for Massachusetts to implement a new constitution—a process that stretched into 1780.

When Adams contemplated the myriad problems involved in shaping Massachusetts's government and society, he shuddered at the example being set by John Hancock. As his contemporaries and historians agree, Hancock cared little for political idealism. He craved the sunshine of public adulation. He sought popularity, which gave him a sense of self-worth. Politically, Hancock resembled a well-oiled weather vane. He easily shifted positions according to the prevailing winds of public opinion. If he could not feel how those winds blew, he wavered and avoided taking a firm position.

Hancock demonstrated his character and values by how he responded to being president of Congress, a largely ceremonial post. He reveled in the visibility and status that accompanied the presidency, and he exploited the office for his own purposes. Upon leaving Congress in the summer of 1778, Hancock insisted on delivering a valedictory address that would, seemingly, require a flattering response from Congress. And, despite manpower problems, Hancock pressed General Washington to provide a military detachment to escort his carriage to Boston. Samuel Adams was appalled. He and his cousin John had sponsored the fabulously wealthy Hancock for the office of president to counter Tory claims about Whigs being a pack of poverty-stricken rabble-rousers. But Hancock was acting like a pompous aristocrat, not a virtuous republican. Moreover, Hancock had already disappointed Samuel by not actively championing independence and by opposing the effort to form an alliance with France. The political friendship between the two, which had been cooling, turned frigid.

Hancock received his military escort and arrived in Boston looking like a very important personage indeed. Once at home, he staged a gala reception and continued a lavish lifestyle. However, it took time for the statement of gratitude he expected from Congress to arrive. It was delayed because of opposition led by—Samuel Adams. The revolutionary politician observed that two others had served as president and neither had "made a parting Speech or received the Thanks of Congress." Congress did eventually vote Hancock a statement of thanks, but only by a six-to-four margin. Worse yet for Hancock, under Adams's leadership, Massachusetts voted *against* issuing the pronouncement. As Robert Finkelstein, a biographer of Hancock, indicated, "this galling insult was not forgotten."

Over the next few months Adams received numerous reports detailing Hancock's aristocratic lifestyle, his hubris, and his quest for popularity. In all these ways, Hancock assaulted what Adams considered republican virtues. It was not mere chance that just as Hancock left Congress, Adams mentioned that he was infinitely more concerned about "the Contagion of Vice" than the power of America's enemies. And it was obvious whom

Samuel had in mind when he denounced Whigs who exhibited an insatiable thirst for "that vanity of vanities," public adulation.

In a September 1778 letter, Samuel Savage, who wanted to reconcile Adams and Hancock, commented on Boston having "become a new City" owing to its "exceeding Gayety of Appearance." That report made Adams livid. He responded by warning that luxury and extravagance would destroy the virtues necessary to preserve the people's liberty and happiness. He was not subtle about blaming the lamentable developments on Hancock. Adams pointed to an extravagant, and he thought perhaps illegal, Boston militia entertainment that featured John Hancock. Samuel rhetorically wondered when they might "again see that Sobriety of Manners, that Temperance, Frugality, Fortitude and other manly Virtues" that had once been "the Glory and Strength of my much lov'd native Town." A month later Adams rebuffed another of Savage's calls for a reconciliation by again carping about Hancock's lavish gatherings. Ostentatious entertainments were, Samuel groused, incompatible with the present serious times, especially since many of the state's citizens could barely subsist. In Adams's mind, Hancock grossly compounded the evil by inviting Tories to his galas and thus blurring the lines between Whigs and Tories. Adams soon depicted John Hancock as the second coming of Thomas Hutchinson.

Adams believed Hancock's vain pursuit of popularity helped unleash a torrent of vices more likely than the British to destroy liberty. It was time, said Adams, for those who wanted to transmit the blessings of liberty to their posterity to unite in support of "public Virtue." In pursuit of that goal, Adams again employed his pen in a lobbying effort that trumpeted the necessity of supporting education. Elaborating on arguments he advanced in 1775, Samuel expressed sorrow that some Massachusetts communities reportedly found maintaining schools too costly. Appealing to pride, Adams said he wished anyone who questioned the necessity of maintaining the education system could hear the comments of sensible and public-minded southerners. They showered compliments on Massachusetts for having always provided instruction for the young. In fact, Virginians had become so convinced of the importance of education that they reportedly planned to establish a public education system. These wise southerners understood that "if Virtue & Knowledge are diffusd among the People, they will never be enslavd. This will be their great Security. Virtue & Knowledge will forever be an even Balance for Powers & Riches."

While Adams glorified virtue and education, Hancock looked for ways to become governor. He began forging a powerful coalition that included archconservatives Adams detested. Hancock did not want Adams's virulent anti-Toryism cutting into his potential power base. Hancock's obscuring of the lines between Whig and Tory, a development that made Adams seethe, paid dividends in the May 1778 elections. Adams's close friend and staunch political ally, James Warren, had been Speaker of the House of Representatives; but, with Tories voting in Plymouth for the first time in seven years, Warren could not even win reelection to the House. Hancock's political strategy aimed to reduce the political influence of any prominent leaders who might oppose him. Part of the plan entailed circulating negative reports about Samuel Adams, including the scurrilous charge that he wanted Washington replaced as commander in chief. Adams argued that the man who "fabricated the Charge did not believe it himself." And when his dearest Betsy mentioned political slanders being hurled at her beloved husband, Samuel comforted her by claiming that every honest and sensible man who knew him would attest to his having acted with honorable consistency. He defiantly added that "the Censure of Fools or Knaves is Applause."

Despite his defiance, Samuel realized that returning to Massachusetts for a while would give him a chance to wash off the political mud that had been pitched at him. But it was not personal political need that convinced him in mid-1779 he should go home for an extended time. Adams believed the interests of Massachusetts, and of America, required him to journey to Boston. He feared that Massachusetts's zealous efforts in the great cause could be jeopardized by the state's continuing inability to form a new constitution, an inability that threatened to plunge the state into chaos. Dissidents in the western counties of Berkshire and Hampshire had shut down courts in 1775, ostensibly because the people had not established the government. In September 1776 the legislators recommended having the next General Court produce a constitution, and nearly 75 percent of the townships agreed. However, some townships maintained that the state's constitution must be drafted by a separate convention elected solely for that purpose. While the legislators rejected this plea, they did stipulate that the proposed constitution would be sent to the towns for their approval. Thus, although not created by a separate convention, the constitution would reflect the bedrock republican ideal of government resting on the consent of the governed. The General Court produced a constitution in 1778, but the overwhelming majority of citizens and townships (147 of 178) rejected it, primarily because it lacked a bill of rights. Facing further threats of violence from the western sections of the state, the General Court admitted defeat in February 1779 by asking if the people wanted a separate constitutional convention. The answer was already apparent. Although he did not say it openly, it seems likely that Adams contemplated helping Massachusetts achieve the new constitution he believed the state had to have for its own good, for the good of the Union, and for the great cause.

Adams arrived in Boston in May of 1779, and the next month the General Court officially authorized holding a constitutional convention. He was promptly elected as a delegate and became deeply involved in creating the Massachusetts Constitution. He served on the convention's thirty-member committee charged with formulating a constitution. The Committee of Thirty turned the job of creating a first draft over to a subcommittee made up of Samuel Adams, John Adams, and James Bowdoin. Unfortunately this Drafting Committee did not keep a record of its deliberations. In fact, the three men did not even preserve a copy of the draft constitution they wrote. The closest available approximation of the subcommittee's document is the constitution the Committee of Thirty forwarded after making revisions.

John Adams asserted, and most analysts have accepted his claim, that he was the "principal" author of the constitution. That may be true, but it would be absurd to think Samuel Adams and James Bowdoin had no significant input. In addition, both the Committee of Thirty and the full convention made modifications, some of them significant. Indeed, John Adams himself claimed that none of the three members on the subcommittee drafted the controversial Article 3 of the Declaration of Rights, which dealt with religion. And, in part because John Adams left for Europe in early November, the task of getting the convention to approve the proposed constitution fell primarily on Samuel. Even more important, the document presented to the Committee of Thirty was undeniably the work of many minds, not just the three-member Drafting Committee. Before any drafting began, the convention delegates emphatically articulated three basic points. The state's constitution must include a declaration of rights; the government must be "a FREE REPUBLIC"; and, "it is the essence of a free republic, that the people be governed by FIXED LAWS OF THEIR OWN MAKING." In addition, the Massachusetts Constitution obviously drew upon earlier documents and political systems. Its Declaration of Rights incorporated ideas and even language from Virginia's influential 1776 Declaration of Rights. The proposed structure of government owed a good deal both to the 1691 charter and the constitution Massachusetts's voters rejected in 1778.

Despite the paucity of evidence, three salient points are indisputable. First, Samuel Adams believed constitution-making required compromise. As "An Address of the Convention . . . to their Constituents" that he coauthored emphasized, when producing constitutions, one's special interests should give way "to essential Principles, and Considerations of general Utility." Second, he approved of the constitution's main features. Third, the constitution of 1780 contained specific, innovative features that reflected Samuel's concerns about protecting the people's liberties by looking to the past and by promoting virtue among the people, especially through education.

The Massachusetts Constitution was thoroughly Whig, thoroughly republican, in its statement of ideals. The document's language proclaimed it "a social compact" voluntarily entered into by the people to provide them "with the power of enjoying, in safety and tranquillity, their natural rights and the blessings of life." If the government failed to protect those rights, "the people have a right to alter the Government, and to take measures necessary for their safety, prosperity, and happiness." The Declaration of Rights stretched to thirty detailed articles. It included the cardinal theoretical statements that all power resides originally in the people and that every member of society had a right "to be protected . . . in the enjoyment of his life, liberty and property, according to standing laws."

The most notable features of the Massachusetts Constitution of 1780 were its separation of powers and its well-developed system of checks and balances. As Samuel, but not John, desperately wanted, elections would occur annually. Voting was restricted to free adult males who were worth £60 or who owned a freehold—land rights—yielding at least £3 a year. The two-branch legislature was again called the General Court. Representatives had to own a £100 freehold or be worth at least £200; senators had to possess a freehold worth at least £300 or be worth £600. To reflect the ideal of "equality," the size of a township's House delegation was based on population. The Senate was limited to forty seats distributed with some attention given to the size of a county's population. The House and Senate had to concur before a bill went to the governor, who was assisted by an advisory Council selected primarily from among the ranks of the Senate. The Committee of Thirty version gave the governor an absolute veto, a provision John Adams adamantly championed. However, as finally approved, the governor's veto could be overridden by a two-thirds vote of the General Court. Judges, who were appointed by the governor with the advice and consent of the Council, were guaranteed reasonable salaries and held their posts "during good behavior."

Two additional sections are especially relevant for trying to understand Samuel Adams's views on the role of virtue in protecting the people's liberties. The first of these especially significant sections, the famous Article 3 of the Declaration of the Rights of the Inhabitants, concerned religion. The constitution required that the governor be a Christian and also stipulated that the people had a "duty" to worship "the SUPREME BEING." Moreover, the constitution justified public support for religion by proclaiming that "Good morals" were "necessary to the preservation of civil society." The Committee of Thirty version said the legislature could authorize using tax moneys to support public worship and could enjoin all citizens to attend religious services, "provided there be any such teacher [i.e., minister] on whose ministry they can conscientiously and conveniently attend." That limitation on public support for religion added weight to the constitution's strong statement on freedom of conscience. It stipulated that anyone who did not "disturb the public peace, or obstruct others in their religious worship" would themselves not be "hurt, molested, or restrained" from worshipping "GOD" according "to the dictates of his own conscience."

The full convention found some of the Committee of Thirty's provisions on religion unacceptable. The existing laws effectively made the Congregational Church the established state religion, and the majority of delegates insisted on keeping it that way. After very long debate, the convention retained the statement on freedom of conscience but revised the mechanics of public support for religion. The revisions to this section, Article 3, effectively kept the Congregational Church as the state church and also restricted public support of religion to Protestant ministers. These revisions seemed to limit—and contradict—the statement on freedom of conscience by saying that peaceful and law-abiding Christians "shall be equally under the protection of the law." Based on his fall 1778 denunciation of a Christian who would "destroy the peace of others . . . because they differ from him in Matters of mere opinion," Adams would have favored the original draft, which, if enacted, would have moved Massachusetts further along the road toward religious toleration. However, to get the proposed constitution through the convention, he apparently accommodated to the majority position. The difficulty of using Article 3 to understand Samuel's views is underscored by John Adams's statement that no one on the three-member Drafting Committee produced Article 3.

The second key section concerning virtue was a noncontroversial article that contained ideas and language Samuel Adams had often employed in promoting education. The constitution lauded the sagacious ancestors for supporting a general education system. It proclaimed that "Wisdom and knowledge, as well as virtue, diffused generally among the body of the people" were "necessary for the presentation of their rights and liberties." To ensure that all persons had the opportunity for education, legislators and magistrates must forever cherish and support the public schools, the town grammar schools, and Harvard College. These provisions reflected Samuel's emphasis on providing education for the many, not just the few.

The Massachusetts Constitution of 1780 did not create a "democratic" government, nor did it truly protect religious freedom. It was, however, thoroughly republican. It was built on the ideal that government must rest on the consent of the governed. It embraced the principle that the people must be governed by "FIXED LAWS OF THEIR OWN MAKING." Annual elections gave the voters a ready check on their elected officials. In addition, when compared to the 1691 charter, the constitution provided a government with better checks and balances. The new government would have what Samuel considered the necessary energy without being likely to endanger the people's liberties. From his perspective, the constitution seemed well worth defending because it was founded on what he called "sober Republican Principles."

A discussion Samuel had in December 1780 with the Marquis de Chastellux, the French major general who was so impressed with Adams when they first met earlier that month, helps elucidate Adams's view of the constitution and politics in general. The lengthy conversation was, the Frenchman said, interrupted only by a glass of Madeira, a dish of tea, and the arrival of another lodger. Chastellux opened the discussion by expressing "anxiety" about the new American state constitutions, especially the Massachusetts document. Chastellux considered it dangerous to let virtually every man vote for the legislators. It might do for now "because every citizen is about equally well-off." But time would produce greater economic inequality and endemic political problems because those with property would have "the real force." The state would then face "the two equally dangerous extremes of aristocracy and anarchy." Chastellux suggested it would have been wiser to allocate power based on ownership of property.

Adams, of course, readily agreed that one should consider future generations, not just the present moment. Yet, while admitting it was not perfect, he heartily defended the constitution. He began by recounting how it was created through a wonderful process that included a specially elected convention, analysis by the voters, and then the return of the document to the delegates for final revisions. "If two-thirds of the voters approved it, it was to have the force of law, and be regarded as the work of the people themselves." It would, in sum, be a republican constitution built on the consent of the governed. Samuel added that, of the twenty-two thousand votes cast in the state, far more than two-thirds favored the new constitution. He proudly asserted that the last time a constitution came into being in such a legal manner occurred in the days of Lycurgus— nine centuries before the birth of Christ! Adams's glorification is open to challenge. Although the evidence is again not fully clear, some sections of the constitution may not have gotten the required two-thirds approval. In counting votes, the delegates may have occasionally used creative accounting. Nevertheless, Adams was right to stress the significance of how Massachusetts formulated its constitution. The eminent constitutional historian Andrew C. McLaughlin maintained that "the fully developed convention" process used in Massachusetts constituted "the greatest institution of government which America has produced." "It answered in itself," said McLaughlin, "the problem of how men could make government of their own free will."

Responding to Chastellux's anxiety about the distribution of political power, Adams explained the logic of the system. Voicing what for him was at the core of the dispute with Great Britain, Adams argued that "a state is never free except when each citizen is bound by no law whatever that he has not approved of, either directly, or through his representatives." Accordingly, "every citizen must . . . have a part in elections." Although Adams claimed the suffrage requirements would not bar any citizen from voting, some citizens, which at the time meant free adult males, could not meet the property requirement. So Adams still accepted the standard contemporary argument that voters should have a material stake in society. In short, they should own property. The commonplace nature of that idea is illustrated by the fact that, when they created new constitutions, none of the American states extended the vote to all adult freemen. Pennsylvania and North Carolina came the closest by letting free male taxpayers vote.

Having maintained that all citizens would have a voice in the laws that governed them, Adams focused on who could represent the people. He stressed that the House of Representatives constituted "the people themselves represented by their delegates." Therefore, the property requirements for serving in the House should not be, and in Massachusetts were not, set too high. According to Adams, "thus far the government is purely democratic." But the democratic power, like all power, must be checked. And the members of the House were especially prone to letting their "passions and whims" influence them. The Senate and the governor, advised by his Council, provided the necessary "moderating power." Here, said Adams, is where the holders of property had a balancing power. Senators could reject a House bill, and it required "considerable property" to serve as a senator. Moreover the governor could veto a bill, although the legislature could, after "fresh examination," override the veto by a two-thirds vote. Adams maintained that this process provided the balance necessary to produce sound legislation without destroying "the authority of the people."

Chastellux marveled at how Adams's pronouncements contradicted his popular image. Adams had often been "reproached with consulting his library rather than present circumstances, and of always proceeding by way of the Greeks and Romans in order to reach the Whigs and Tories." However, said Chastellux, Adams's studies of the ancients did not keep him from being pragmatic or from paying close attention to present circumstances. The French general also commented upon what he considered the revolutionary politician's amazing transformation. Adams had supposedly moved from being "the most extravagant partisan of democracy" to being a person who stressed the importance of a mixed government. Chastellux was right to emphasize that Adams planned for the future by looking to the past, that he was sensitive to present circumstances, and that he could be politically flexible and pragmatic. But the Frenchman missed important subtleties, and he was wrong about Adams having undergone a political metamorphosis.

Samuel Adams had "democratic" tendencies. They were reflected in his glorification of the people's role in creating the Massachusetts Constitution, in his strident insistence that the people had a right to elect public servants who were duty bound to work for the public good, and in his stress on the importance of annual elections. His defense of what he called the "simple Democracies" of New England's towns reflected his democratic proclivities. But if one defines democracy as all citizens having equal voting rights and an equal right to run for office, Adams was no democrat. He never argued that propertyless people should have the vote. He even tempered the "democratic" notion of majority rule. While he emphasized that the majority must govern, he never argued that the majority was always right. If the majority acted on what he called "their first emotions," they might well take inappropriate action or produce poor legislation. The unreasonable will of the majority must be checked just as the potential tyrant must be checked. His praise for the careful checks and balances of the Massachusetts Constitution reflected his belief that "a Power without any restraint is Tyranny" and that liberty could be assailed by the many as well as by the few.

In July 1780 Samuel said the "great Business" of ratifying Massachusetts's new frame of government "was carried through with much good Humour among the People, and even in Berkshire," which had been a disruptive force since 1775. As the months went by, Samuel continued to report that the new constitution met with general approval. Still, he saw the adoption of a constitution as merely a first step toward creating the virtuous society he considered essential to preserving liberty. Because he believed history proved that legislators and magistrates "have always had a mighty Influence on the People," he placed great importance on the upcoming special elections scheduled for September. In a letter written to try to influence those elections, Adams asserted that the first politicians elected under the new constitution, and especially the first governor, "may probably stamp the moral as well as political Character of the People." Clearly trashing Hancock, Adams fretted that the people might select politicians who liked "Levity," "Foppery," "Vanity & the Folly of Parade." He considered "Pomp & Show" tools of aristocracies and monarchies. Adams knew the kind of men he wanted to hold public office. Massachusetts would be set on a solid footing and flourish provided the elected officials were "Men of Wisdom & Knowledge, of Moderation & Temperance, of Patience Fortitude & Perseverance, of Sobriety & true Republican Simplicity of Manners, of Zeal, for the Honor of the Supreme Being & Welfare of the Common Wealth." He expected a great deal!

Shifting political coalitions, rather than organized political parties, waged electoral battles in the Massachusetts of the 1780s. In 1780, announcements in the press made it clear that Hancock and James Bowdoin were the principal candidates for the governor's post. Before returning to Congress, Adams made his views—which did not favor Hancock—known to anyone who asked. When he learned that Hancock had won the election easily, Adams was distressed. Nevertheless, he put the best face on the result. If Hancock became "a wise & virtuous" governor, Adams would salute him and happily see him reelected. And if Hancock proved a poor choice, the people would see their error and avoid making the same mistake again. Despite these evenhanded comments, the letters Adams sent home in the fall of 1780 bristled with allusions to Hancock acting like a monarch.

For personal reasons Adams found the special elections that launched the new government disconcerting. He adhered to the view that people should not put themselves forward as candidates for political posts. He prided himself on never asking for votes and on doing his duty without considering whether he might benefit materially. He also blasted plural officeholding as a pernicious practice that must be curbed. Nevertheless, in addition to his elected posts, he had since July 1775 served as secretary of state of Massachusetts, an appointive post that made him responsible for producing state documents. He retained the position even though he spent most of his time in Congress and therefore had to employ a deputy who performed the secretary's duties in Massachusetts. When it came to plural officeholding during the war, it turned out that Adams sinned much less than most leading Massachusetts Whigs. It is also true, using a standard Adams applied, that the post of secretary did not necessarily conflict with Adams's other duties. These points do not, however, change the fact that when it came to *his* plural officeholding, Adams had been ignoring his own argument about cutting deep to remedy the evil.

When the post of secretary of state became an elective position in 1780, Adams's political friends assumed the voters would keep him in the office. However, John Avery, the man who had actually done most of the secretary's work, won the September election. Moreover, Adams was for the first time in years not elected to a single Massachusetts political office. The only post he now held was that of congressman. Adams's friends rightly blamed Hancock for conspiring against him, and Samuel himself was clearly knocked off stride by the public's seeming lack of faith in him. Although he spoke of "that Retirement from publick Cares, which my Country seems to point out for me," he quickly regained his balance. Samuel said he regarded Avery highly and would hold no grudge against him, and he meant it. More important, Adams analyzed his own political loss in a way that revealed his keen grasp of human nature and simultaneously illuminated his ideal of public service. When James Warren informed Adams that "the Tongue of Malice" was employed against him, Samuel figuratively turned the other cheek. The slanderous comments would, he said, merely make him all the more careful to avoid doing anything that could justly be criticized. Revealing judicious insight, he added the observations: "We are apt to be partial in our own Judgment of our selves. Our Friends are either blind to our Faults or not faithful enough to tell us of them." Adams's understanding of human nature helps explain his extraordinary ability to work with others to fashion political agreements.

His loss in the secretary of state election also caused Adams to reflect philosophically on how a politician should view public service. Responding to Elizabeth's anger over the slights he had received, Samuel maintained that in a free republic the people possessed the absolute right of voting for any candidate they pleased. No person should expect a government post merely because he had held office before. What a public servant had was a duty to do everything possible for "promoting the Cause of Liberty & Virtue." If the people wanted to replace him, the public servant should accept that decision and gracefully retire to private life. The revolutionary politician believed he had adhered to those standards. Thinking of his fellow citizens of Boston and of Massachusetts, Samuel added that "in their Service, I began my political Race. I have ever kept their Interest in View."

Samuel Adams was anxious to return home from Congress in 1781 in part because he thought that the "Interest" of Boston and Massachusetts required his personal services to help fight the growing level of vice he believed John Hancock did so much to foster. Adams put the issue bluntly when writing to James Warren. Observing that "Power is intoxicating" and implying that the new governor was already tipsy, Samuel stated that "our Country will stand in Need of its experienced Patriots to prevent its Ruin." Deeply worried about how Governor John Hancock's high-living lifestyle might undermine republican virtue, Adams began working immediately to secure Hancock's defeat in the first regular election under the new state constitution, which was scheduled for April. Before leaving Philadelphia, Samuel drafted two essays for the *Boston Gazette*. The first of the commentaries, each styled "Extract of a Letter from the Southward," appeared in print on April 2, 1781—election day in Massachusetts.

The election-day letter, clearly part of Adams's continuing efforts to promote and protect a government based on "the Principles of Liberty," constituted a primer on voting in "free Republics." Adams's analysis highlighted a concern many Americans shared: the fear that political factions and political parties would form and consequently destroy good government. Adams offered the readers advice on how to ensure that Massachusetts would "never sink into the Violence and Rage" that came with political parties. The responsibility rested with the citizens, who when voting exercised "one of the most solemn Trusts in human Society." The voters must be devoted to the constitution, not to persons. For the benefit of the republic, the voters, and their posterity, Adams hoped that "the great Business of Elections will never be left by the Many, to be done by the Few." Accentuating the ideal of virtuous republicanism, he spoke of embracing "that Simplicity which is the Ornament and Strength of a free Republick." Making a thinly veiled reference to Hancock, he wrote that political servants who still reveled in monarchical pomp or who thirsted after "Adulation" were unworthy candidates for public office. Adams drove that point hard by celebrating the fact that annual elections let people correct their "Mistakes."

If Adams thought his first letter would affect the elections, he misjudged badly. Hancock and his candidate for lieutenant governor, Thomas Cushing, romped to victory in all parts of the commonwealth. Hancock got every vote cast in Boston; Cushing garnered over 96 percent of Boston's votes. Adams could not have been shocked by Hancock's victory, only by its magnitude. Samuel knew that the ideal of achieving consensus still exerted real influence in Massachusetts. He was also well aware of Massachusetts's tradition of reelecting public officials. There was some truth in

James Warren's bitter lament that being elected once amounted to being elected for life. So, realistically, Adams could not have expected the voters to dump Hancock. Still, given his views on promoting republican virtue, Adams had to try to influence the 1781 election.

The second essay Adams forwarded to the *Boston Gazette* demonstrated his understanding of the political realities. The letter was written before the elections occurred but not published until after the results became known. Adams added to his primer on voting by saying he trusted that each voter had expressed his honest views rather than having "prostituted" his vote to please a friend or a patron. Adams devoted most of his energy to trumpeting his often stated ideal that the people's vigilance could check evil office-holders. Citizens must, he said, monitor their public servants by inquiring "freely, but decently," into their conduct. Adams offered a detailed example from Swedish history to illustrate that even good men might abuse their power if they were not watched carefully. He literally highlighted his basic thought: *"There is no restraint* [on politicians] *like the pervading eye of the virtuous citizens."*

Adams planned to follow his own advice about keeping careful watch on public servants, especially Governor Hancock. He also intended to reform a Boston that James and Mercy Otis Warren, Elbridge Gerry, and the Reverend Samuel Cooper described as being awash in gaiety. They reported that the Bostonians, especially "the Gentry" and even ministers, were, alas, eagerly adopting the gaudy social trappings of monarchy. Because he believed Massachusetts's liberty was not yet set on a firm foundation and was in grave danger from the likes of Hancock, Samuel Adams's political race had not yet run its course by the time he retired from Congress and returned to Boston in the spring of 1781.

9

"The Consistent Republican"

$\mathcal{S}$amuel Adams did indeed remain politically active after retiring from Congress. During the 1780s, he immersed himself in Boston politics and often served as moderator of the town meeting. He also continually served in the Massachusetts Senate, a majority of the time as its president. In 1789, he became lieutenant governor and then held the governorship from mid-1794 through mid-1797 before finally leaving public office at the age of seventy-four. At times during the 1780s and 1790s, city-, state-, and continental-level constitutions that, in Adams's view, defended the people's liberties and gave them a constitutional means to redress their grievances faced severe challenges. He showed flexibility when confronting the challenges, but he never wavered from his lifelong commitment to safeguarding republican constitutions against *any* threat. And, holding firm to his view that a free republic like Massachusetts needed a virtuous citizenry to survive, Adams continued to act on his belief that the people must turn away from decadence. As he called for promoting virtue, especially through education, he did more than celebrate the importance of expanding educational opportunities for all children. He played a central role in achieving significant educational advancements both in Boston and the commonwealth. In all these ways, the revolutionary politician strove to promote ideas of the Revolution that he believed would serve posterity. In fact, from the time he retired from Congress through the rest of his political life, Samuel Adams fought above all else, as he put it, "to secure the blessings of equal liberty to the present and future generations." He was, as political supporters described him, "the consistent Republican."

When Samuel Adams arrived back in Boston in 1781, his own eyes convinced him that simple republican virtue was not a hallmark of his beloved native city. Assembly balls and other fashionable amusements, extravagant displays of wealth, and even gambling enjoyed widespread popularity. Although he sought to quell the growing profligacy, he did not share the enthusiasm some displayed for using proscriptive legislation to promote piety. Instead, he continued to emphasize the importance of promoting virtue by providing a public education to all children. In December 1781, the Boston Town Meeting appointed him chairman of a committee charged with assessing the city's public school system. Five days later he remarked that one of the committee's interests was "the better Education of female Children." Samuel was apparently speaking only for his committee; the town meeting had not mentioned educating females. Boston put an additional member on the Adams committee in March 1782 and sharpened its charge by asking the group to determine whether some new arrangement would improve the public school system.

Two years elapsed before the Adams committee presented its analysis to the town meeting. When it finally appeared, the report bore Adams's imprint. It opened by applauding the wisdom of the people's venerable ancestors for fashioning an extensive education system that ranged from simple writing schools to Harvard College. Turning the colonial founders into education democrats, the committee report proclaimed that "Our free schools seem to have been intended for the Benefit of the Poor and the Rich." Indeed, the founders supposedly wanted to place all children on an equal footing by giving them equal educational opportunities. The report emphasized that these original goals, which benefited the whole community, should still guide Boston's actions.

The Adams committee attributed its slowness in presenting a plan to the difficulty of determining how many children attended Boston's schools and, accordingly, recommended conducting a school census. The town meeting approved. The committee also maintained that truancy was a problem and that some of the absent children injured their minds and virtue by gambling. The town meeting accepted the committee's proposal that it deal with these problems by carefully investigating the moral character of anyone seeking to open a private school. The committee's investigation also found that some public school teachers shortened the instructional hours so they could earn extra income tutoring. The committee said the practice of shortening instructional hours should be halted but balanced that by declaring that Boston must pay its teachers a living wage. Again the town meeting concurred.

The Adams committee report of March 1784 addressed two potentially divisive topics: providing education for the poor and for females. The committee recommended that, pending the completion of the school census, the Overseers of the Poor assist the poor so even the most destitute child could attend school. This program would have applied to all children, including females. Aware that controversy swirled around the idea of offering females a general education, the Adams committee approached the issue gingerly by merely saying the question of educating females "required particular Consideration." The members trod no further than suggesting that females would become more useful members of society if they received schooling. The town meeting sidestepped these controversial proposals by deferring them for possible future action. In the next few months of 1784, the meeting increased teachers' salaries and also agreed to establish a new school in the city's southern section. Thus, although the Adams committee successfully pushed some education reforms, it had not realized the goal of ensuring that all the city's children could receive instruction in the public schools.

By mid-1785, even though some were promoting plays, a form of amusement he believed undermined republican virtues, Samuel thought the prospect for reforming society was improving. John Hancock had decided to retire, at least temporarily, from the governorship and left office in 1785. James Bowdoin, the man Samuel supported in the first governor's race, defeated Hancock's handpicked replacement, Thomas Cushing. Governor Bowdoin earned Adams's praise by quickly issuing a proclamation "for the Encouragement of Piety, Virtue, Education and Manners and for the Suppression of Vice." Admitting he had long wished to see Hancock leave the governor's chair, Adams allowed himself to hope that, with a new chief magistrate and others setting a better example, the people "may *perhaps* restore our Virtue."

Samuel Adams nurtured that restoration of virtue above all by continuing to emphasize the importance of providing every child with a public education. It took another four years, but in 1789, Adams and his allies achieved stunning support for, and transformations in, the education systems first of Massachusetts and then of Boston. In June the General Court passed one of the most influential education acts in American history. Sections of the act read like a compilation of arguments Adams had been trumpeting for years. Reestablishing the kind of colonial education system Adams so praised, the legislature decreed that all towns with at least fifty families must maintain a town school; larger communities must also support grammar schools. As in Boston, government officials were to ensure that only persons of good moral character became teachers. This 1789 act did not address the question of educating females; but, in the fall of that year, Boston's town meeting finally faced the issue. Spurred by a petition calling for reform that would include educating both sexes, the meeting appointed a Committee of Twelve, one from each ward, to report on the petition. When Bostonians held high executive state posts, they were not expected to serve on town meeting committees. Samuel, who by then was the state's lieutenant governor, did the unexpected. Reflecting his long-standing commitment to expanding educational opportunities in Boston, "His Honor Sam¹. Adams, Esq." represented the city's Ninth Ward.

The Committee of Twelve recommended creating an elected school committee that would run an education system open to girls as well as boys. Three "reading schools" would teach reading and the proper use of English; three "writing schools" would offer the instruction in writing and arithmetic usually taught in the town schools. These schools, open to all children ages seven through fourteen, would be located to serve the northern, central, and southern sections of Boston. Another school would prepare students for university studies. Stressing that these innovations would require little increased spending, the committee boldly asserted that the great and obvious advantages that children in general, and females in particular, would derive from the plan "would abundantly compensate & Justify a far greater expence." Despite its plea for educating both sexes, the committee did not advocate full equality. Boys would attend school all year round; girls would only receive instruction for six months each year. And the report's language suggested that the college preparatory school would only be open to males.

In October 1789, the town meeting approved the committee's plan and authorized developing Boston's "new School system." Despite offering females less-than-equal educational opportunities, after a lengthy effort in which Samuel Adams figured prominently, Boston had taken the greatest strides yet made in a major American city toward providing free public education for both sexes. Few contemporary American political leaders supported creating a public education system; far fewer advocated providing a general education to girls as well as boys. Adams's strong efforts on behalf of educating all children illustrated his firm commitment to his often stated belief that education was crucial to perpetuating a republican government. Upon reflection, it is hardly surprising that he championed education for females. He had always prized and lauded the influence his elder sister, Mary, had on him. Even more important, from the 1760s on, at a time when many of New England's adult women were not literate, Samuel knew the joys of a wife who could read and write. Moreover, he had come to rely on Elizabeth as a partner in political endeavors as well as in those things normally considered within the "sphere" of women.

Samuel Adams thought that giving all children a virtuous education would make them better custodians of liberty. He and the other promoters of a virtuous republican lifestyle could not, however, always set the political agenda in Boston. In the very period when the Adams committee first began achieving educational reform in the mid-1780s, Adams had to deflect efforts to alter—to destroy—Boston's own constitution. For more than a century, Boston had been governed by town meetings, a system that gave the citizens a direct vote in determining how their city functioned. But as proponents of incorporation had noted long before, the town meeting, which functioned through elected committees, could often be less than efficient. In 1784, several leading citizens decided the inefficiency must stop. They submitted a petition saying Boston should be incorporated and run by a mayor and aldermanic system. This request came at a time when many urban elites in America touted the glories of incorporating cities. But those who trumpeted the people's right to participate actively in governance typically considered incorporation schemes aristocratic power grabs. As a local political author put it, those seeking to change Boston's "present democratic plan" aimed to replace it with an aristocratic form of government. Samuel Adams, truly a man of the town meeting, believed that Boston's government gave the people the power to preserve their liberties. Refusing to let Boston's republican constitution be ripped apart in the name of efficiency, Adams led the anti-incorporation forces. He did it not merely to defend his beloved native town but also to safeguard town meeting government throughout New England. As he said when writing to a citizen of Connecticut, he believed that the people could not be enslaved or even significantly injured so long as they retained and made "good Use" of "those simple Democracies in all our Towns that are the Basis of our State Constitutions."

No one could rival Samuel Adams's knowledge of how to make "good Use" of a town meeting's democratic features. In this case, his power came as chairman of committees that evaluated the ideal of incorporation. With Adams warning that incorporation "might . . . be instrumental to the introduction of aristocracy," the first incorporation effort quickly fizzled. When another incorporation effort was mounted in the fall of 1784, Adams again chaired the evaluating committee. Stressing that it had held three meetings and "fully considered the Matter," the Adams committee reported that it could find nothing wrong with Boston's constitution. The town meeting voted its approval and politely, but firmly, told the incorporation petitioners to withdraw their request. Although the incorporation forces did not give up, their efforts were long thwarted; Boston was not finally incorporated as a city until 1822.

Samuel Adams believed that the loyalists who had abandoned America during the Revolution represented yet another threat to a virtuous republican society. As he contemplated the refugees, Adams adhered to the strident positions enunciated during the 1760s and early 1770s. Time and again, especially when promoting economic warfare, the town meeting had said those who undermined the cause should be ostracized *forever.* Adams's actions proved that, for him, the prewar diatribes were not mere propagandistic bombast. Adams considered the refugees anti-American, antirepublican, and politically dangerous. He prophesied that, if allowed to return, Tory refugees would join forces with evil demagogic politicians and undermine republican government. Moreover, if the loyalist wretches came back, "Mutual Hatred and Revenge" would produce "perpetual Quarrels between them & the people & perhaps frequent Bloodshed." Some of the vile but cunning refugees might gradually regain public standing and form factions in support of one or another foreign nation. Believing that America might already be in danger from such factions, Adams told his diplomat cousin, John, that every effort must be taken to counter the Tories' "evil Effects." Because he both hated Tories and considered them dangerous, Adams expressed joy when he saw that the peace treaty ending the war could be interpreted as giving individual states the right to bar loyalist refugees from returning. He labored to make that a reality. As the head of a town meeting committee appointed at the end of the war, he persuaded Boston to endorse strong anti-Tory positions. The town meeting proclaimed that, whether they fought for the king or merely sought the shelter of his forces, Tories were "Conspirators against the Rights and Liberties of America and of Mankind." The "Traitors" who had fled America should "never" be taken back.

The actions of American military men helped fuel Adams's concern about loyalist refugees joining political factions. In May 1783, officers of the Continental Army formed a "Society of Friends" and named it for Lucius Quinctius Cincinnatus, the famous Roman general who, after leading the armies to victory, refused any special honors and returned to his life as a farmer. While any Continental army or French officer could join the Society of the Cincinnati, militia officers were not automatically entitled to membership. The society could, whenever it chose, bestow honorary membership on individuals. As an initiation fee, members had to contribute a month's pay to the society's coffers. The local branches could, if they wished, levy additional financial tithings.

Adams and others who denounced the society maintained that it debauched the ideal of Cincinnatus. The group adopted regalia that included a gold eagle medal and a wide blue ribbon so its members could "be known and distinguished." The society embraced hereditary primogeniture by letting a member's eldest son join. Worse yet, the constitution of the Cincinnati, as most called the group, suggested it would become politically active. The society's mix of aristocracy and militarism terrified Adams and others, including Thomas Jefferson, John Adams, Elbridge Gerry, and James Warren. Supplying his cousin John with ammunition, Samuel depicted the district and state conventions of the Cincinnati as trying to usurp the powers of the state legislatures, the Congress, and other government officials. Samuel warned that, "being an Order of *Military* Men," the Cincinnati might soon try to enforce their resolutions and in the process possibly destroy America's free governments.

As a consistent republican who believed one must ardently defend established constitutions that guarded the people's freedom, Samuel Adams became an anti-Cincinnati activist. He was instrumental in convincing the Massachusetts legislature to denounce the Cincinnati as an aristocratic threat to republicanism. To spread the message, in April 1784 he dispatched letters to Elbridge Gerry, an equally ardent opponent of the Cincinnati, who was serving in Congress. Samuel ominously noted that the formation of the Cincinnati constituted "as rapid a stride towards an hereditary military nobility as ever was made in so short a time." Since it would be politically unwise to disparage the officers as nothing more than power-hungry aristocrats, Adams claimed he was sure few, if any, of the Cincinnati's founders had evil intentions. The real danger would come from the officers' posterity, who might want to transform the pageantry of nobility into the real thing. For individuals who might dismiss these arguments, Adams conjured up a frightening scenario. By letting foreigners into their ranks, the Cincinnati increased the danger that "a foreign Influence might prevail in America."

Since the revered George Washington endorsed the Cincinnati, and since Adams respected and trusted Washington, he carefully noted that Washington must not think the Cincinnati posed a danger to liberty. And, when the anti-Cincinnati firestorm erupted, the general responded by quickly recommending several changes in the society's constitution. The hereditary features should be eliminated; anything that had "a political tendency" should be expunged; provisions should guarantee that the group's money could not be used for political purposes. In May 1784 the first general meeting of the Cincinnati endorsed Washington's recommendations.

Although anti-Cincinnati sentiment quickly subsided, Adams and many others were not reassured. Writing to Gerry in 1785, Samuel evoked an image he had used in the 1760s against the British. He declared that the changes approved at the 1784 general meeting made the Cincinnati *more* dangerous because the society "is the same serpent still, but it hides its sting." Moreover, the state Cincinnati organizations rejected the alterations Washington recommended and the first general meeting approved. So, despite Washington's efforts, the Cincinnati retained its dangerous militaristic and aristocratic features and, in Adams's view, stood ready to unleash its power to influence and possibly control America's legislatures. Adams and Gerry kept trying to convince Congress it must go on record as opposing the Cincinnati. Congress did not act, and in time the Cincinnati proved that the extreme fears raised by its foes were wrong. Nevertheless, in the early 1780s, fervent republicans could not foresee that the Society of the Cincinnati would be benign. So, given his cardinal rule that one must watchfully defend the people's rights and the people's republican constitutions, Adams's anti-Cincinnati campaign made sense.

Although decidedly unhappy about Congress's failure to oppose the Cincinnati, Adams consistently advocated the necessity of backing the confederation government. His ardent support for the central government stemmed from the fact that it was a confederation of sovereign states. Adams, who considered himself a citizen of both the United States and Massachusetts, had a well-developed sense of dual citizenship. Thus, while he constantly referred to Massachusetts as his "Country," he could also tell a South Carolinian that "We are Citizens of the United States & our Interest is *one.*" Given this view, he regularly expressed concern for upholding "the honour of congress" because Congress "is and must be the cement of the union of the states."

Adams's support for the confederation government was especially evident in the positions he took on the volatile issue of giving America's military officers pensions. While he was still a congressman, Congress debated the question at length before finally, in 1780, offering half pay for life to officers who would serve for the duration of the war. During the war, Adams zealously supported most proposals that bolstered the revolutionaries' military power, and the half-pay-for-life resolution aimed to keep experienced officers in the field. But Adams, whose fear of a military establishment was legendary, balked at what he considered a dangerous bow to the military. He voted against the pensions.

Once the war was safely won, strong sentiment welled up for reneging on the proffered officers' pensions. The anger festered even after March 1783 when the Congress "commuted" the lifetime pensions to full pay for five years. In September, as protests over "commutation" flared, especially in Connecticut, Adams responded to a question about where he stood on the matter. Although he had opposed the pensions in 1780, Adams now backed Congress unflinchingly. Knowing his comments would be used in the commutation fight, Samuel offered reasons for supporting Congress's actions. He intimated that five-year pensions were preferable to lifetime pensions in part because they were less likely to perpetuate militaristic attitudes. Moreover, on the basis of the claim that officers supposedly missed economic opportunities open to "their fellow citizens at home," the pensions seemed "just & reasonable." In addition, commutation would probably be cost effective when measured against the original promise of half pay for life. For Adams, such considerations mattered less than the principle of defending Congress when it exercised legitimate constitutional powers. Congress had been created, he pointed out, so the "joint wisdom" of the states could protect "our just rights and liberties." When an army became necessary because Britain waged war against those rights, Congress had the constitutional responsibility of deciding how to support the army, and a congressional majority voted for the pensions. The states, therefore, must support Congress's actions even if the actions seemed inappropriate. Adams added the forceful reminder that "an *honest* man" would understand that "States as well as individual persons are equally bound to fulfill their engagements."

While he consistently advocated the importance of backing Congress, Adams's responses to possibly altering how Congress functioned sprang from a basic principle. He measured every suggestion by the question: will it perhaps undermine liberty? If his answer was yes, he opposed it. Thus, early in the war, he voted to create boards of war, ordnance, navy, and finance that would be run by skilled persons who were not members of Congress. He did so because he believed the change would improve efficiency without endangering liberty. However, in 1781, he voted against a congressional plan that effectively shifted major responsibilities from congressional committees to executive departments headed by a powerful superintendent. He was especially leery of creating a superintendent of finance and pleaded with his fellow congressmen to oppose the idea. He feared a superintendent of finance might gain a "highly dangerous" and "undue influence" both in Congress and in state legislatures. Alluding to the extraordinary power the British finance minister wielded, Adams predicted that even an angel-like financier might become so influential he could control Congress. A proponent of the new system countered by saying that "the breath of congress could annihilate the financier." Adams shot back, "the time might come, and if they were not careful it certainly would, when even congress would not dare to blow that breath." To protect the people's liberty, he preferred keeping the clumsy and often inefficient committee system rather than risk having power consolidated in one person's hands. A majority of Adams's fellow congressmen disagreed. They voted the executive system into existence.

Whenever the question of revising the Articles surfaced, Adams thus tempered his desire to ensure that the continental government could function effectively with a similar concern about not undermining liberty. By the time he left Congress in mid-1781, it was already painfully evident that Congress could not rely on the states for the funds necessary to run the Union's government. Adams found that disconcerting in part because he considered it "sound Policy" for governments to discharge their debts "with all possible Speed" so future generations would not be encumbered. Accordingly, Adams supported the 1781 and 1783 proposals to give Congress a measure of financial security by letting it levy impost duties. Indeed, although justifiably famous for being politically upright, Adams was accused of underhanded shenanigans in support of the 1783 proposal. In a letter Gerry sent to a legislative committee Adams chaired, Massachusetts's congressmen proposed that the state refuse to approve the impost unless Congress adopted several positions favorable to the state. In effect, the delegates recommended blackmailing Congress. An Adams committee member pocketed the unsavory letter, and Massachusetts approved the impost proposal in October 1783. Soon thereafter politicos charged that Adams and the other two members of the committee purposefully suppressed the letter. The legislature launched an investigation, and Adams apologized profusely. He maintained that the crush of his work as Senate president, his ill health, and the fact that Congressman Stephen Higginson had already briefed the General Court on the delegates' ideas explained his failure to ensure that the legislators received the letter. Adams escaped censure; the committeeman who pocketed the letter did not. Adams told Gerry that "mere forgetfulness" caused the problem and that the complaints against him sprang from political animus and would evaporate as soon as the next election was over. Gerry accepted his friend's explanation. Adams was, in fact, seriously ill when the incident occurred in September 1783, and, as he predicted, it did him no lasting harm. Nevertheless, when all allowances have been made, the fact remains: his behavior, which did support the effort to increase Congress's powers, was at best negligent and possibly devious.

Although they garnered strong support, the 1781 and 1783 impost proposals both foundered because any one state could scuttle the amendment
process. So Congress remained financially impotent. It also could not effectively regulate the Union's commerce. Once peace returned, Americans fell
into old buying habits and resumed trading with Britain. As Adams lamented, the British consequently refused to negotiate a commercial treaty since
they already had the benefit of America's trade without making concessions. In part to give Congress leverage against the British, many Americans
advocated granting Congress the kind of commercial power Britain once
exercised. Formal proposals on the matter surfaced beginning in 1783.
Adams supported granting Congress commercial powers. In the fall of
1785, he noted that, while Massachusetts and New Hampshire tried to use
navigation acts to force nations to enter commercial treaties with the United States, neighboring states had not taken similar action. This left the two
activist states "suffering by their own honest exertions for the general interest." Thus Congress's inability to regulate commerce had exacerbated economic woes in Massachusetts. It seemed obvious that Congress should have
"sufficient Power to regulate the Trade of the States with foreigners."

Some Americans insisted that the confederation should not be granted
any additional powers. Others thought that only a vigorous consolidated
national government could meet America's needs. Adams belonged to neither camp. He was willing, even anxious, to give the confederation government the power it needed to function. But he also assessed each recommended change by asking himself if it might undermine the Articles'
objective of promoting "liberty." Thus, in 1785, when he called for giving
Congress commercial powers, he held that Congress could be granted
"properly guarded" powers "without endangering the Principles of the
Confederation." However, when the idea of undertaking a full revision of
the Articles surfaced, he balked. Adams feared such a revision might transform the central government into a dangerous monolith. In one of the
numerous political letters he sent for Gerry's use in 1785, Adams averred
that "a general revision" of the Articles seemed unnecessary and "dangerous." He warned that the confederation's commitment to liberty could be
"lost" in at least two possible ways. If the people were not watchful and
attentive, a few scheming men might grasp the government. Or, if the frame
of government were revised, it might be couched in "ambiguous Terms"
and then interpreted in ways that would harm or even destroy liberty.

Samuel Adams's desire to modify rather than totally revise the Articles
ran into problems that touched him personally as he strove to preserve
Massachusetts's constitutional government. The problems were rooted in
economic difficulties. The war thoroughly disrupted the Massachusetts
economy. Nevertheless, the people, particularly farmers, derived some economic benefit from the presence of the American and French armies.
However, the military market shrank dramatically in 1780 as the fighting

shifted to the South. The economic dislocations touched all, but western farmers, many living on the economic margin, felt especially squeezed by the loss of markets. The General Court appeared to exacerbate the economic woes. Starting in 1779 and continuing into 1780, the legislature levied heavy taxes to meet financial obligations to its own citizens and to Congress. Although the policy of heavy taxation pinched the people, Adams considered the pinch necessary. The Revolutionary generation must not shirk its duty; it must not burden posterity with a massive debt.

Citizens, particularly in the westernmost counties, did more than grumble. Facing hard times and in many cases imminent bankruptcy, people flooded the General Court with petitions in 1780. They pressed for tax relief and insisted that the supply of money be increased. In 1781 and into 1782, extralegal conventions met to demand action. By the spring of 1782, crowd actions disrupted some government functions in western Massachusetts. In April a crowd shut down courts in Hampshire County. One of the crowd leaders, Samuel Ely, reportedly urged the people on with the cry "Come on my brave boys, we will go to the wood pile and get clubs enough, and knock their gray wigs off, and send them out of the world in an instant." Some citizens defended the judges, and bloodshed was averted. However, the efforts to capture and punish Ely raised the possibility that violence might bubble up again.

The General Court responded with a hard fist encased in a soft glove. In midsummer 1782, the legislators suspended habeas corpus for six months but also declared that, for one year, certain goods—including livestock, grain, and marketable lumber—would be legal tender. In addition, the General Court dispatched three legislators, headed by Senate president Samuel Adams, to hear the westerners' complaints. During July and August of 1782, the legislature's committee attended town meetings and then met with a special convention of towns. Westerners aired their grievances and called for redress. But the convention also thanked the General Court for listening and, more important, called upon everyone to support constitutional government. Given this development, the legislature applauded the Adams committee and enacted a general pardon that excluded only Ely. Major uprisings were averted, but sporadic crowd action continued to flare, and ad hoc conventions began springing up in the eastern as well as the western sections of the state. The gatherings did more than criticize the Massachusetts government. They often opposed giving Congress the right to levy an impost, and many harsh words were uttered about the impropriety of Congress granting pensions to military officers.

Although Adams believed that the people's grievances should be considered, his response to the ongoing challenges to constitutional government was predictable. While he regarded citizen watchfulness as "a political Virtue" and "one of the greatest Securities of publick Liberty," he also observed that some men, under the guise of being "watchful Patriots," were assaulting everything the governments did and using conventions to stir up "Discord & Animosity. " Adams, who feared anarchy as much as tyranny, stressed that, while citizen watchfulness was vital, it was equally true that "there is Decency & Respect due to Constitutional Authority." Adams also pointed out that, while the methods being used in the 1780s were methods he had employed in the 1760s, there was a fundamental difference. In the 1760s the people used county conventions and popular committees to defend the right of being governed only by laws fashioned by their own representatives. Now the people had a constitution that guaranteed their legislators and other public officials would be annually selected in free elections; therefore, county conventions and popular committees challenged, rather than defended, constitutional rights.

By 1785, in part owing to an improving economic situation, the danger posed by demagogues such as Samuel Ely and by ad hoc bodies appeared to have subsided. The quiet was misleading, though, especially in western Massachusetts, where large numbers of people still labored under a heavy burden of debt. In 1786, when the General Court refused to issue paper money and also enacted a hefty tax hike, open rebellion erupted. The rebels, who had their greatest strength in the two westernmost counties of Berkshire and Hampshire, organized themselves into military units led by veterans of the war. One of the principal rebel commanders was Daniel Shays, a former Continental Army captain, and the uprising became known as Shays's Rebellion. The first spasm of violence occurred in late August when armed men shut down the courts in Northampton in Hampshire County. Adams and the Boston Town Meeting tried to halt the violence. In September, with Adams serving as moderator, the meeting appointed a committee, headed by Adams, to draft a circular letter. The lengthy missive was designed to convince the dissidents that they should renounce violence and support constitutional government. The Adams group emphasized that any real grievances could be—and to protect the rights of posterity must be—redressed by using the established constitutional process.

Words proved ineffective. The uprising spread. In January 1787, about fifteen hundred rebels commanded by Shays threatened to capture the federal arsenal at Springfield. They might have succeeded had not Massachusetts fielded an army of more than four thousand that stopped them, but only after an exchange of fire left the blood of two dozen rebel farmers soaking into the snow. Four were killed, twenty wounded. Organized resistance sputtered on into February, and fear of a renewal of violence lingered well into the summer. For Samuel Adams, Shays's Rebellion constituted perhaps the ultimate horror: the people waging war against a constitution that protected their liberties and provided them with legal means to redress grievances. Once the rebellion was crushed, most politicians, sensing that the public wanted mercy, endorsed clemency for the rebels. Adams refused to pander to the popular mood. He wanted the ringleaders hanged because, as he reportedly said, "in monarchies, the crime of treason and rebellion may admit of being pardoned or lightly punished; but the man who dares to rebel against the laws of a republic ought to suffer death."

Shays's Rebellion played a crucial role in the eventual destruction of the Articles of Confederation and the subsequent creation of a truly national government. American politicians who wanted to revamp the Union's government skillfully exploited the fear that accompanied Shays's Rebellion. Exaggerated reports of rebellion brewing throughout New England helped convince George Washington, the most admired and trusted man in the Union, to attend the convention Congress authorized to recommend changes in the Articles. The convention that met in Philadelphia from May into September 1787 disregarded its instructions and drafted a totally new Constitution. Congress, which by then rarely had enough members to function, followed the convention's recommendation and called upon the states to have elected ratification conventions vote on the proposed Constitution. The people of Massachusetts, like those throughout the Union, disagreed sharply over the merits of the new governmental framework. In fact, opinion in the Union divided about equally on the question of adopting it. In Massachusetts, a state that the pro-Constitution forces knew they had to carry, a majority of the citizens favored rejecting the convention's document.

Believing he would oppose the new Constitution, its staunch Massachusetts supporters contemplated trying to block Adams's election to the state's ratifying convention. They abandoned the idea in part, as Christopher Gore noted, because "those who are in favor of the Constitution feared the consequences of opposing S.A.'s election." They reasoned, said Gore, that if Adams were not a delegate, he might openly attack the Constitution and also surreptitiously influence groups of delegates. If he attended, his arguments could be countered more easily. Moreover, as Gore admitted, Adams could not be defeated at the polls. So supporters of the Constitution plotted to neutralize Adams. In January 1788, just before the ratifying convention opened, almost four hundred Boston artisans and tradesmen who favored the Constitution met and proclaimed that no delegate should even think about trying to amend, much less oppose, the new Constitution. That message was, supporters of the proposed Constitution emphasized, designed above all to try to influence one man: Samuel Adams.

Adams did dislike the proposed Constitution. He expressed his general views in a letter to his old political friend Richard Henry Lee in early December 1787. "I confess, as I enter the Building I stumble at the Threshold. I meet with a National Government, instead of a Federal Union of Sovereign States." Adams was right. The framers of the Constitution had replaced a federal constitution with one that, while it retained some federal features, created a national government. However, in a brilliant propaganda maneuver, the nationalists appropriated the popular term "Federalist" for themselves while tarring anyone who raised questions about the new Constitution with the derisive label "Anti-Federalist."

Adams used basic Anti-Federalist arguments against the Constitution. After suggesting that America was too vast and the interests of its people too diverse to be governed effectively by a single national legislature, Adams played the aristocracy card. Maintaining that "the Seeds of Aristocracy" lay "like a Canker Worm . . . at the Root of free Governments," he asserted that those seeds began germinating before the war ended. The clear implication was that the new Constitution sprang from an ongoing aristocratic plot to subvert free republican governments. Having attempted to place Federalists on the wrong side of basic rights issues, Adams pitched the idea of amending rather than annihilating the Articles. He did that by elaborating on the essential points he had made in 1785 when arguing against a general revision of the Articles. Adams maintained that, with adjustments, the Articles, which protected America's liberty, would serve the people well. Going to the extreme of adopting a new frame of government was, he argued, unnecessary and dangerous.

Despite his strictures against the proposed Constitution, Adams knew the confederation government was woefully underpowered. In addition, he could not deny that the process being used to replace the Articles was the same republican process he glorified when it was used to create the Massachusetts Constitution. Therefore he could not simply reject the new Constitution.

He told Gore in early January that he planned to attend the convention with an open mind. In fact, Gore noted that Adams said that, *if the document were amended,* a government could be formed from the proposed Constitution. Gore, an intense Federalist, dismissed Adams's comments. He should not have. Adams listed moderation among the republican virtues and had acted with moderation when he helped create the Massachusetts Constitution. He had also urged the people to exercise moderation when considering the proposed state constitution. Indeed, whenever he approached the question of forming a government, Adams had always shown a willingness to compromise where it could be done without endangering liberty. Moreover, he always stressed the impossibility of achieving either perfection or everything one wanted in a government. Had Gore not been so closed-minded, he would have realized that Adams would likely be open-minded and judicious at the ratifying convention. Gore's own recent experience with Samuel should have underscored that thought. Christopher's father, John Gore, a painter and color merchant, had left his family behind and fled Boston with the British forces in March 1776. He returned in 1785 and in June 1787 petitioned the legislature asking to be naturalized and granted American citizenship; that request, supported by patriotic notables including James Bowdoin, was granted. Despite his detestation of loyalists, Samuel did not oppose John Gore's request because Gore's two sons had supported the Revolution and the wife and daughters John had abandoned. Samuel later told Christopher that, because of his "pure regard" for him, he was "always willing" to allow John Gore to return. Had Christopher considered Samuel's reasonableness in the case of his loyalist father, he would have offered a better forecast of how Samuel would behave at the ratifying convention.

For most of the convention, which opened on January 9, 1788, Adams stayed out of the debates and functioned, as he put it, more as "an auditor than an objector." Nathaniel Gorham, a committed Federalist delegate to the ratifying convention, seemed to acknowledge that fact on January 20. He apparently placed Adams on a list of delegates "who appear to be determined to hear all that can be said on the subject—& then vote as they think right." Another ardent Federalist, Henry Knox of New York, used almost identical language when he said that Adams was on that list of thoughtful swing voters. Adams's actions at the convention support that judgment and his own claim about being an auditor, not an objector. When he did participate in the convention's activities, Samuel evenhandedly followed precedents established during the process of drafting and adopting the Massachusetts Constitution. He successfully urged the delegates to invite Elbridge Gerry, who had attended the Philadelphia convention, to answer delegates' questions about how the Constitution came into being. Federalists interpreted that as a hostile action because Gerry had refused to sign the Constitution and had publicly explained why. In urging that Gerry attend, Adams was, in fact, following precedent. When the Boston Town Meeting discussed the proposed Massachusetts Constitution in 1780, it had asked constitutional convention delegates to attend so they could answer the citizens' queries.

While passionate Federalists disliked his position on bringing Gerry into the ratifying convention, fervent Anti-Federalists disliked Adams's response to one of their tactics. When they began deliberations, the delegates agreed to discuss the proposed Constitution paragraph by paragraph. However, as the convention progressed, leading Anti-Federalists tried to change the rules. Realizing they had the votes to defeat the Constitution and not wanting to risk slippage in their ranks, they moved to stop debating each paragraph. Adams opposed the motion, and it lost. His position not only supported the idea of fair play but also adhered to the town meeting precedent of going over a proposed constitution paragraph by paragraph before voting on it.

On two additional occasions when he spoke, Adams displayed an evenhandedness that again favored the Federalists. When a pro-Constitution speaker commented upon the "anarchy" of Shays's Rebellion, an opponent attempted to silence him by claiming that the discussion was not germane. Adams was among those who disagreed, and the pro-Constitution speaker was allowed to continue. Similarly, Anti-Federalists tried to exploit the fact that the Constitution stipulated that the slave trade could be outlawed by

Congress, but only after a twenty-year interval. They chastised the framers of the Constitution for not banning the slave trade immediately. Adams was one of the delegates who, because the framers had set a specific date for potentially voting the slave trade out of existence, "rejoiced that a door was now to be opened for the annihilation of this odious, abhorrent practice in a certain time."

As the convention progressed, Adams thus demonstrated a judicious, fair-minded, and pragmatic approach. The problem for devout Federalists and Anti-Federalists was that neither camp wanted to compromise. Each side desperately wanted to win because each thought that the ultimate fate of the Constitution depended on what happened in Massachusetts. Federalists were especially averse to admitting that the Constitution might contain any fundamental defects lest that admission open the door for holding a second constitutional convention. Many Anti-Federalists throughout the Union were calling for that second gathering as a means of killing the proposed new government.

Believing they must carry Massachusetts, Federalists swallowed hard and compromised. They struck a deal with the very popular John Hancock. He had been elected president of the convention but had not attended, supposedly because his gouty condition forced him to stay in bed. As cynics noted, by not attending the convention, Hancock avoided having to take a position. According to Rufus King, an influential and fervent Federalist, the pro-Constitution forces trolled for Hancock's support in part by dangling the possibility that he might become the first president of the new United States government. After all, if the Anti-Federalist–leaning Virginia did not ratify, George Washington would be ineligible. Hancock bit, and the Federalists reeled him on board. Federalists considered Adams's support vital, and they did convince Adams to support the compromise arrangements. But, intriguingly, King did not mention any offers being made to catch him. Adams apparently joined in the arrangement on the basis of the merits of the case. Under the compromise, Federalists pledged to exert their "influence" to have a group of amendments added to the Constitution. In exchange for that pledge, Hancock and Adams would advocate outright, rather than conditional, ratification. Federalists hoped that, with "the weight" of both Hancock and Adams, they could secure ratification.

John Hancock left his sickbed and attended the convention for the first time on January 30, 1788. The next day he dramatically recommended approving the Constitution, but with the understanding that amendments would be added once the new government began functioning. Hancock offered nine amendments. By prearrangement, Adams moved that Hancock's proposals be adopted. Adams focused on the first proposed amendment, which said that "it be explicitly declared that all powers not expressly delegated to Congress, are reserved to the several States." This was, for Adams, the crucial amendment. It would, as much as possible, ensure that the new Constitution would meet the standard he had enunciated in 1785. The Union's frame of government should not be couched in ambiguous language that might be construed in ways that would threaten liberty.

Knowing many Anti-Federalists faulted the proposed Constitution for its failure to include a bill of rights, Adams proclaimed that Hancock's first amendment "appears, to my mind, to be a summary of a bill of rights." In endorsing the compromise, Adams reminded the delegates that, when considering great and controversial issues of government, a person had to show respect for differing views. One had to weigh all the facts and be guided by "mature judgment." He added that if Massachusetts ratified the Constitution with the understanding that amendments would be added, other states would probably follow suit. Thus, the country could reap the immediate benefit of a more vigorous central government while also anticipating that the Constitution would be altered to alleviate the concerns of those who, like himself, had serious reservations about it.

Days later, just before the ratification vote, Adams tried to protect basic liberties even more explicitly. He moved that the proposed amendment limiting the national government to the powers "expressly" delegated to it be expanded by adding: "And that the said Constitution be never construed to authorize Congress to infringe the just liberty of the Press, or the rights of Conscience; or to prevent the people of the United States who are peaceable citizens, from keeping their own arms; or to raise standing armies, unless when necessary for the defence of the United States, or of some one or more of them; or to prevent the people from petitioning in a peaceable and orderly manner, the Federal Legislature, for redress of grievances; or to subject the people to unreasonable searches and seizures of their persons, papers, or possessions." This lengthy addition, which amounted to a bill of rights, reflected Adams's concern that a good constitution must protect the people's liberties. However, after considerable debate, the proposal failed to garner support, and Adams withdrew it.

Even with the backing of Hancock and Adams, the pro-Constitution forces feared they might not win. Their anxiety was justified; the final vote proved agonizingly close. With both Hancock and Adams voting to ratify, Massachusetts approved the Constitution 187 to 168. Leading Federalist delegates conceded that they probably would have failed had they not obtained the support of the famous patriots. Although the vote was tight, once the votes were in, a number of Anti-Federalist delegates said that, since the majority had approved it, they would now support the Constitution.

Adams swung over to the pro-ratification group for several intertwining reasons. He always believed that government must have the power needed to perform its constitutional duties. And no one could deny that the piecemeal efforts to revise the Articles had repeatedly failed—and would probably continue to fail. Even more important, Adams firmly believed that the people had the right to alter or abolish a constitution. And, although the

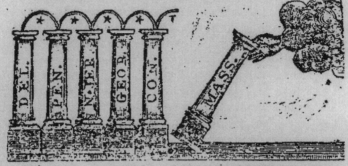

States—like the gen'rous vine fupported live,
The ftrength they gain is from th'embrace they giv
THE FEDERAL PILLARS.

UNITED THEY STAND—DIVIDED FALL.

A veffel arrived at Cape-Ann, after a fhort paf-
fage from Georgia, confirms the pleafing intelligence announced in our laft, that that State has u-
nanimoufly ratified the Federal Conftitution. Thus
is a FIFTH PILLAR added to the glorious fabrick.
May Maffachufetts rear the SIXTH.

As we predicted in our laft, fo it happened—
Monday morning, was ufhered in with the ring-
ing of bells in this metropolis, on account of the
pleafing intelligence received by Saturday night's
mail, that the State of Connecticut had added a
FOURTH PILLAR to that GRAND REPUB-
LICAN SUPERSTRUCTURE, the FEDERAL
CONSTITUTION.

"The Federal Pillars" from the *Massachusetts Sentinel* (January 16, 1788).

framers violated both the Congress's instructions and the instructions of the
Massachusetts legislature, in part by bypassing the amending provisions of
the Articles of Confederation, the Constitution would be subjected to a
thoroughly republican ratifying process. So, if ratified, the new frame of
government would rest on the consent of the governed. But what mattered
most to Adams was the fact that Massachusetts Federalists had agreed to
help add amendments that would, he hoped, wring the ambiguity out of
the Constitution. Moreover, since it seemed certain other states would follow Massachusetts's lead, Adams had good reason to think the new Constitution would be amended to protect the people's liberties.

As he helped move Massachusetts toward approving a Constitution that transformed the nature of America's government, Adams's own life was, unfortunately, also being transformed. On January 17, just over a week after the ratifying convention began deliberations, his son died at the age of thirty-seven. The younger Samuel's health had declined while he was serving in the war, and he returned home to live in semiretirement. Given Samuel Adams's emphasis on fashioning a society and government for the benefit of one's posterity, given his reference to parents hoping their children would outlive them, the loss of his only son devastated Samuel. Some attributed Adams's general silence at the convention to the trauma of his son's death. That probably was not the case, but as of January 1788, Adams's own posterity consisted of his daughter Hannah and her children. The death of Samuel Jr., ironically, provided Samuel and Elizabeth with the greatest financial security they had known in their married life. He willed the certificates he had earned in the war to his father, and they were soon worth approximately $12,000, a huge sum for that day.

At the same time he lost his only son, Samuel was reestablishing a political partnership with John Hancock. Adams's antagonism toward Hancock had been softening, perhaps because Hancock did not exert the determining influence on society Adams thought the first governor might. By the time the new Constitution was proposed in 1787, Samuel and John had reconciled socially. Their political reconciliation stemmed from their similar views on the new Constitution. Elbridge Gerry expressed the crucial point when he remarked that, "with all his foibles," Hancock was "yet attached to the whig cause." Samuel agreed, and soon he and Hancock were once again functioning as a political team.

J. P. Brissot de Warville, a French traveler who visited Boston in July 1788, documented the rapprochement. He observed that Adams "is the best supporter of the party of Governor Hancock." While the Frenchman did not attempt to explain why the two men had formed a close alliance, he offered hints. Although Hancock craved popularity, he still possessed the "spirit of patriotism" he had displayed at the start of the Revolution. Brissot de Warville, who like Chastellux before him found Adams remarkable, also ventured a comment on what motivated Adams. "If ever a man was sincerely an idolater of republicanism," Brissot de Warville maintained, "it is Samuel Adams." The Frenchman marveled that he had never known of any man who so exemplified the characteristics of his stated political persuasion. Adams "has the excess of republican virtues, untainted probity, simplicity, modesty, and, above all, firmness; he will have no capitulation with abuses; he fears as much the despotism of virtue and talents, as the despotism of vice."

Brissot de Warville was right to hearken back to the patriotism of the struggle against Britain. From Adams's perspective, something of a similar struggle went on from the ratification of the new Constitution through the rest of his active political career. Adams had wrestled with the British serpent because he believed it threatened to kill America's liberties. Adams reunited with Hancock because both men, whatever else motivated them, feared the new national government might emulate the British government and attack basic rights. Together they would make Federalists live up to their promises to defang the Constitution by attaching language that would limit the potentially sweeping powers of the national government.

Adams's concerns about the Constitution forced him to reconsider his retirement from national office. He let his name be put forward as a candidate for the United States House of Representatives. In that December 1788 election, Adams was opposed by Fisher Ames, a bright, articulate, but very young lawyer. Adams's supporters, confident of victory, stressed that "this venerable patriot" was an able and experienced politician who would give Massachusetts real weight in the new Congress and also protect the people's economic interests. The young Ames, they said, could not measure up. Adams was depicted as a friend of the poor, and *"if he has a prejudice in his politicks, it leans to the rights and privileges of the common people."* Ames's proponents hammered at the idea that Adams's support for the Constitution was suspect and that their brilliant candidate was no younger than Adams when he first served in the legislature.

The election results proved shocking. Ames did more than win; he beat Adams 445 to 439 in Boston. Adams's backers howled about the voters' ingratitude and poor judgment in spurning the *"American* Cato." However, the results made sense. Bostonians, like the people in America's other major cities, overwhelmingly supported the Constitution. Urbanites of all classes wanted a powerful central government that could promote their economic interests. Since Adams seemed more concerned about shackling the power of the new government than exploiting it, Ames's views on the Constitution more closely matched the views of his new constituents. Also, the low turnout—less than 900 voters in Boston—probably made a real difference. Just five months later, over 1,800 people voted in Boston. In that hotly contested election, Hancock and Adams ran as a team for governor and lieutenant governor, and each amassed more than 1,200 votes, a 2-to-1 victory margin in Boston. Adams took office as lieutenant governor in June 1789 and was annually reelected for the next four years. When Hancock died in October 1793, Adams assumed the duties of governor and then won the 1794 governor's race. He held the governorship until he retired in the spring of 1797.

Even though he lost the race for the House of Representatives in 1788, Adams continued to pursue a twofold objective in national politics. He wanted to make the Constitution a document worth defending because it protected the people's rights. For Adams that required amending it, ideally by limiting the national government to the powers expressly delegated to it. At the same time, he believed in the rule of law. He had, after all, voted to ratify the Constitution. So Adams's dual goal included protecting the Constitution even as he sought to modify it.

In 1789, as Congress considered possible amendments, Adams employed the well-established tactic of using private letters to achieve political ends. He wrote to Richard Henry Lee and Elbridge Gerry, who were both serving in the United States Congress, and laid out the case for supporting alterations. Knowing some Federalists used the argument that the Constitution might be cluttered up with multitudes of special-interest amendments, Adams stressed that no amendments should be added to suit "partial or local considerations." What he sought, Adams said, were amendments that applied to every American. He called, above all, for eliminating the "ambiguous Expressions" in the Constitution that might, in time, be used to subvert liberty. He also stressed that, as much as possible, state sovereignty must be retained because it was the safeguard of the citizens' private and personal rights.

The campaign to amend the Constitution ultimately produced the Bill of Rights, which was added to the Constitution in December 1791. Adams could have gloated, and his political supporters certainly did, that the lengthy amendment he proposed at the Massachusetts ratifying convention contained most of the guarantees found in the Bill of Rights. However, for Adams the crucial Tenth Amendment was defective. Rather than limiting the central government to those powers expressly delegated to it, the amendment merely said that the powers not delegated to the national government were reserved to the states or the people. The failure to include that one word—"expressly"—created the constitutional ambiguity Adams loathed and the opportunity to enlarge national powers he feared. To get it ratified in 1787–88, leading Federalists, including Alexander Hamilton, claimed the Constitution created a limited government with circumscribed powers. However, by 1791, with Hamilton leading the way, nationalists changed their minds and conveniently determined that the Constitution contained "implied" powers. Their argument came under heavy attack and still remains a matter of controversy more than two centuries later. Nevertheless, the proponents of implied powers carried the day.

As the battle over implied powers unfolded, Samuel Adams seemingly confronted a dilemma about accepting or attacking the Constitution that ardent nationalists were twisting into a document more to their liking. However, he had voted for the Constitution, and it had been approved by the people's representatives in ratifying conventions. In addition, as promised by its Massachusetts proponents, the document had been amended to include a Bill of Rights. Adams considered the amendments deficient, but they had been added. Given the fact that the Constitution rested on the consent of the governed, given his firm commitment to the rule of law when the people possessed a constitution that gave them the means to redress perceived grievances, Adams actually did not face a dilemma. He

H. R. Hall engraving after John Johnston's 1795 painting of Governor Samuel Adams. Courtesy of the Frick Art Reference Library.

would support the Union's new government while continuing to keep careful watch lest it turn into a liberty-destroying serpent.

In January 1794, Adams used the occasion of his first address to the General Court as governor of the commonwealth to accentuate the importance of protecting the people's rights. He emphasized his cardinal belief that the people had a duty "to secure the blessings of equal liberty to the present and future generations." Drawing upon Lockean concepts of governments being formed by the mutual consent of people seeking to protect their "natural rights," Adams linked fundamental political principles directly to America's governments. He did more than quote an ideal of the Declaration of Independence, which he rendered as "all men are created equal, and are endowed by their Creator with certain unalienable rights." He asserted that, since the Declaration was "ratified by all the States," it followed that "the doctrine of Liberty and Equality is an article in the political creed of the United States." That was good because, if liberty and equality were missing, a person could not have the necessary "tranquillity of mind" that came from knowing "that his own personal safety and rights are secure." He paid special homage to the Massachusetts Constitution for exemplifying the American political creed by conspicuously promoting liberty and equality. Adams coupled this glorification of liberty and equality with equally emphatic praise for the rule of law under a republican constitution. He stressed that, as governor, "the Constitution must be my rule." He also espoused the philosophy of limited powers by saying he was delighted that the Massachusetts Constitution gave him only limited and circumscribed powers. He added to that pronouncement by describing himself as a mere agent of the people.

Turning his attention to the central government, Adams again coupled protection of freedom with the need for the rule of law. Faced with what he saw as the growing threat from the advocates of implied powers, Adams emphasized that "all powers not vested in Congress, remain in the separate States." Nevertheless, he manifested balance and a commitment to the rule of law by saying that "unremitting caution" should be used to ensure that neither the federal government nor the state governments encroached on the other's constitutional rights. It is doubtful that Adams feared that the states would subvert liberty by somehow overwhelming the central government. Still, his words reiterated the fundamental point that both the Massachusetts and the United States Constitutions must be protected. The rule of law must prevail.

Samuel Adams's response to the Whiskey Rebellion that occurred later in 1794 demonstrated his commitment to defending constitutional government. Angered by what they considered an outrageously unfair national excise tax, people in western Pennsylvania terrorized tax collectors, stopped mail deliveries, and disrupted court proceedings. By this time, national political parties were forming. Leaders of the emerging Federalist Party, which championed the ideal of implied powers and building a vigorous national government, proclaimed that the anarchy in Pennsylvania must be stopped. President Washington agreed, and the national government dispatched a huge army of more than ten thousand to crush the uprising. By the time the army arrived, though, the rebellion had evaporated. These developments gave those who opposed the expansion of national powers an opportunity to tar the government and the Federalist Party. The opponents of Federalists went by various names. In Massachusetts they called themselves "Republican Federalists" and "Real Republicans"; nationally, they came to be known as the Democratic Republicans. Samuel Adams was seen as the group's leader in Massachusetts, while Thomas Jefferson was the acknowledged head of the emerging national party. Jefferson sarcastically dismissed the Whiskey Rebellion with the airy observation that "an insurrection was announced, and proclaimed and armed against, but could never be found." Adams responded differently. He voiced the same ideals he had articulated when confronting Shays's Rebellion. In an official address, Governor Adams observed that the whiskey "insurrection" challenged "an act of the Federal Government." That was unacceptable because, however much people might detest the legislation, it "is constitutionally an act of the people, and our Constitutions provide a safe and easy method to redress any real grievances." He trumpeted that idea even more loudly when he stated what, for him, was the fundamental principle of democratic republicanism: "no people can be more free [than] under a Constitution established by their own voluntary compact, and exercised by men appointed by their own frequent suffrages." Given that, Adams bluntly asked, "what excuse then can there be for forcible opposition to the laws?" If real grievances existed, the people's freely elected representatives would find "a constitutional remedy." These pronouncements made it clear why Governor Adams praised the vigorous actions taken by President Washington and why Adams also asserted that those measures were "supported by the virtue of citizens of every description."

Adams's commitment to supporting a republican constitution amendable by the people led him, over time, to embrace the Constitution more warmly. Adams, an acknowledged master politician, had always been sensitive to the tone as well as the precise meaning of words. In the early 1790s, he was fastidious about describing the central government as the "Federal Government." Doing so underscored his commitment to preserving the ideal of state sovereignty as much as he could. But in his fall 1795 thanksgiving proclamation, Governor Adams asked the people to thank God "that he hath in his Good Providence united the several States under a National Compact formed by themselves, whereby they may defend themselves against external Enemies, and maintain Peace and Harmony with each other."

By the time he addressed the General Court in January 1796, Adams lavished real praise on the United States Constitution. He stressed that the United States and Massachusetts Constitutions were founded upon the same principles, including "the great fundamental political truth that all power is derived from the people." Later that same year, again speaking to the legislators, Adams referred to the Constitution's preamble ideal of establishing a more perfect Union and invoked what for him was a sacred political concern, the duty to posterity. He asserted that the American people had a duty to preserve the Union "and transmit it unbroken to posterity." He clasped the Constitution even more firmly by saying it was also in the people's "lasting interest" as well as "their public safety and welfare" to preserve the more perfect Union. That fall in the traditional thanksgiving proclamation, Adams again celebrated the fact that both the state and national constitutions possessed the vital ingredients of democratic republicanism. Both constitutions were "formed by ourselves, and administered by Men of our own *free Election*."

Adams's increasing praise of the Constitution reflected political reality. Once the Bill of Rights had been added, no wise politician would dare suggest the Constitution be overthrown. Still, the question of adding yet more amendments remained very much alive. So, even as he embraced the Constitution more firmly, Adams invited the people to consider changing it. In the 1796 address in which he praised the Constitution, he also opined that America's Revolutionary governments must be considered *"experiments"* and "wisdom" dictated that the people should often think about "first principles." If they discovered their rights being undermined by either the state or the national constitution, the people should alter the offending document. Looking again to the needs of posterity, he prophetically warned that if either the federal or state governments "infringed" on the other's "Constitutional rights" for any period of time, America might eventually experience "such convulsions as may shake the political ground upon which we now happily stand." The revolutionary politician never lost his zeal for trying to ensure that the Constitution would be a bulwark "to secure the blessings of equal liberty to the present and future generations," not a potential political serpent.

Although he continued to seek alterations to the United States Constitution, Adams did not think the Massachusetts Constitution, which kept earning not only his but general approbation, was in any way materially defective. As a state executive, Adams focused on what he considered crucial issues for promoting liberty and equality and securing them for posterity. He demonstrated his concern about protecting basic rights—and his ability to acknowledge personal error—by how he dealt with the question of selecting replacement presidential electors. In 1796 the General Court passed a resolution allowing the state's presidential electors to replace any of their number who might die or resign. Adams signed the resolution the day he received it but soon reconsidered. As best he could, he erased his name from the resolution. The next day he explained his actions. Saying he had approved the resolution "prematurely," he maintained that permitting electors to fill vacancies in their own ranks "appears to be dangerous to the Liberties of the People, and ought not to form a precedent in a free government." He urged the legislators to find a way to deal with the problem that was more consistent with the spirit of Massachusetts's republican government. Two days later, Adams returned to the issue by emphasizing that he sought to avoid establishing "a dangerous Precedent." He added that if the legislators thought differently, he would, having honestly admitted his error in signing the resolve, be content with their decision. Adams was up to old tricks. He was clearly attempting to force the legislators to rescind their resolution by placing them on the wrong side of a basic rights issue. He failed to move the legislators.

As governor, Adams also tried to convince the legislators to follow the principle of equality when it came to staffing the militia. Over the years, the Massachusetts legislators had crafted laws exempting large numbers of men from serving in the state militia. The exemptions, as such exceptions normally do, favored the wealthier and more prominent. In 1797, as he prepared to end his public service, Governor Adams tried to call the members of the General Court back to first principles. He asked them to eliminate those parts of the militia statutes that created what he labeled "invidious exemptions." Adams proclaimed that militia service "should equally apply to all the active citizens, within the age prescribed by law." The legislators did not share his ardor for the equality that would accompany universal militia service. They did not recast the militia laws.

In addition to continuing his lifelong goal of protecting the people's essential rights, as governor, Adams continued his quest to promote virtue. As he grew older and contemplated facing God's final judgment, Adams alluded ever more frequently to the importance of religion in shaping a virtuous citizenry. He often pointed out that the state constitution said public officials should promote piety, religion, and morality because these virtues were essential to maintaining free republican government. But, as he had since the days before independence was declared, Adams continued to single out education as the linchpin to attaining a virtuous republican society.

The four inaugural addresses Adams gave as governor when opening the General Court sessions were, in essence, state of the state messages. In each address, Adams stressed education's vital role and reiterated ideas and even language stretching back to the early 1780s when he headed Boston's education committee. Given his repeated appeals about implementing the constitution's call for cherishing education, the returning members of the General Court probably smiled knowingly when, in his last state of the state address in 1797, Governor Adams observed that he had "frequently" reminded the legislators of "the great importance of education from town schools through the university." And he proceeded to do it yet again. Education should do more than promote "the pursuit of useful science." It should serve a moral purpose by impressing on children's minds "a strong sense of the duties they owe to their God, their instructors, and each other."

Samuel Adams wanted to ensure that the public education system would be based on the essential principles of liberty and equality. His concern for equality even led him to question the value of academies, privately run institutions that typically prepared youths for university studies. The 1790s marked a great period of academy founding in Massachusetts, and Adams's constant reminders to the General Court about its constitutional duty to promote education probably helped fuel that development. The General

Court typically provided a land grant to help establish an academy. Adams might have been expected to applaud the rise of academies; instead, he viewed them questioningly. He told the General Court that the dramatic expansion of academies could injure the town grammar schools, which provided education to rich and poor on an equal basis. The problem with the academies, said Adams, was that in general only "the more wealthy" could attend. If the wealthy focused their attention and influence on developing such schools, support for the town schools might diminish. If that happened, useful learning and a sense of social cohesion "may cease to be so equally and universally disseminated." As a group, Massachusetts's legislators did not share Adams's assessment. They responded to his pleas by preparing a lengthy report on academies. It did not, however, emphasize the need for a fully integrated and egalitarian system of public education at the secondary level; rather, the legislators' main concern was ensuring that academies were created throughout the state and received support in the form of state land grants. Despite his efforts, it would take decades for Massachusetts to create the system of free, universal education Adams deemed so essential to preserving republicanism. Still, by the time he left public office in 1797, Boston and Massachusetts had, in no small part through his efforts, tremendously expanded the educational opportunities available to all children.

During the 1790s, Samuel Adams's work protecting the people's rights and helping build a virtuous republican society became enmeshed in the partisan political wrangling that grew more vicious over the decade. As acting governor and then as governor and leader of the Massachusetts Democratic Republicans, Samuel Adams functioned as a lightning rod for Federalist Party anger. When the annual April elections neared, the Federalist press bristled with increasingly virulent, partisan invective. Adams came under widespread attack. Old charges were recycled. Critics dredged up his failures as a tax collector, his periodic fallings-out with John Hancock, and his supposed animosity toward Washington. The voters heard that Adams was much too friendly with Revolutionary France, especially when the vital interests of the two nations clashed. Opponents lambasted him for overstepping his bounds by using his position as governor to speak out in January 1796 against the immensely unpopular commercial treaty John Jay had negotiated with Great Britain. Now in his seventies, Adams was described as too old and infirm to function as governor. These kinds of charges were routinely leveled in a state that was increasingly becoming a bastion of Federalist Party strength.

Despite the political mudslinging, Samuel Adams easily won reelection in 1795 and 1796. He did fail in his effort to win election as a presidential elector for Thomas Jefferson in 1796, but then the other chief candidate for president was a native son of Massachusetts, Samuel's cousin John Adams. And given Massachusetts's voting traditions, Samuel likely could have continued to occupy the governor's chair. But he was approaching his seventy-fifth birthday, and that made him think about retiring to private life. Events soon turned his thoughts into conviction. In September 1796, President Washington said he would retire. That announcement convinced Samuel that he too should finally leave public office. In January 1797, he informed the General Court that he would not allow his name to be offered as a candidate. He displayed the sense of humor he was noted for in personal life by wryly alluding to the attacks on his age. "The infirmities of age," he observed, "render me an unfit person in my own eyes, and very probably in the opinion of others, to continue in this station." He noted that he had served Massachusetts "in various stations to the best of my ability, and I hope with general approbation." Having grown old in the service of Massachusetts, the revolutionary politician voiced his sense of duty by adding that "when released from the burdens of my public station, I shall not forget my country.—Her welfare and happiness, her peace and prosperity, her liberty and independence will always have a great share in the best wishes of my heart."

Epilogue: "The Patriarch of Liberty"

*S*amuel Adams always enjoyed children and in retirement spent many hours with his grandchildren, his posterity. He also loved reminiscing about the Revolutionary days. Perhaps he thought occasionally of how, years before, John Adams had his son John Quincy, then age eighteen, carry a letter to Samuel. John's letter reminded Samuel that when John Quincy was but a child, Samuel had taken him onto the Boston Common "to see with detestation the British troops, and with pleasure the Boston militia." John indicated the lessons had not been lost. John Quincy, his father said, "thinks of . . . peace and civil life" and wanted to pursue the law. Samuel had responded, "That *Child* whom I led by the Hand with a particular Design, I find is now become a promising youth." "If I was instrumental at that Time of enkindling the Sparks of Patriotism in his tender Heart," Samuel added, "it will add to my Consolation in the latest Hour."

As Samuel enjoyed his posterity and reminisced about the Revolution, he and Elizabeth no longer had money worries. The 1788 bequest of Samuel Jr. had given them financial security, and wise investments in land increased their wealth. By the mid-1790s the Adamses could accurately be called "rich." Wealth did not change Samuel's plain style of living. He exhibited the simple republican frugality for which he had long been famous. He still dressed plainly in the style of the Revolutionary era. The Adamses did not keep a carriage. Their home suggested that in some ways plain living could blend into indifference. The family's frame house on Water Street was decidedly weather-beaten. Only old-timers could attest to its once having been yellow. As the century turned, Samuel got his earthly affairs in order. The last vestiges of the old family homestead, which the British had trashed during the war, were sold off in 1802. Samuel had already made a will that revealed his love and respect for Elizabeth, his dearest Betsy. He made Elizabeth and her brother, his daughter Hannah's husband, his executors.

Samuel always considered his cousin John a friend and in 1797 wrote to President Adams as "Your Old and unvaried Friend." John responded in kind. Nevertheless, Samuel was pleased when John lost the election of 1800 because Thomas Jefferson replaced him. Jefferson offered a revealing tribute to the man he praised as the one person who might be called the helmsman of the American Revolution. When he took office, the new president delivered a justifiably famous inaugural address that invited all Americans of whatever political party to celebrate what united them: a commitment to the same fundamental political values, above all a commitment to majority rule and the rule of law under the Constitution. But he also added that all Americans "will bear in mind this sacred principle, that though the will of the majority is in all cases to prevail, that will, to be rightful, must be reasonable; that the minority possess their equal rights, which equal laws must protect, and to violate would be oppression." Jefferson forwarded a copy to Samuel and said: "in mediating the matter of that address, I often asked myself, is this exactly in the spirit of the patriarch of liberty, Samuel Adams? Is it as he would express it? Will he approve of it?" Jefferson phrased the ideal of majority rule tempered by reasonable consideration of minority rights more elegantly than Samuel Adams had, but, as Jefferson suggested, Adams had articulated and lived by those ideals. Samuel approved.

President Jefferson, who profoundly respected Adams from their early days together in the Continental Congress onward, added that he had recently received reports of Samuel being "avoided, insulted, frowned on." Jefferson observed that all he could think of when he received those reports was "'Father, forgive them, for they know not what they do.'" The new president stressed that he counted on receiving Adams's wise counsel. Samuel responded with thanks but added, "it is not in my power dear friend to give you council." Still, "though an Old Man cannot advise you, he can give you a Blessing."

Even though Adams had retired from politics, the Jeffersonian Republicans, as they were now known, found ways to have him defend what he had called "the principles of Democratic Republicanism." In 1802, Boston publishers who had long supported Adams and Jefferson printed a series of four letters Samuel and John Adams had exchanged a dozen years before. John initiated a philosophical discussion by asking, "is the millennium commencing?" In his two lengthy responses, Samuel offered commentary that, when matched with the words and deeds of his long political life, shows how consistently he strove to protect constitutional liberties and promote liberty for posterity. Samuel maintained that "the Love of Liberty is interwoven in the soul of Man, and can never be totally extinguished." To protect their liberty, the people needed a republican form of government that possessed "a mixture of Powers to check the human passions" and stop them from rushing to extremes. When John suggested that in a republic "the People have an essential *share* in the sovereignty," Samuel gently but firmly chided him by asking, "Is not the *whole* sovereignty, my friend, essentially in the People?" For Samuel, what made America's constitutions magnificent was the fact that the people had created them and under those constitutions the people had the power, through frequent elections, to retain or replace their public servants.

Although he glorified the American constitutions, Samuel Adams believed that even the best man-made constitution would contain defects and so something more was necessary to preserve good republican government. That something was a virtuous education. He proclaimed that "to renovate the Age," leaders must realize "the importance of educating their *little boys,* and *girls."* Education must be "universal"; it should draw the rich and the poor together and make no distinction among them. He wanted all children to learn the importance of "the fear, and Love of the Deity, and universal Phylanthropy" as well as love of country and "the Art of *self* government, without which they can never act a wise part in the Government of Societys, great, or small." Samuel again lauded Massachusetts's ancestors for having founded an educational system "by which means Wisdom, Knowledge, and Virtue have been generally diffused among the people." It had enabled the people "to form and establish a civil constitution calculated for the preservation of their rights and liberties."

Samuel Adams's last known letter revealed how he continued to see morality as essential to America and how, at the same time, he defended religious liberty. In the fall of 1802 he wrote to another old Revolutionary, Thomas Paine. While praising him for his great work in bringing about the decision for American independence, Adams chastised Paine for reportedly having undertaken "a defence of infidelity." The people of New England, Adams insisted, would never turn their backs on God. However, Samuel also maintained that "we ought to think ourselves happy in the enjoyment of opinion, without the danger of persecution by civil or ecclesiastical law." And speaking of the need for honesty and civility in public life, he stressed that "neither religion nor liberty can long subsist in the tumult of altercation, and amidst the noise and violence of faction." Those words reflected Adams's anger about President Jefferson being "calumniated for his liberal sentiments" and being libeled "without the least shadow of proof." The revolutionary politician could retire from public office, but he could never fully retire from politics.

As 1802 turned into 1803, friends noticed that Samuel, now eighty, was growing weaker. He ventured out of doors less and less often. What Adams had called "the latest Hour" came on Sunday, October 2, 1803. The next edition of Boston's *Independent Chronicle,* the city's leading Jeffersonian Republican paper, carried a black bordered announcement: "SAMUEL ADAMS Is Dead!" The editors bemoaned the loss of "the consistent and inflexible Patriot and Republican" who was "our *political parent."* The man they called "the Father of the American Revolution" had been, they stressed, "the undeviating friend of civil and religious liberty." A week later the editors filled their front page and much of the second with a biographical tribute written by Judge James Sullivan, an old friend and political ally. Saying he had produced "but a gazette sketch" of Adams, Sullivan asserted that "to give his history at length, would be to give an history of the American revolution."

The praise these Jeffersonian Republicans draped over Samuel Adams sounds excessive. Yet the Reverend William Bentley of Salem, a man who had had very harsh things to say about Adams, expressed remarkably similar thoughts in his diary just one day after Adams died. Observing that Adams's "religion & manner were from our ancestors" and that he "was a puritan in his manners always," Rev. Bentley asserted that "No man contributed more towards our revolution." Samuel Adams "had an impenetrable secrecy, & a great popular influence by his inflexibility & undaunted courage." He "preserved through life in his Republican principles without any conformity to parties, influence or times." And Adams's politics, said Bentley, rested on his beliefs that "rulers should have little, the people much" and that "the rank of the rulers is from the good they do, & the difference among the people only from personal virtue. No entailments, not privileges. An open world for genius & industry."

As the tributes to Samuel Adams poured forth, Jeffersonian Republicans took umbrage when nine United States senators refused to wear black crepe in honor of Adams and Edmund Pendleton, who had also recently died. One of the nine was John Quincy Adams, the now grown child Samuel had taken to the Boston Common to scorn the redcoats and salute the local militia. Even in death Samuel Adams could not escape the growing "noise and violence" of party politics.

Samuel Adams ran his political race for more than half a century, and he stood in the political glare from the mid-1760s until the dawn of the nineteenth century. He was arguably America's first professional and first modern politician. He made politics his lifelong occupation, and he pioneered ways of drawing the people into the political process. His call for installing a gallery in the Massachusetts House, his leadership of mass meetings, his regular use of newspapers to distribute propaganda, his development and use of committees of correspondence, and his personal interaction with an extraordinary number of ordinary people all helped transform the political process. More than any other American, he did merit the title "the Father of the American Revolution."

Adams's lengthy political life, as his contemporaries often emphasized, was notable for its philosophical consistency. He acted on the belief that everyone had duties to posterity, above all that of promoting and protecting liberty and equality. Reasonable people would, he argued, protect the rights of others lest their own rights be trampled. But, following John Locke as he so often did, Adams observed that humans were not always reasonable, and so they needed constitutions—republican constitutions—to protect their fundamental rights. Early in life he determined that a constitution that protected the people's liberty and provided them with the means to seek legal redress should be steadfastly safeguarded. And he always trumpeted the view that the people, the legitimate source of power, should keep a watchful eye on their public servants. Yet, he also stressed that the people should treat their public servants with decency, and he insisted that the people must obey the laws. Indeed, the revolutionary politician argued that even unconstitutional laws should be opposed through legal means. He never wavered from a commitment to the rule of law. If the people had the constitutional means to obtain redress of grievances, they must, he insisted, not resort to violence. Open rebellion, as Locke had observed, was justified *only* if tyrants gave an injured people no alternative but to fight or be enslaved.

As he helped nudge America toward independence, Adams added a consuming desire to build a virtuous society to his lifelong quest of protecting constitutional liberties. He did that because he believed that God intended people to live under a republican form of government and that, to preserve that government, the people must be virtuous. Over the last two decades of his political career, Samuel Adams labored to convince the people to embrace republican virtues, and he placed extraordinary faith in the ability of education to produce a virtuous society. His words and deeds marked him as a true proponent of public education for all children, for posterity.

Although born to a life of promise, Samuel Adams was in his forties before it seemed that promise might be fulfilled. He finally realized it by devoting himself to a political life built on the premise that a citizen had a duty "to secure the blessings of equal liberty to the present and future generations." He can fairly be faulted for shoddy tax collecting, for winking at his own plural officeholding, and perhaps for how he mishandled the letter from the congressmen who wanted to blackmail Congress. But, as his harshest critics admitted, even if backhandedly, he was a remarkably upright man and politician who most certainly was motivated neither by a desire to enrich himself nor by a desire for popularity. What he did desire, and most ardently, was to be remembered by posterity as a defender of liberty.

In the midst of the War for American Independence, America's revolutionary politician had summed up his ideals of public service when he observed, "It would be the Glory of this Age, to find Men having no ruling Passion but the Love of their Country, and ready to render her the most arduous and important Services with the Hope for no other Reward in this Life than the Esteem of their virtuous Fellow Citizens." It was the glory of Samuel Adams that his life so closely matched that high standard.

Selected Bibliography

Major Primary Sources

This biography is rooted in an analysis of primary sources. Harry A. Cushing, ed., *The Writings of Samuel Adams,* 4 vols. (New York, 1904–8), is essential but less than complete. Cushing could not include every important thing Adams wrote because Samuel occasionally destroyed correspondence, as he put it, to protect his friends. In addition, credible eyewitness reports indicate that many Adams papers disappeared after his death, some falling prey to autograph hunters. Moreover, because Adams followed the established practice of using pen names for the newspaper essays he composed and because some political documents were multiauthored efforts, no editor could identify and publish all that he wrote. However, Cushing added to the inherent problems, especially by limiting himself to materials found in the Samuel Adams Papers (hereafter SA Papers) housed in the New York Public Library. Since that collection does not include *anything* Adams penned before 1764, his pre-Revolutionary era writings cannot be found in *The Writings.* In addition, if Adams material had already been published elsewhere, Cushing often merely noted that rather than including the item in *The Writings.* Finally, following what was then a common editorial practice, Cushing sought to publish only the writings, not the papers, of Samuel Adams..Thus Cushing excluded letters written to Samuel Adams even if they were part of the SA Papers. So, while Cushing let only a few transcription errors slip by, he did not even include all of the writings—some of real importance—found in the SA Papers. (I worked with the microfilm edition of the SA Papers available from Scholarly Resources.)

Fortunately, some of the deficiencies in *The Writings* can be circumvented. Wells, Hosmer, and Miller—authors of Adams biographies noted below—each identified some of Adams's pre-Revolutionary writings. In addition, volumes of particular value because they contain Adams letters Cushing skipped or correspondence sent to Adams include: Massachusetts Historical Society, *Warren-Adams Letters,* 2 vols. (Boston, 1917, 1925); Richard Frothingham, *Life and Times of Joseph Warren* (Boston, 1865); Richard Henry Lee, ed., *Life of Arthur Lee,* 2 vols. (Boston, 1829); James T. Austin, *The Life of Elbridge Gerry,* 2 vols. (Boston, 1828–29); Charles Francis Adams, ed., *The Works of John Adams . . .,* 10 vols. (Boston, 1850–56); C. Harvey Gardiner, ed., *A Study in Dissent: The Warren-Gerry Correspondence, 1776–1792* (Carbondale, Ill., 1968); Edmund C. Burnett, ed., *Letters of Members of the Continental Congress,* 8 vols. (Washington, D.C., 1921–36); Paul H. Smith, ed., *Letters of Delegates to Congress 1774–1789,* 25 vols. (Washington, D.C., 1976–98), which is available in CD-ROM format issued by Historical Database. (The collections edited by Burnett and by Smith are especially valuable for correcting the erroneous claim—contained in *The Writings* and elsewhere—that Adams authored the important 1778 propaganda piece signed "An American.") An examination of the SA Papers yielded additional vital material, most especially letters Samuel received from his second wife. In addition, since he corresponded with numerous people during the era of the American Revolution, many items related to Adams can be found in manuscript collections and in the published papers of many leading figures of that era.

Government publications that are important for uncovering Adams's role in Massachusetts political bodies include the volumes commonly known as the Boston Town Records. For this study, the most important were: *A Report of the Record Commissioners of the City of Boston containing Boston Town Records 1700 to 1728* (Boston, 1883); *A Report of the Record Commissioners of the City of Boston, containing the Boston Town Records from 1729 to 1742* (Boston, 1885); *A Report of the Record Commissioners of the City of Boston, containing the Boston Town Records, 1742 to 1757* (Boston, 1885); *A Report of the Record Commissioners of the City of Boston, containing the Boston Town Records, 1758 to 1769* (Boston, 1886); *A Report of the Record Commissioners of the City of Boston, containing the Boston Town Records, 1770 through 1777* (Boston, 1887); *A Report of the Record Commissioners of the City of Boston, containing the Boston Town Records, 1778 to 1783* (Boston, 1895); *A Volume of the Records relating to the Early History of Boston containing Boston Town Records, 1784 to 1796* (Boston, 1903). Although not a government publication, Robert F. Seybolt's *Town Officials of Colonial Boston 1634–1775* (Cambridge, Mass., 1939) is based on Boston town records. Descriptions of the duties of individual posts can be found in Samuel Freeman, *The Town Officer* . . . (Portland, Mass., 1791).

The pre-Revolution journals of the Massachusetts House of Representatives should be consulted in the Historical Society of Massachusetts facsimile reprint editions, which contain instructive introductions. See *Journals of the House of Representatives of Massachusetts* [for 1715–1779], 55 vols., totaling 65 parts (Boston, 1919–90). On the extralegal gatherings that effectively superseded the colonial legislature, see *Journals of the Provincial Congress of Massachusetts in 1774 and 1775, and of the Committee of Safety* . . . (Boston, 1838). The relevant later house records, examined via the microfiche publication of the Evans bibliography cited below, are much more truncated and thus less informative than the earlier house journals. The journals of the Massachusetts Senate for the 1780s when Adams served in that body are in manuscript and are so skimpy they do not even contain any roll call vote information. The scattered reports on 1780s General Court proceedings occasionally contained in contemporary media publications are similarly too skimpy to be of real help. The official Massachusetts records of constitutional conventions Adams attended are contained in *Journal of the Convention for Framing a Constitution of Government for the State of Massachusetts* . . . (Boston, 1832) and *Debates and Proceedings in the Convention of the Commonwealth of Massachusetts Held in the Year 1788* (Boston, 1856). For Adams's work as a congressman, the basic primary source is Worthington C. Ford et al., eds., *Journals of the Continental Congress, 1774–1789*, 34 vols. (Washington, D.C., 1904–37).

Numerous collections of official correspondence, official political documents, and political tracts are of special importance for understanding Adams's efforts and actions in Massachusetts. In addition such works, like others cited in this bibliography, often contain introductions, headnotes, and analytical footnotes that are especially useful. Important collections include: Edward Channing and Archibald C. Coolidge, eds., *The Barrington-Bernard Correspondence and Illustrative Matter 1760–1770* (Cambridge, Mass., 1912); Francis S. Drake, ed., *Tea Leaves* (Boston, 1884); Frederic Kidder, *History of the Boston Massacre, March 5, 1770* (Albany, 1870); Alan Bradford, ed., *Speeches of the Governors of Massachusetts 1765–1775 . . .* (Boston, 1818); Oliver M. Dickerson, comp., *Boston under Military Rule (1768–1769) as Revealed in A Journal of the Times* (Boston, 1936); "Proceedings of the North End Caucus," in *The Life of Colonel Paul Revere,* by Elbridge H. Goss, 2 vols. (Boston, 1891), 2: 635–44; *Letters to the Ministry from Governor Bernard, General Gage, and Commodore Hood* (Boston, 1769); Philip S. Foner, ed., *The Democratic-Republican Societies, 1790–1800* (Westport, Conn., 1976); Robert J. Taylor et al., eds., *Papers of John Adams,* 10 vols. to date (Cambridge, Mass., 1977–); L. Kinvin Worth and Hiller B. Zobel, eds., *Legal Papers of John Adams,* 3 vols. (Boston, 1965); Oscar Handlin and Mary Handlin, eds., *The Popular Sources of Political Authority: Documents on the Massachusetts Constitution of 1780* (Cambridge, Mass., 1966); *Law in Colonial Massachusetts 1630–1800,* Publications of The Colonial Society of Massachusetts, vol. 62 (Boston, 1984); Albert Matthews, "The Solemn League and Covenant, 1774," in *Transactions 1915–1916,* Colonial Society of Massachusetts (Boston, 1917), 103–22; Robert J. Taylor, ed., *Massachusetts, Colony to Commonwealth: Documents on the Formation of Its Constitution, 1775–1780* (Chapel Hill, N.C., 1961); Clarence E. Carter, comp. and ed., *The Correspondence of General Thomas Gage . . . 1763–1775,* 2 vols. (New Haven, Conn., 1931–33); John P. Kaminski and Gaspare J. Saladino, eds., *Ratification of the Constitution by the States: Massachusetts,* vols. 4–7 of *The Documentary History of the Ratification of the Constitution* (hereafter *DHRC*), (Madison, Wisc., 1997–2001).

More general collections of political correspondence, political documents, or political tracts also proved essential. Works of this nature include Merrill Jensen, ed., *English Historical Documents: American Colonial Documents to 1776* (London, 1955); Edmund S. Morgan, ed., *Prologue to Revolution: Sources and Documents on the Stamp Act Crisis* (Chapel Hill, N.C., 1959); Bernard Bailyn, ed., *Pamphlets of the American Revolution 1750–1776,* 1 vol. to date (Cambridge, Mass., 1965–); Merrill Jensen, ed., *Constitutional Documents and Records, 1776-1787,* vol. 1 of *DHRC* (Madison, Wisc., 1976); Edgar E. Hume, ed., *General Washington's Correspondence concerning the Society of the Cincinnati* (Baltimore, 1941).

Instructive analysis offered by non–Americans, ranging from private travelers to ambassadors, who dealt with Adams can be found in: Marquis de Chastellux, *Travels in North America in the Years 1780, 1781, and 1782,* trans. and ed. Howard C. Rice Jr., 2 vols. (Chapel Hill, N.C., 1963); J. P. Brissot de Warville, *New Travels in the United States of America* (London, 1792); Mary A. Giunta et al., eds., *The Emerging Nation: A Documentary History of the Foreign Relations of the United States under the Articles of Confederation, 1780–1789,* 3 vols. (Washington, D.C., 1996).

Relevant contemporary diaries, correspondence, and other documentary accounts that did not focus on Adams include Anne Hulton, *Letters of a Loyalist Lady: Being the Letters of Anne Hulton, Sister of Henry Hulton, Commissioner of Customs at Boston, 1767–1776* (Cambridge, Mass., 1927); L. H. Butterfield, ed., *Diary and Autobiography of John Adams,* 4 vols. (Boston, 1961); Anne Rowe Cunningham, ed., *Letters and Diary of John Rowe Boston Merchant 1759–1762, 1764–1779*

(Boston, 1903); William Duane, ed., *Extracts from the Diary of Christopher Marshall, .
. . 1774–1781* (Albany, N.Y., 1877); L. H. Butterfield, ed., *Adams Family Corre-
spondence [1761–1778]*, 2 vols. (Boston, 1963); Abram E. Brown, *John Hancock: His
Book* (Boston, 1898); Charles R. King, ed., *The Life and Correspondence of Rufus
King*, 6 vols. (New York, 1894–1900); Frank Moore, ed., *The Diary of the Revolution*
(Hartford, Conn., 1876); Leonard W. Labaree et al., eds., *The Papers of Benjamin
Franklin*, 36 vols. to date (New Haven, 1959–); Thomas Jefferson Randolph, *Mem-
oirs, Correspondence, and Miscellanies from the Papers of Thomas Jefferson*, 4 vols. (Char-
lottesville, Va., 1829); Paul L. Ford, ed., *The Writings of Thomas Jefferson*, 10 vols.
(New York, 1892–99); Julian P. Boyd et al., eds., *The Papers of Thomas Jefferson*, 28
vols. to date (Princeton, N.J., 1950–); William Bentley, *The Diary of William Bentley,
D.D.: Pastor of the East Church Salem, Massachusetts*, ed. authority of the Essex Insti-
tute, 4 vols. (Salem, Mass., 1905–14); Peter O. Hutchinson, ed., *The Diary and Letters of His Excellency Thomas Hutchinson, Esq.*, 2 vols. (London, 1883–86). A unique
and extraordinarily significant eyewitness account of aspects of the anti-tea activities of 1773 is available in L. F. S. Upton, "Proceedings of Ye Body Respecting the
Tea," *William and Mary Quarterly* (hereafter *WMQ*) 22 (April 1965): 287–300.

Histories, or focused commentary, produced by people who knew Adams and
who worked with or against him are invaluable. The analysis of three men who
detested Samuel and his politics are particularly revealing. For Thomas Hutchinson,
see his *The History of the Colony and Providence of Massachusetts-Bay*, ed. Lawrence S.
Mayo, 3 vols. (Cambridge, Mass., 1936), which should be used in conjunction with
Catherine B. Mayo, ed., "Additions to Thomas Hutchinson's 'History of Massachusetts Bay,'" *American Antiquarian Society Proceedings* 59, part 1 (April, 1949): 11–74
and Thomas Hutchinson, *The History of the Providence of Massachusetts Bay, from 1749
to 1774 . . .*, ed. John Hutchinson (London, 1828). Peter Oliver's colorful invective
appears in Douglas Adair and John A. Schutz, eds., *Peter Oliver's Origin and Progress
of the American Rebellion: A Tory View*, rev. ed. (Stanford, Calif., 1967). For the views
of Joseph Galloway, see his *Historical and Political Reflections on the Rise and Progress
of the American Rebellion* (London, 1780); and Thomas Balch, ed., *The Examination of
Joseph Galloway, Esq. by a Committee of the House of Commons* (Philadelphia, 1855).
Of the contemporary pro-Revolution historians, the most important for this work
were William Gordon, *The History of the Rise, Progress, and Establishment, of the Independence of the United Sates of America*, 4 vols. (London, 1788); and Mercy Otis Warren, *History of the Rise, Progress and Termination of the American Revolution interspersed
with Biographical, Political and Moral Observations*, ed. Lester H. Cohen, 2 vols. (Indi-
anapolis, 1989; originally published in 3 vols., Boston, 1805).

Contemporary newspapers yielded a wide range of crucial information such as
election returns, commentary, and descriptions of events. While newspapers published in other areas were occasionally consulted for material on specific topics, the
most useful newspapers were all published in Boston. In order of their founding
date, they include *Boston News-Letter*, 1704–76; *Boston Gazette*, 1719–98; *Boston
Post-Boy*, 1734–75; *Boston Evening-Post*, 1735–75; *The Independent Advertiser*,
1748–1749; *Boston Chronicle*, 1767–1770; *Independent Chronicle*, 1776–1804+; *Massachusetts Centinel*, 1784–90; *Columbian Centinel*, 1790–1804+. *Boston Magazine*
(1783–86) contains reports of some of the proceedings of the General Court, but,
as noted, the coverage is thin. David O. Murdoch, ed., *Rebellion in America: A Con-

temporary British Viewpoint, 1765–1783 (Santa Barbara, Calif., 1979) provides fac-simile reprintings of the sections of the *Annual Register* that dealt with American issues.

A wide variety of nonserial contemporary publications were examined by using the American Antiquarian Society microfiche edition of works in the Evans Collection. The guides and indexes to this irreplaceable source include Charles Evans, Clifford K. Shipton, and Roger P. Bristol, eds., *American Bibliography*, 14 vols. (Chicago and Worcester, Mass., 1903–59); Clifford K. Shipton and James E. Mooney, *National Index of American Imprints through 1800: The Short-Title Evans*, 2 vols. (Worcester, Mass., 1969); Roger P. Bristol, *Supplement to Charles Evans' American Bibliography* (Charlottesville, Va., 1970); Roger P. Bristol, *Index to Supplement to Charles Evans' American Bibliography* (Charlottesville, Va., 1971).

The Biographers' Samuel Adams

In the first half of the nineteenth century, from the time James Sullivan's glowing obituary appeared in the *Independent Chronicle* in 1803, Samuel Adams was often depicted as *the* hero of the movement for independence and second only to Washington in the overall struggle to win independence from Great Britain. Adams's less-than-ardent support for the Constitution of 1787, however, was typically seen as a flaw or a lapse that required explanation. Although he did not produce an individual Adams biography, by midcentury the extraordinarily influential historian George Bancroft had set the tone in his *History of the United States, from the Discovery of the American Continent*, 10 vols. (Boston, 1834–74). Bancroft's Adams figured prominently as a highly influential hero of the quest for American independence. Other authors of the day echoed that interpretation. So William V. Wells, Adams's great-grandson, was not breaking new ground when he published his laudatory *The Life and Public Services of Samuel Adams*, 3 vols. (Boston, 1865, with an unrevised 2d ed. in 1888). The work of Bancroft, like many other American writers of the era, suffered from an extensive—one could call it a blind—American patriotism; authors often simply assumed that the Americans had righteousness on their side in the struggle against British rule. Although he too decried Bancroft's American chauvinism, Edmund S. Morgan rightly emphasized that no one knew the primary sources as well as Bancroft. Indeed, the SA Papers in the New York Public library formed part of the magnificent document collection Bancroft gathered on the American Revolution.

William V. Wells, like Bancroft before him, exhibited an unbending pro-American view. He also had a propensity to assume that Samuel was always upright and noble. Nevertheless, a comparison of materials in the SA Papers and other sets of documents with Wells's volumes deepens the tie to Bancroft's approach. Like Bancroft, Wells obviously pored over the records with an impressive diligence. And he brought a thoughtful scholarly concern to the vital question, what did Samuel Adams author? Indeed, assuming readers arm themselves against the obvious biases—for example, Adams's views of Thomas Hutchinson are paraded as the simple truth—Wells's biography of Adams is arguably the best ever produced. It is weakest where the biographies have traditionally been weakest: in the years after independence was declared and especially in the period after the War of American Independence concluded in 1783.

The writing of James K. Hosmer occupies a transition position between the nineteenth century's generally favorable view of Adams and the more critical interpretation that gained prominence in the twentieth century. In his brief *Samuel Adams, The Man of the Town-Meeting* (Baltimore, 1884), Hosmer outlined what became basic themes in his lengthy biography of Adams: (1) Adams represented the noble Anglo-Saxon "Folk-mote" tradition of community-based democracy; and (2) Samuel Adams was second only to George Washington in importance in achieving American independence. Hosmer developed these themes with greater detail in *Samuel Adams* (Boston, 1885; and a minimally revised ed., Boston, 1898). The full biography, which blended praise of ordinary people's actions in the town meeting with the assertion that Adams skillfully managed the workings of the town meeting, was notable for Hosmer's determined effort to challenge the patriotic excess of earlier writers, particularly William V. Wells. So, even as he trumpeted Adams's importance and gloried in his commitment to town meeting democracy, Hosmer foreshadowed what would become a dominant negative interpretation. Sounding like Adams's contemporary enemies, Hosmer maintained that, in an ungentlemanly way, Samuel distorted material based on a philosophy of "the ends justify the means." Advancing the idea that Tories, especially Thomas Hutchinson, deserved respect, Hosmer asserted that Hutchinson's "one mistake . . . was disloyalty to the folk-mote" (1885, p. 280; 1898, p. 253). In addition, Hosmer began what became an unfortunate tradition among biographers: he treated Adams's post-1776 career quickly and dismissively; only one of the twenty-three chapters in Hosmer's book covered Adams's post-1776 years.

Jaded by the experience of World War I, anxious about modern revolutions, and influenced by trendy forms of psychoanalysis, Ralph V. Harlow drew an even less favorable picture in *Samuel Adams—Promoter of the American Revolution: A Study in Psychology and Politics* (New York, 1923). Rejecting any notion of the people's inherent democratic abilities, folkmote or otherwise, Harlow argued that the Great War demonstrated that the masses—that public opinion—could be manipulated easily. Harlow, who accepted Thomas Hutchinson's views of Adams almost as uncritically as Wells accepted Adams's views of Hutchinson, depicted Adams as a demagogic zealot who twisted reality and savaged truth to foment opposition to Great Britain. And what motivated Samuel Adams? As his subtitle suggested, Harlow offered a psychological analysis: Adams was probably a neurotic, and he obviously suffered from an "inferiority complex." It was Adams's need for success, said Harlow, that turned him into a political agitator who was supposedly driven by emotion rather than logical reflection. Saying that the skills of a political agitator were hardly conducive to building new states gave Harlow the excuse to sketch Adams's post–Declaration of Independence life as quickly as Hosmer did, and even more derisively. Although Harlow rode his thesis much too hard, he should be credited—or blamed—for articulating the core of what soon became the prevailing interpretation of the man he called "promoter of the American Revolution."

John C. Miller, whose influential *Sam Adams: A Pioneer in Propaganda* (Boston, 1936) became the standard modern biography, wrote at a time when the evils of political propaganda and political dictators preyed on the minds of Americans. He, too, denigrated Adams and ordinary people. Employing the views of ardent Adams opponents such as Thomas Hutchinson, Peter Oliver, and Governor Bernard, Miller depicted Adams as the dictator of Boston who controlled a trained mob. Aided by repeated British blunders and often using underhanded methods, Adams, said Miller, adroitly played a prime role in moving America toward independence. In addition to asserting that Adams sought independence because he distrusted British imperial authority and intentions, Miller held that Adams wanted to restore the manners and morals of an earlier Puritanism. In offering this analysis, Miller too facilely assigned controlling power to Adams; Miller also, on little or no evidence, assigned anonymous writings, especially those dealing with religious themes, to Adams. Like most other biographers, Miller rushed through the post-1776 period. As he rushed, Miller became even more inclined to present partisan political attacks on Adams as the truth, and he put words in Adams's mouth that appeared in anonymous publications. In addition, Miller slighted important topics such as the extensive effort Adams poured into expanding educational opportunities. Miller's distorted image extended to his use of "Sam" rather than "Samuel." Even Adams's enemies habitually referred to him as Samuel Adams, not as Sam Adams.

Stewart Beach dealt with the issue of Adams's post-1776 career by skimming over it in a brief epilogue and by candidly titling his work *Samuel Adams: The Fateful Years, 1764–1776* (New York, 1965). Still, that title is somewhat misleading because Beach was less interested in providing an analytical biography of Adams than in using him as a central figure in constructing a narrative of how events in Boston helped produce the American Revolution. As he told the story, Beach also highlighted the role of "the mob," but he was less deterministic than Miller in asserting that Adams controlled and directed such crowd actions.

Another modern biography appeared while this volume was in preparation. See William M. Fowler Jr., *Samuel Adams: Radical Puritan* (New York, 1997).

As its title indicates, Richard D. Brown's *Revolutionary Politics in Massachusetts: The Boston Committee of Correspondence and the Towns, 1772–1774* (Cambridge, Mass., 1970) is not an Adams biography. But it deserves special note because, as a "biography" of Boston's committee of correspondence, it elucidates Adams's crucial role in a vital organization that pushed the revolutionary movement forward.

In addition to the book-length biographies, many scholars have published brief sketches of Samuel Adams or included him as one of the principals in a limited collective biography. While a discussion of the many works of this kind is beyond the scope of a selective bibliographical note, two brief biographical sketches merit special mention. Clifford K. Shipton's short biography of Adams, offered in *Biographical Sketches of Those Who Attended Harvard College in the Classes 1736–1740* (Boston, 1958), provides valuable information on Adams's early years and is especially useful in correcting the often repeated erroneous claim that Adams was a brewer. But Shipton's analysis is most notable for the venomous loathing he poured over this member of the class of 1740. One might almost think that Thomas Hutchinson or Peter Oliver—Harvard graduates much more to Shipton's liking— penned the entry. Pauline Maier presented a far more complimentary, and more convincing, analysis in "A New Englander as Revolutionary: Samuel Adams," a revision of her 1976 *American Historical Review* essay, which formed part of her book *The Old Revolutionaries: Political Lives in the Age of Samuel Adams* (with a new introduction, New York, 1990; originally published 1980), 3–50. Maier, who included a useful brief historiography in her essay, emphasized that Adams acted on "consistent principles" (p. 18).

Works containing vital information on Samuel Adams, family members, or special aspects of Adams's career include J. Gardner Bartlett, comp., *Henry Adams of Somersetshire, England, and Braintree, Mass.* (New York, 1927); Clifford K. Shipton, *Biographical Sketches of Those Who Attended Harvard College in the Classes 1768–1771* (Boston, 1975); Forrest McDonald, *We the People: The Economic Origins of the Constitution* (Chicago, 1958); Andrew H. Ward, "Notes on Ante-Revolutionary Currency and Politics," *New England Historical and Genealogical Register* 14 (July 1862): 261–64; Richard Frothingham, "The Sam Adams Regiments in the Town of Boston," *Atlantic Monthly,* June 1862, 701–20; August 1862, 179–203; November 1863, 595–616; Charles Warren, "Samuel Adams and the Sans Souci Club in 1785," in *Proceedings,* Massachusetts Historical Society, 1926–27 (Boston, 1927), 318–44; Samuel Elliot Morison, "Two 'Signers' on Salaries and the Stage, 1789," in *Proceedings,* Massachusetts Historical Society, 1928–29 (Boston, 1930), 55–63; William Pencak, "Samuel Adams and Shays's Rebellion," *New England Quarterly* (hereafter *NEQ*) 62 (March 1989): 63–74.

Key sources for understanding—and dismissing—the spurious charge that Adams was part of a cabal to replace George Washington as commander in chief include Bernard Knollenberg, *Washington and the Revolution: A Reappraisal—Gates, Conway, and the Continental Congress* (New York, 1940); Edmund C. Burnett, *The Continental Congress* (New York, 1941); Douglas S. Freeman, *George Washington: A Biography—Leader of the Revolution* (New York, 1951); L. H. Butterfield, "Rush and Washington," in *Letters of Benjamin Rush,* ed. L. H. Butterfield, 2 vols. (Princeton, N.J., 1951), 2: 1197–1208; H. James Henderson, *Party Politics in the Continental Congress* (New York, 1974).

In addition to published works, the following dissertations on Samuel Adams were consulted: Matthew Seccombe, "From Revolution to Republic: The Later Political Career of Samuel Adams, 1774–1803" (Ph.D. diss., Yale University, 1978); Arthur Lee Smith Jr., "Samuel Adams' Agitational Rhetoric of Revolution" (Ph.D. diss., University of California, 1968); Owen R. Stanley, "Samuel Adams: A Case Study in the Strategies of Revolution" (Ph.D. diss., Washington State University, 1975).

Other Secondary Sources

However much they may differ on what weight to give to Samuel Adams in analyzing the era of the American Revolution, few authors who touch on the topic fail to at least mention him. In addition, works that might give Adams little or even no attention or that focus on areas other than Boston or Massachusetts can be important in helping shape one's analysis. Given these points, the list that follows is far from exhaustive. Rather, it indicates works that were actively used in preparing this biography. Although individual works are noted only once, a given item might reasonably fit in more than one category because authors often cover a range of topics.

General works on the evolving nature of the British Empire and on issues that bedeviled the empire on the way to the Revolution include: Oliver M. Dickerson, *The Navigation Acts and the American Revolution* (Philadelphia, 1951); John L. Bullion, *A Great and Necessary Measure: George Grenville and the Genesis of the Stamp Act* (Columbia, Mo., 1982); Lawrence H. Gipson, *The Coming of the Revolution, 1763–1775* (New York, 1954), and *The Triumphant Empire: The Rumbling of the Coming Storm, 1766–1770* (New York, 1967); Gary B. Nash, *The Urban Crucible: Social Change, Political Consciousness, and the Origins of the American Revolution* (Cambridge, Mass., 1979); David Ammerman, *In the Common Cause: American Response to the Coercive Acts of 1774* (Charlottesville, Va., 1974); John Sainsbury, *Disaffected Patriots: London Supporters of Revolutionary America, 1769–1782* (Kingston, Ont., 1987); Peter D. G. Thomas, *The Townshend Duties Crisis: The Second Phase of the American Revolution 1767–1773* (Oxford, 1987), and *Tea Party to Independence: The Third Phase of the American Revolution 1773–1776* (Oxford, 1991); Arthur M. Schlesinger, *The Colonial Merchants and the American Revolution* (New York, 1918) and *Prelude to Independence: The Newspaper War on Britain, 1764–1776* (New York, 1958); Thomas C. Barrow, *Trade and Empire: The British Customs Service in Colonial America, 1660–1775* (Cambridge, Mass., 1967); Ian R. Christie and Benjamin W. Labaree, *Empire or Independence, 1760–1776: A British-American Dialogue on the Coming of the American Revolution* (New York, 1976); John Shy, *Toward Lexington: The Role of the British Army in the Coming of the American Revolution* (Princeton, N.J., 1965); Philip Davidson, *Propaganda and the American Revolution* (Chapel Hill, N.C., 1941); Pauline Maier, *American Scripture: Making the Declaration of Independence* (New York, 1997); Sydney V. James, *Colonial Rhode Island: A History* (New York, 1975); David S. Lovejoy, *Rhode Island and the American Revolution, 1760–1776* (Providence, R.I., 1958); Edmund S. Morgan, "Colonial Ideals of Parliamentary Power, 1764–1766," *WMQ* 5 (July 1948): 311–41, and corresponding letters to the editor in *WMQ* 6 (January 1949): 162–70.

Works dealing with Massachusetts or Massachusetts-based topics that emphasize the colonial era include Benjamin W. Labaree, *Colonial Massachusetts: A History* (Millwood, N.Y., 1979); Robert E. Brown, *Middle-Class Democracy and the Revolution in Massachusetts, 1691–1780* (Ithaca, N.Y., 1955); Stephen E. Patterson, *Political Parties in Revolutionary Massachusetts* (Madison, Wisc., 1973); Richard L. Bushman, *King and People in Provincial Massachusetts* (Chapel Hill, N.C., 1985); Andrew M. Davis, *Currency and Banking in the Province of Massachusetts-Bay: Part 1, Currency* (Cambridge, Mass., 1900), and *Currency and Banking in the Province of Massachusetts-Bay: Part 2, Banking* (Cambridge, Mass., 1901); Ellen E. Brennan, *Plural Office-Holding in Massachusetts, 1760–1780: Its Relation to the "Separation" of Departments of Government* (Chapel Hill, N.C., 1945); Donald C. Lord and Robert M. Calhoon, "The Removal of the Massachusetts General Court from Boston, 1769–1772," *Journal of American History* 55 (March 1969): 735–55.

Works dealing with Boston or Boston-based topics that emphasize the colonial era include Carl Bridenbaugh, *Cities in Revolt: Urban Life in America, 1743–1776,* rev. ed. (New York, 1971; originally published 1955); G. B. Warden, *Boston, 1689–1776* (Boston, 1970); Walter M. Whitehall, *Boston: A Topographical History,* 2d enlarged ed. (Cambridge, Mass., 1968); Samuel A. Drake, *Old Landmarks and Historic Personages of Boston* (Boston, 1876); Alan Day and Katherine Day, "Another

Look at the Boston 'Caucus,'" *Journal of American Studies* 5 (April 1971): 19–42; G. B. Warden, "The Caucus and Democracy in Colonial Boston," *NEQ* 43 (March 1970): 19–45; Charles M. Andrews, "The Boston Merchants and the Non-Importation Movement," *Transactions 1916–1917,* Colonial Society of Massachusetts (Boston, 1918), 159–259.

Works that emphasize crowd actions, including works that are especially important for the theory of crowd actions and the "inarticulate," include Edmund S. Morgan and Helen M. Morgan, *The Stamp Act Crisis: Prologue to Revolution* (with a new introduction, Chapel Hill, N.C., 1995; 1st ed. 1953, and rev. ed. 1962); Benjamin W. Labaree, *The Boston Tea Party* (New York, 1964); Hiller B. Zobel, *The Boston Massacre* (New York, 1970); Pauline Maier, *From Resistance to Revolution: Colonial Radicals and the Development of American Opposition to Britain, 1765–1776* (New York, 1972); Dirk Hoerder, *Crown Action in Revolutionary Massachusetts, 1765–1780* (New York, 1977); John P. Reid, *In a Rebellious Spirit: The Argument of Facts, the Liberty Riot, and the Coming of the American Revolution* (University Park, Pa., 1979); Alfred F. Young, *The Shoemaker and the Tea Party: Memory and the American Revolution* (Boston, 1999); George G. Wolkins, "The Seizure of John Hancock's Sloop *Liberty,*" in *Proceedings,* Massachusetts Historical Society, October 1921–June 1922 (Boston, 1923), 239–84; Albert Matthews, "Joyce Junior," *Transactions 1902–1904,* Colonial Society of Massachusetts (Boston, 1906), 90–104; George P. Anderson, "Ebenezer Mackintosh: Stamp Act Rioter and Patriot," "Pascal Paoli, An Inspiration to the Sons of Liberty," and "A Note on Ebenezer Mackintosh," in *Transactions 1924–1926,* Colonial Society of Massachusetts (Boston, 1927), 15–64, 180–210, 348–61; R. S. Longley, "Mob Activities in Revolutionary Massachusetts," *NEQ* 6 (March 1931): 98–130; Robert E. Moody, "Samuel Fly: Forerunner of Shays," *NEQ* 5 (January 1932): 105–34; Jesse Lemisch, "New York's Petitions and Resolves of December 1765: Liberals vs. Radicals," *New-York Historical Society Quarterly* 49 (October 1965): 313–26; Jesse Lemisch, "Jack Tar in the Streets: Merchant Seamen in the Politics of Revolutionary America," *WMQ* 25 (July 1968): 371–407; Jesse Lemisch and John K. Alexander, "The White Oaks, Jack Tar, and the Concept of the 'Inarticulate,'" *WMQ* 29 (January 1972): 109–34; John K. Alexander, "The Fort Wilson Incident of 1779: A Case Study of the Revolutionary Crowd," *WMQ* 31 (October 1974): 589–612, and "Deference in Colonial Pennsylvania and That Man from New Jersey," *Pennsylvania Magazine of History and Biography* 102 (October 1978): 422–36; Alfred F. Young, "George Robert Twelves Hewes (1742–1840): A Boston Shoemaker and the Memory of the American Revolution," *WMQ* 38 (October 1981): 561–623; Barbara Clark Smith, "Food Rioters and the American Revolution," *WMQ* 51 (January 1994): 3–38; Barbara Clark Smith, "The Politics of Price Control in Revolutionary Massachusetts, 1774–1780" (Ph.D. diss., Yale University, 1983); Beverly O. Held, "'To Instruct and Improve . . . to Entertain and Please': American Civic Protests and Pageants 1765–1784," 2 vols. (Ph.D. diss., University of Michigan, 1987).

Works that deal primarily with military and political developments in the new nation include George Bancroft, *History of the Formation of the Constitution of the United States,* 2 vols. (New York, 1882); Claude H. Van Tyne, *The Loyalists in the American Revolution* (New York, 1902); Merrill Jensen, *The Articles of Confederation: An Interpretation of the Social-Constitutional History of the American Revolution,*

1774–1781 (with additional prefaces, Madison, Wisc., 1970; originally published 1940); Elisha P. Douglass, *Rebels and Democrats: The Struggle for Equal Political Rights and Majority Rule during the American Revolution* (Chapel Hill, N.C., 1955); Howard H. Peckham, *The War for Independence: A Military History* (Chicago, 1958); Jackson Turner Main, *The Antifederalists: Critics of the Constitution, 1781–1788* (Chapel Hill, N.C., 1961); Don Higginbotham, *The War of American Independence: Military Attitudes, Politics, and Practice, 1763–1789* (New York, 1971); Willi Paul Adams, *The First American Constitutions: Republican Ideology and the Making of the State Constitutions in the Revolutionary Era*, trans. Rita Kimber and Robert Kimber (Chapel Hill, N.C., 1973; expanded ed., Madison, Wisc., 2000); Jon C. Teaford, *The Municipal Revolution in America: Origins of Modern Urban Government, 1650–1825* (Chicago, 1975); Jack N. Rakove, *The Beginnings of National Politics: An Interpretive History of the Continental Congress* (Baltimore, 1979) and *Original Meanings: Politics and Ideas in the Making of the Constitution* (New York, 1996); John K. Alexander, *The Selling of the Constitutional Convention: A History of News Coverage* (Madison, Wisc., 1990); Marc W. Kruman, *Between Authority and Liberty: State Constitution Making in Revolutionary America* (Chapel Hill, N.C., 1996).

Works that illuminated Massachusetts topics, especially of the postindependence era, include George R. Minot, *The History of the Insurrections in Massachusetts*, 2d ed. (Boston, 1810); Anson E. Morse, *The Federalist Party in Massachusetts to the Year 1800* (Princeton, N.J., 1901); Richard Frothingham, *History of the Siege of Boston . . .*, 6th ed. (Boston, 1903); James H. Stark, *The Loyalists of Massachusetts and the Other Side of the American Revolution* (Boston, 1910); Robert J. Taylor, *Western Massachusetts in the Revolution* (Providence, R.I., 1954); Paul Goodman, *The Democratic-Republicans of Massachusetts: Politics in a Young Republic* (Cambridge, Mass., 1964); Van Beck Hall, *Politics without Parties: Massachusetts, 1780–1791* (Pittsburgh, 1972); Ronald M. Peters Jr., *The Massachusetts Constitution of 1780: A Social Compact* (Amherst, Mass., 1978); Stanley K. Schultz, *The Culture Factory: Boston Public Schools, 1789–1860* (New York, 1973); Robert A. Gross, ed., *In Debt to Shays: The Bicentennial of an Agrarian Rebellion* (Charlottesville, Va., 1993); Peter S. Field, *The Crisis of the Standing Order: Clerical Intellectuals and Cultural Authority in Massachusetts, 1780–1833* (Amherst, Mass., 1998); Arthur Lord, "Some Objections Made to the State Constitution, 1780," and Samuel Elliot Morison, "The Struggle over the Adoption of the Constitution of Massachusetts, 1780," in *Proceedings*, Massachusetts Historical Society, 1916–1917 (Boston, 1917), 54–60, 353–411; David E. Maas, "The Massachusetts Loyalists and the Problem of Amnesty, 1775–1790," in *Loyalists and Community in North America,* ed. Robert M. Calhoon et al. (Westport, 1994), 65–74; Kathryn K. Sklar, "The Schooling of Girls and Changing Community Values in Massachusetts Towns, 1750–1820," *History of Education Quarterly* (hereafter *HEQ*) 33 (Winter 1993): 511–42; Joel Perlmann, Silvana R. Siddali, and Keith Whitescarver, "Literacy, Schooling, and Teaching among New England Women, 1730–1820," *HEQ* 37 (Summer 1997): 117–39; John Witte Jr., "'A Most Mild and Equitable Establishment of Religion': John Adams and the Massachusetts Experiment," *Journal of Church and State* 41 (Spring 1999): 213–52.

Biographical studies include John Eliot, *A Biographical Dictionary . . .* (Boston, 1809); Thomas C. Amory, *Life of James Sullivan: with Selections from his Writings*, 2 vols. (Boston, 1859); John A. Schutz, *Legislators of the Massachusetts General Court,*

1691–1780: A Biographical Dictionary (Boston, 1997); William Tudor, *The Life of James Otis of Massachusetts . . . 1760 to 1775* (Boston, 1823); Henry S. Randall, *The Life of Thomas Jefferson*, 3 vols. (New York, 1858); Esther Forbes, *Paul Revere and the World He Lived In* (Boston, 1942); John R. Alden, *General Gage in America: Being Principally a History of His Role in the American Revolution* (Baton Rouge, La., 1948); John Cary, *Joseph Warren: Physician, Politician, Patriot* (Urbana, Ill., 1961); John A. Schutz, *William Shirley: King's Governor of Massachusetts* (Chapel Hill, N.C., 1961); Ward L. Miner, *William Goddard, Newspaperman* (Durham, N.C., 1962); John J. Waters Jr., *The Otis Family in Provincial and Revolutionary Massachusetts* (Chapel Hill, N.C., 1968); Helen R. Pinkney, *Christopher Gore: Federalist of Massachusetts, 1758–1827* (Waltham, Mass., 1969); Bernard Bailyn, *The Ordeal of Thomas Hutchinson* (Boston, 1974); Gordon E. Kershaw, *James Bowdoin: Patriot and Man of the Enlightenment* (Lanham, Md., 1991); John Ferling, *John Adams: A Life* (Knoxville, Tenn., 1992); David H. Fischer, *Paul Revere's Ride* (New York, 1994); Rosemarie Zagarri, *A Woman's Dilemma: Mercy Otis Warren and the American Revolution* (Wheeling, W. Va., 1995); Ellen E. Brennan, "James Otis: Recreant and Patriot," *NEQ* 12 (December 1939): 691–725; Gregory H. Nobles, "'Yet the Old Republicans Still Persevere': Samuel Adams, John Hancock, and the Crisis of Popular Leadership in Revolutionary Massachusetts, 1775–1790," in *The Transforming Hand of Revolution: Reconsidering the American Revolution as a Social Movement*, ed. Ronald Hoffman and Peter J. Albert (Charlottesville, Va., 1995), 258–85; Robert Z. Finkelstein, "Merchant, Revolutionary, and Statesman: A Re-Appraisal of the Life and Public Services of John Hancock, 1737–1793" (Ph.D. diss., University of Massachusetts, 1981).

Material on the nature of society and culture in eighteenth-century America is, even if not explicitly stated, often linked to topics and questions raised in J. Franklin Jameson, *The American Revolution Considered as a Social Movement* (Princeton, N.J., 1926). A summary of some findings through the mid-1990s is available in Alfred F. Young, "American Historians Confront 'The Transforming Hand,'" in *The Transforming Hand of Revolution*, ed. Hoffman and Albert, 346–492. Works on the nature of society and culture that were of particular use for this study include Nancy F. Cott, *The Bonds of Womanhood: "Women's Sphere" in New England, 1780–1835*, 2d ed. (New Haven, Conn., 1997); Linda K. Kerber, *Women of the Republic: Intellect and Ideology in Revolutionary America* (with an added preface, New York, 1986; originally published 1980); Mary Beth Norton, *Liberty's Daughters: The Revolutionary Experience of American Women, 1750–1800* (with added preface, Ithaca, N.Y., 1996; originally published 1980); Carol Berkin, *First Generations: Women in Colonial America* (New York, 1996); Ronald Hoffman and Peter J. Albert, eds., *Women in the Age of the American Revolution* (Charlottesville, Va., 1989); Benjamin Quarles, *The Negro in the American Revolution* (Chapel Hill, N.C., 1960; with a new foreword by Thad W. Tate and a new introduction by Gary B. Nash, 1996); Arthur Zilversmit, *The First Emancipation: The Abolition of Slavery in the North* (Chicago, 1967); Edgar J. McManus, *Black Bondage in the North* (Syracuse, N.Y., 1973); Colin G. Calloway, *The American Revolution in Indian Country: Crisis and Diversity in Native American Communities* (Cambridge, Mass., 1995); John K. Alexander, *Render Them Submissive: Responses to Poverty in Philadelphia, 1760–1800* (Amherst, Mass., 1980); Rosemarie Zagarri, "The Rights of Man and Woman in Post-Revolutionary America," *WMQ* 55 (April 1998): 203–30.

Index

Within entries, Samuel Adams is abbreviated SA.

21–23; comparison to SA, 22–24, 30–31; at Massachusetts convention of 1768, 62–64; in Massachusetts House, 21–22, 31, 39, 44, 52, 53, 54, 55; mental illness of, 76, 78; political inconsistency, 23–24, 31,43, 56, 97; popularity of, 21, 76; relationship with SA, 22, 24, 28, 30–31, 39, 48, 52, 53, 58, 59, 60, 63, 70, 73, 74, 75, 76, 97, 99, 109; and Stamp Act Congress, 24, 31
Otis, James, Sr., 43
Overseers of the Poor, 192

Paine, Robert Treat, 84–85, 135
Paine, Thomas, 148, 153, 158, 161, 221
palsy, 100, 167
Paoli, Pascal, 61
paper money. *See* currency
Parliament: attitudes toward America, 17–18, 49–50, 61; representation in, 32, 36–37; —, SA on, 20–21, 32, 36–37, 51, 52; supremacy of, British views on, 17–18, 37, 75, 93; —, Hutchinson and General Court debate, 112–14; —, James Otis Jr. on, 21, 31; —, SA on, 20, 32–33, 55, 56, 112–13, 114, 120–21, 129, 138; taxing powers of, SA on, 19–21, 24, 30, 36–37, 45, 47, 49, 51, 69, 103, 138. *See also* individual topics
patriotism, shifting meaning of term, 74
Pemberton, Samuel, 84
Pendleton, Edmund, 222
Pennsylvania, 138, 158, 184, 213
Pennsylvania Evening Post, 153
pensions, 54, 71, 74, 197–98
petition, right of, 55, 78, 108–9, 207
Philadelphia: 34, 49, 50–51, 59, 61, 70, 75, 91, 128, 131, 132, 139, 148; Tea Act and, 120, 122, 124, 126; as seat of central government, 136, 137, 142, 143, 147, 158, 159, 169
Phillips, William, 84
Pierce, Joseph, 23

Pitt, William, 37
Plan of Union, 140
plays, 193
plural officeholding, 39–40, 43, 175, 186–87, 223
Plymouth, 95, 109, 180
political parties: national, 213–14, 217, 222; in state of Massachusetts, 186, 188, 213–14, 217–18, 220. *See also* popular party; court party
Pollard, Benjamin, 11
poor, the, 16 27–28, 57, 85, 163; education of, 192–93. *See also* commonality
"Pope's Day," 33, 56
popular party (Massachusetts), 5, 6, 13, 29, 41, 44, 47, 48, 54, 58, 63. 74
postal systems, 128–29, 213
posterity, duty to, 95–96, 102, 132, 172, 173, 188, 191, 201, 202, 209, 212, 214, 215
poverty. *See* poor, the
power, love of, 174, 188
power of the purse, 2–3, 16, 21, 96, 101, 103, 106. *See also* salaries
preferment, 41, 43, 48, 100, 136
presidential electors, 215–16
Preston, Thomas, 81, 84, 94
price regulation, 163
Princeton, Battle of, 158
Privy Council, 47
propaganda: British, 104–5; campaigns of SA, 27, 28, 68–69, 70–71, 76, 79–80, 87, 94–95, 99, 100–3, 106–7, 117–19, 160–61, 173–75, 179, 188–89, 225–26
prostitution, 68
Psalm 35, 139
public works, 85, 137
Puritan, 176, 222

Quartering Act (1765), 45, 47, 52, 67, 73
Quebec, 144
Quincy, Josiah, 84, 88, 142

About the Author

John K. Alexander is professor of history at the University of Cincinnati. An associate editor of *American National Biography* (1999), he is also the author of *Render Them Submissive: Responses to Poverty in Philadelphia, 1760–1800* (1980) and *The Selling of the Constitutional Convention: A History of News Coverage* (1990).